# ADOBE® FLASH® CS4 PROFESSIONAL

**Fl**

# CLASSROOM IN A BOOK®

The official training workbook from Adobe Systems

as3 queries

Adobe®

Adobe Press books are published by Peachpit, a division of Pearson Education located in Berkeley, California. For the latest on Adobe Press books, go to www.adobepress.com. To report errors, please send a note to errata@peachpit.com. For information on getting permission for reprints and excerpts, contact permissions@peachpit.com.

Writer: Russell Chun
Editor: Rebecca Gulick
Production Coordinator: Kate Reber
Copyeditor: Anne Marie Walker
Proofreader: Liz Welch
Technical Editor: Jeremy Rue
Compositor: WolfsonDesign
Indexer: FireCrystal Communications
Cover design: Eddie Yuen
Interior design: Mimi Heft

Printed and bound in the United States of America

ISBN-13: 978-0-321-57382-7

ISBN-10: 0-321-57382-X

9 8 7 6 5 4 3 2

# WHAT'S ON THE DISC

**Here is an overview of the contents of the Classroom in a Book disc**

## Lesson files ... and so much more

The *Adobe Flash CS4 Professional Classroom in a Book* disc includes the lesson files that you'll need to complete the exercises in this book, as well as other content to help you learn more about Adobe Flash CS4 and use it with greater efficiency and ease. There is also a PDF of the book's appendix to allow you to view the true RGB rendering of the hexadecimal color codes onscreen. The diagram below represents the contents of the disc, which should help you locate the files you need.

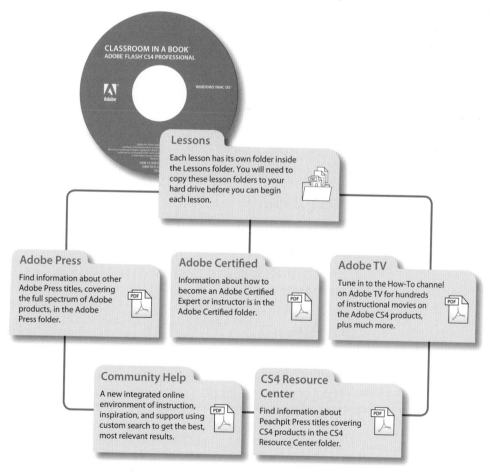

**Lessons**

Each lesson has its own folder inside the Lessons folder. You will need to copy these lesson folders to your hard drive before you can begin each lesson.

**Adobe Press**

Find information about other Adobe Press titles, covering the full spectrum of Adobe products, in the Adobe Press folder.

**Adobe Certified**

Information about how to become an Adobe Certified Expert or instructor is in the Adobe Certified folder.

**Adobe TV**

Tune in to the How-To channel on Adobe TV for hundreds of instructional movies on the Adobe CS4 products, plus much more.

**Community Help**

A new integrated online environment of instruction, inspiration, and support using custom search to get the best, most relevant results.

**CS4 Resource Center**

Find information about Peachpit Press titles covering CS4 products in the CS4 Resource Center folder.

*to make movies*

# CONTENTS

# GETTING STARTED

Adobe® Flash® CS4 Professional provides a comprehensive authoring environment for creating interactive Web sites and digital animation. Flash is widely used to create engaging applications that are rich with video, sound, graphics, and animation. You can create original content in Flash or import it from other Adobe applications, quickly design simple animations, and use Adobe ActionScript 3.0 to develop sophisticated interactive projects.

## About Classroom in a Book

*Adobe Flash CS4 Professional Classroom in a Book* is part of the official training series for Adobe graphics and publishing software. The lessons are designed so that you can learn at your own pace. If you're new to Flash, you'll learn the fundamental concepts and features you'll need to use the program. *Classroom in a Book* also teaches many advanced features, including tips and techniques for using the latest version of the Flash application.

The lessons in this book include opportunities to use new features, such as the new motion tween model and the Motion Editor, to create armatures with inverse kinematics, to work in 3D, to use the Adobe Media Encoder, and more.

## Prerequisites

Before you begin to use *Adobe Flash CS4 Professional Classroom in a Book*, make sure that your system is set up correctly and that you've installed the required software. You should have a good working knowledge of your computer and operating system. You should know how to use the mouse and standard menus and commands, and also how to open, save, and close files. If you need to review these techniques, see the printed or online documentation included with your Microsoft Windows or Apple Mac OS software.

## Installing Flash

● **Note:** You can download the latest version of Apple QuickTime from www.apple.com/quicktime/download.

You must purchase the Adobe Flash CS4 software either as a stand-alone application or as part of the Adobe Creative Suite. Both products come with Adobe Media Encoder CS4, Adobe Extension Manager CS4, Adobe Device Central CS4, and Adobe Bridge CS4, in addition to the actual Adobe Flash CS4 application. Flash CS4 requires Apple QuickTime 7.1.2 or later. For system requirements and complete instructions on installing the Flash software, see the Adobe Flash ReadMe.html file on the application DVD.

Install Flash from the Adobe Flash CS4 application DVD onto your hard disk. You cannot run the program from the DVD. Follow the onscreen instructions.

Make sure that your serial number is accessible before installing the application. You can find the serial number on the registration card or on the back of the DVD case.

## Optimizing Performance

Creating animations is memory-intensive work for a desktop computer. Flash CS4 Professional requires a minimum of 512 MB of RAM; 1 GB or more is recommended. The more RAM that is available to Flash, the faster the application will work for you.

## How to Use These Lessons

● **Note:** Many aspects of the Flash application can be controlled by multiple techniques, such as a menu command, a button, dragging, and a keyboard shortcut. Only one or two of the methods are described in any given procedure so that you can learn different ways of working, even when the task is one you've done before.

Each lesson in this book provides step-by-step instructions for creating one or more specific elements of a real-world project. Some lessons build on projects created in preceding lessons; most stand alone. All the lessons build on each other in terms of concepts and skills, so the best way to learn from this book is to proceed through the lessons in sequential order. In this book, some techniques and processes are explained and described in detail only the first few times you perform them.

The organization of the lessons is also design oriented rather than feature oriented. That means, for example, that you'll work with symbols on real-world design projects over several lessons rather than in just one chapter.

# Copying the Lesson Files

The lessons in *Adobe Flash CS4 Professional Classroom in a Book* use specific source files, such as image files created in Adobe Illustrator and Adobe Photoshop, video files created in Adobe After Effects, audio files, and prepared Flash documents. To complete the lessons in this book, you must copy these files from the *Adobe Flash CS4 Professional Classroom in a Book* CD (located inside the back cover of this book) to your computer.

1   On your computer, create a new folder in a convenient location and name it **FlashCS4_CIB**, following the standard procedure for your operating system:

   • Windows. In Explorer, select the folder or drive on which you want to create the new folder and choose File > New > Folder. Then type the new name.

   • Mac OS. In the Finder, choose File > New Folder. Type the new name and drag the folder to the location you want to use.

   Now you can copy the source files onto your hard disk.

2   Copy the Lessons folder (which contains folders named Lesson01, Lesson02, and so on) from the *Adobe Flash CS4 Professional Classroom in a Book* CD onto your hard disk by dragging it to your new FlashCS4_CIB folder.

When you begin each lesson, navigate to the folder with that lesson number. In the folder, you will find all the assets, sample movies, and other project files you need to complete the lesson.

If you have limited storage space on your computer, you can copy each lesson folder individually as you need it, and delete it afterward if desired. Some lessons build on preceding lessons; in those cases, a starting project file is provided for you for the second lesson or project. You do not have to save any finished project if you don't want to or if you have limited hard disk space.

## About Copying the Sample Movies and Projects

You will create and publish SWF animation files in some lessons in this book. The files in the End folders (01End, 02End, and so on) within the Lesson folders are samples of the completed project for each lesson. Use these files for reference if you want to compare your work in progress with the project files used to generate the sample movies. The end project files vary in size from relatively small to a couple of megabytes, so you can either copy them all now if you have ample storage space or copy just the end project file for each lesson as needed, and then delete it when you finish that lesson.

# Additional Resources

*Adobe Flash CS4 Professional Classroom in a Book* is not meant to replace documentation that comes with the program or to be a comprehensive reference for every feature in Flash CS4. Only the commands and options used in the lessons are explained in this book. For comprehensive information about program features, refer to any of these resources:

- Adobe Flash CS4 Community Help, which you can view by choosing Help > Flash Help. Community Help is an integrated online environment of instruction, inspiration, and support. It includes custom search of expert-selected, relevant content on and off Adobe.com. Community Help combines content from Adobe Help, Support, Design Center, Developer Connection, and Forums— along with great online community content so that users can easily find the best and most up-to-date resources. Access tutorials, technical support, online product help, videos, articles, tips and techniques, blogs, examples, and much more.

- Adobe Flash Support Center, where you can find and browse support and learning content on Adobe.com. Visit www.adobe.com/support/flash/.

- Adobe TV, where you will find programming on Adobe products, including a channel for professional photographers and a How To channel that contains hundreds of movies on Flash CS4 and other products across the Adobe CS4 lineup. Visit http://tv.adobe.com/.

Also check out these useful links:

- The Flash CS4 product home page at www.adobe.com/products/flash/.

- Flash user forums at www.adobe.com/support/forums/ for peer-to-peer discussions of Adobe products.

- Flash Exchange at www.adobe.com/cfusion/exchange/ for extensions, functions, code, and more.

- Flash plug-ins at www.adobe.com/products/plugins/flash/.

# Adobe Certification

The Adobe Certified program is designed to help Adobe customers and trainers improve and promote their product-proficiency skills. There are four levels of certification:

- Adobe Certified Associate (ACA)
- Adobe Certified Expert (ACE)
- Adobe Certified Instructor (ACI)
- Adobe Authorized Training Center (AATC)

The Adobe Certified Associate (ACA) credential certifies that individuals have the entry-level skills to plan, design, build, and maintain effective communications using different forms of digital media.

The Adobe Certified Expert program is a way for expert users to upgrade their credentials. You can use Adobe certification as a catalyst for getting a raise, finding a job, or promoting your expertise.

If you are an ACE-level instructor, the Adobe Certified Instructor program takes your skills to the next level and gives you access to a wide range of Adobe resources.

Adobe Authorized Training Centers offer instructor-led courses and training on Adobe products, employing only Adobe Certified Instructors. A directory of AATCs is available at http://partners.adobe.com.

For information on the Adobe Certified program, visit www.adobe.com/support/certification/main.html.

# 1 GETTING ACQUAINTED

## Lesson Overview

In this lesson, you'll learn how to do the following:

- Create a new file in Flash
- Adjust Stage settings in the Property inspector
- Add layers to the Timeline
- Manage keyframes in the Timeline
- Work with imported images in the Library
- Move and reposition objects on the Stage
- Open and work with panels
- Select and use tools in the Tools panel
- Preview your Flash animation
- Search for topics in Flash Help
- Access online resources for Flash

 This lesson will take less than an hour to complete. Copy the Lesson01 folder from the *Adobe Flash CS4 Professional Classroom in a Book* CD onto your hard drive if it's not already there.

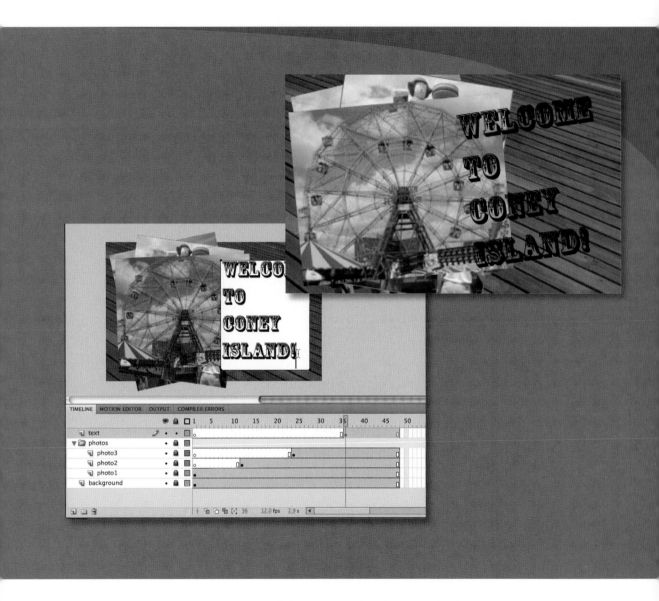

In Flash, the Stage is where the action takes place,
the Timeline organizes frames and layers, and other
panels let you edit and control your creation.

## Starting Flash and Opening a File

The first time you start Flash you'll see a Welcome screen with links to standard file templates, tutorials, and other resources. In this lesson, you'll create a simple animation to showcase a few vacation snapshots. You'll add the photos and a title, and in the process you'll learn about positioning elements on the Stage and placing them along the Timeline.

● **Note:** You can also start Flash by double-clicking a Flash (*.fla) file.

1 Start Adobe Flash. In Windows, choose Start > All Programs > Adobe Flash CS4. In Mac OS, double-click Adobe Flash CS4 in the Applications folder or the Dock.

2 Choose File > Open. In the Open dialog box, select the 01End.swf file in the Lesson01/01End folder and click Open to preview the final project.

An animation plays. During the animation, several overlapping photos appear one by one, ending with a title.

3 Close the preview window.

4 Choose File > New. In the New Document dialog box, choose Flash File (ActionScript 3.0).

ActionScript 3.0 is the latest version of Flash's scripting language, which you use to add interactivity. ActionScript 3.0 requires your browser to have Flash Player 9 or later. In this lesson, you will not be working with ActionScript, but you still must choose with which version your file is compatible.

5   Choose File > Save. Name the file **01_workingcopy.fla** and save it in the 01Start folder. Saving your file right away is a good working habit and ensures your work won't be lost if the application or your computer crashes. You should always save your Flash file with the extension .fla to identify it as the Flash source file.

# Getting to Know the Work Area

The Adobe Flash work area includes the command menus at the top of the screen and a variety of tools and panels for editing and adding elements to your movie. You can create all the objects for your animation in Flash, or you can import elements you've created in Adobe Illustrator, Adobe Photoshop, Adobe After Effects, and other compatible applications.

By default, Flash displays the menu bar, Timeline, Stage, Tools panel, Property inspector, and a few other panels. As you work in Flash, you can open, close, dock, undock, and move panels around the screen. To return to the default workspace, choose Window > Workspace > Essentials.

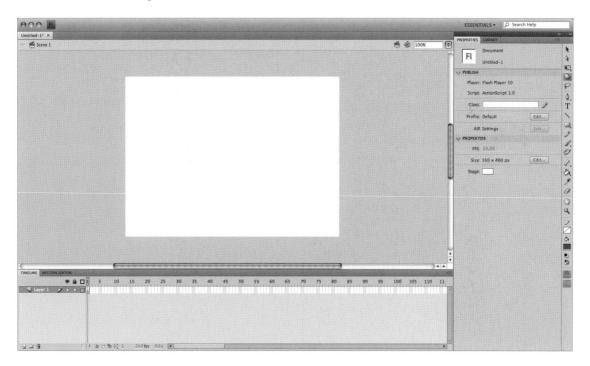

## About the Stage

The big white rectangle in the middle of your screen is called the Stage. As with a theater stage, the Stage in Flash is the area that viewers see when a movie is playing. It contains the text, images, and video that appear on the screen. Move elements on and off the Stage to move them in and out of view. You can use the rulers (View > Rulers) or grids (View > Grid > Show Grid) to help you position items on the Stage. Additionally, you can use the Align panel and other tools you'll learn about in the lessons in this book.

By default, you'll see the gray area off the Stage where you can place elements that won't be visible to your audience (because they are off the Stage). The gray area is called the Pasteboard. To just see the Stage, choose View > Pasteboard to deselect the option. For now, leave the option selected.

To scale the Stage so that it fits completely in the application window, choose View > Magnification > Fit in Window. You can also choose different magnification view options from the pop-up menu just above the Stage.

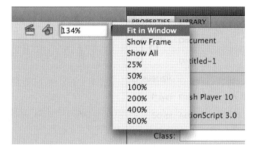

## Changing the Stage Properties

You'll first want to set the color and the dimensions of the Stage. These options are available in the Property inspector, which is the vertical panel just to the right of the Stage.

1 At the bottom of the Property inspector, note the dimensions of the current Stage is set at 550 x 400 pixels. Click the Edit button.

The Document Properties dialog box appears.

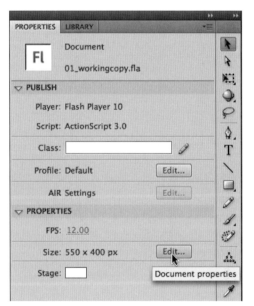

2  In the Width and Height boxes, enter new pixel dimensions. Enter **400** for the Width and **250** for the Height.

3  Click the Background color button and choose a new color for the Stage. Choose dark gray (#333333).

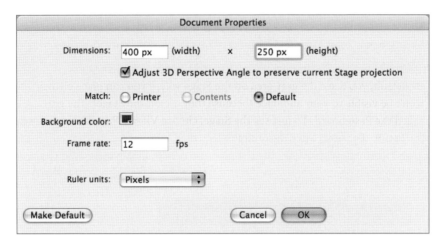

4  Click OK. Your Stage is now a different dimension and color. You can also change the Stage color by clicking the Stage button in the Property inspector. You can change the Stage properties at any time.

# Working with the Library Panel

The Library panel is accessible from a tab just to the right of the Property inspector. The Library panel is where you store and organize symbols created in Flash, as well as imported files, including bitmaps, graphics, sound files, and video clips. Symbols are often-used graphics used for animation and for interactivity.

● **Note:** You'll learn much more about symbols in Lesson 3.

## About the Library Panel

The Library panel lets you organize library items in folders, see how often an item is used in a document, and sort items by type. When you import items into Flash, you can import them directly onto the Stage or into the library. However, any item you import onto the Stage is also added to the library, as are any symbols you create. You can then easily access the items to add them to the Stage again, edit them, or see their properties.

To display the Library panel, choose Window > Library, or press Ctrl+L (Windows) or Command+L (Mac OS).

## Importing an Item to the Library Panel

Often, you'll be creating graphics directly with Flash's drawing tools and saving them as symbols, which are stored in the Library. Other times you'll be importing media such as JPEG images or MP3 sound files, which are also stored in the Library. In this lesson, you'll import several JPEG images into the Library to be used in the animation.

1 Choose File > Import > Import to Library. In the Open dialog box, select the background.jpg file in the Lesson01/01Start folder, and click Open.

2 Flash will import the selected JPEG image and place it in the Library panel.

3 Continue importing all the other JPEG images in the 01Start folder.

4 The Library panel will display all the imported JPEG images with their filenames and a thumbnail preview. These images are now available to be used in your Flash document.

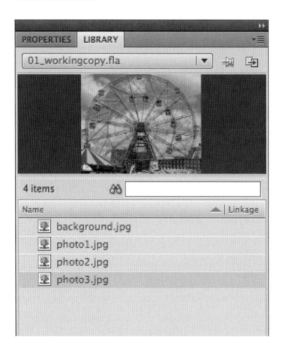

## Adding an Item from the Library Panel to the Stage

To use an imported image, simply drag it from the Library panel onto the Stage.

1 Choose Window > Library to open the Library panel if it isn't already open.

2 Select the background.jpg item in the Library panel.

**3** Drag the background.jpg item onto the Stage and place it approximately in the center of the Stage.

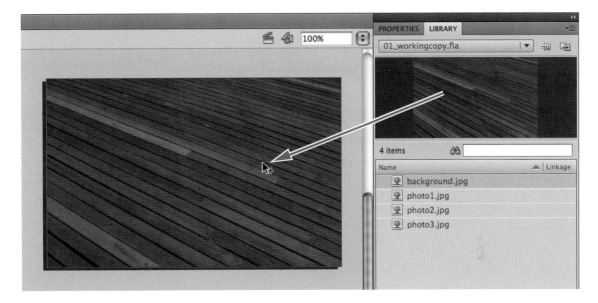

## Understanding the Timeline

The Timeline is located below the Stage. Like films, Flash documents measure time in frames. As the movie plays, the playhead, shown as a red vertical line, advances through the frames in the Timeline. You can change the content on the Stage for different frames. To display a frame's content on the Stage, move the playhead to that frame in the Timeline.

At the bottom of the Timeline, Flash indicates the selected frame number, the current frame rate (how many frames play per second), and the time that has elapsed so far in the movie.

The Timeline also contains layers, which help you organize the artwork in your document. Think of layers as multiple film strips stacked on top of each other. Each layer contains a different image that appears on the Stage, and you can draw and edit objects on one layer without affecting objects on another layer. The layers are stacked in the order in which they appear in the Timeline, so that objects on the bottom layer in the Timeline are on the bottom of the stack on the Stage. You can hide, show, lock, or unlock layers. Each layer's frames are unique, but you can drag them to a new location on the same layer or copy or move them to another layer.

## Renaming a Layer

It's a good idea to separate your content on different layers and name each layer to indicate its contents so that you can easily find the layer you need later.

1 Select the existing layer in the Timeline.

2 Double-click the name of the layer to rename it and type **background**.

3 Click outside the name box to apply the new name.

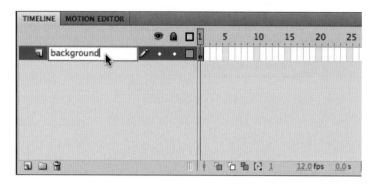

4 Click the black dot below the lock icon to lock the layer. Locking a layer prevents you from accidentally making changes to it.

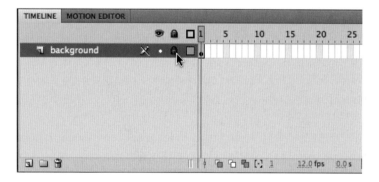

## Adding a Layer

A new Flash document contains only one layer, but you can add as many layers as you need. Objects in the top layers will overlap objects in the bottom layers.

1 Select the background layer in the Timeline.

**2** Choose Insert > Timeline > Layer. You can also click the Add New Layer button below the Timeline. A new layer appears above the background layer.

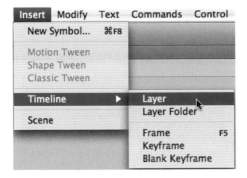

**3** Double-click the new layer to rename it and type **photo1**. Click outside the name box to apply the new name.

Your Timeline now has two layers. The background layer contains the background photo, and the newly created photo1 layer above it is empty.

**4** Select the top layer called photo1.

**5** Choose Window > Library to open the Library panel if it isn't already open.

**6** Drag the Library item called photo1.jpg from the Library on to the Stage.

The photo1 JPEG appears on the Stage and overlaps the background JPEG.

**7** Choose Insert > Timeline > Layer or click the Add New Layer button (  ) below the Timeline to add a third layer.

**8** Rename the third layer **photo2**.

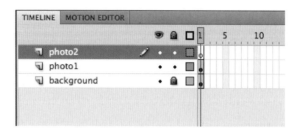

## Working with Layers

If you don't want a layer, you can easily delete it by selecting it and then clicking the Delete Layer button below the Timeline.

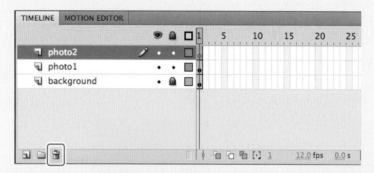

If you want to rearrange your layers, simply click and drag any layer to move it to a new position in the layer stack.

## Inserting Frames

So far, you have a background photo and another overlapping photo on the Stage, but your entire animation exists for only a single frame. To create more time on the Timeline, you must add additional frames.

**1** Select frame 48 in the background layer.

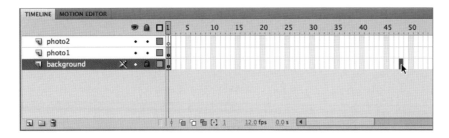

2   Choose Insert > Timeline > Frame (F5). You can also right-click (Windows) or Ctrl-click (Mac OS) and choose Insert Frame from the context menu that pops up.

Flash adds frames in the background layer up to the selected point, frame 48.

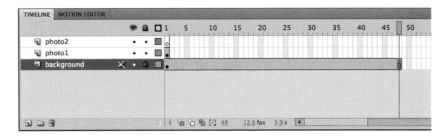

3   Select frame 48 in the photo1 layer.

4   Choose Insert > Timeline > Frame (F5). You can also right-click/Ctrl-click and choose Insert Frame from the context menu.

Flash adds frames in the photo1 layer up to the selected point, frame 48.

5   Select frame 48 in the photo2 layer and insert frames to this layer.

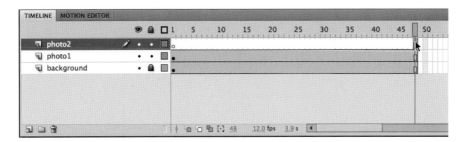

You now have three layers, all with 48 frames on the Timeline. Since the frame rate of your Flash document is 12 frames per second, your current animation lasts 4 seconds.

## Creating a Keyframe

A keyframe indicates a change in content on the Stage. Keyframes are indicated on the Timeline as a circle. An empty circle means there is nothing in that particular layer at that particular time. A filled-in black circle means there is something in that particular layer at that particular time. The background layer, for example, contains a filled keyframe (black circle) in the first frame. The photo1 layer also contains a filled keyframe in its first frame. Both layers contain photos. The photo2 layer, however, contains an empty keyframe in the first frame, indicating that it is currently empty.

You'll insert a keyframe in the photo2 layer at the point in time when you want the next photo to appear.

1   Select frame 18 on the photo2 layer. As you select a frame, Flash displays the frame number beneath the Timeline.

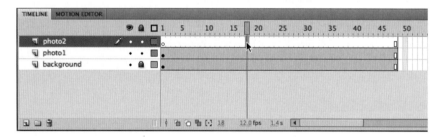

2   Choose Insert > Timeline > Keyframe (F6).

A new keyframe, indicated by an empty circle, appears in the photo2 layer in frame 18.

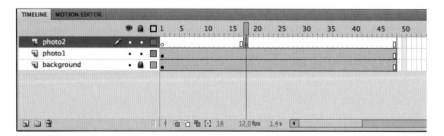

**3** Select the new keyframe at frame 18 in the photo2 layer.

**4** Drag the photo2.jpg item from your library onto the Stage.

The empty circle at frame 18 becomes filled, indicating there is now a change in the photo2 layer. At frame 18, another photo appears on the Stage. You can click and drag the red playhead from the top of the Timeline to "scrub," or show what's happening on the Stage at any point along the Timeline. You'll see that the background photo and photo1 remain on the Stage throughout the Timeline while photo2 appears at frame 18.

Understanding frames and keyframes is essential for mastering Flash. Be sure you understand how the photo2 layer contains 48 frames with 2 keyframes—an empty keyframe at frame 1 and a filled keyframe at frame 18.

## Moving a Keyframe

If you want your photo2.jpg to appear later or earlier, you need to move the keyframe in which it appears later or earlier along the Timeline. You can easily move any keyframe along the Timeline by simply selecting it and then dragging it to a new position.

**1** Select the keyframe in frame 18 on the photo2 layer.

**2** Move your mouse cursor slightly and you'll see a box icon appear near your cursor indicating that you can reposition the keyframe.

**3** Click and drag the keyframe to frame 12 in the photo2 layer.

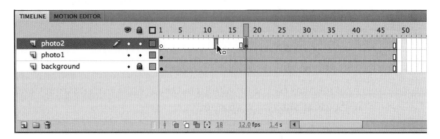

The photo2.jpg now appears on the Stage much earlier in the animation.

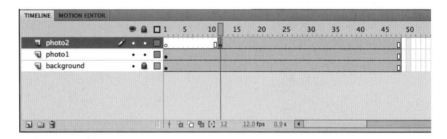

## Removing Keyframes

If you want to remove a keyframe, do not press the Delete key! Doing so will delete the contents of that keyframe on the Stage. Instead, select the keyframe and choose Modify > Timeline > Clear Keyframe (Shift+F6). Your keyframe will be removed from the Timeline.

# Organizing Layers in a Timeline

At this point, your working Flash file has only three layers: a background layer, a photo1 layer, and a photo2 layer. You'll be adding additional layers for this project, and like most other projects, you'll end up having to manage multiple layers. Layer folders help you group related layers to keep your Timeline organized and manageable. Think of it as making folders for related documents on your desktop. Although it may take some time to create the folders, you'll save time later because you'll know exactly where to look for a specific layer.

## Creating Layer Folders

For this project, you'll continue to add layers for additional photos, and you'll place those layers in a layer folder.

1   Select the photo2 layer and click the Add New Layer button ( ![icon] ).

2   Name the layer **photo3**.

3   Insert a keyframe at frame 24.

4   Drag the photo3.jpg from the library on to the Stage.

    You now have four layers. The top three contain photos of scenes from Coney Island that appear at different keyframes.

5   Select the photo3 layer and click the Insert Layer Folder icon ( ![icon] ).

    A new layer folder appears above the photo3 layer.

6   Name the folder **photos**.

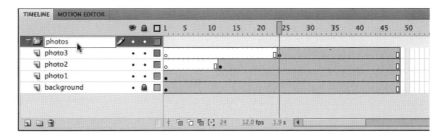

## Adding Layers to Layer Folders

Now you'll add the photo layers to the photo folder. As you arrange layers, remember that Flash displays the layers in the order in which they appear in the Timeline, with the top layer at the front and the bottom layer at the back.

1   Drag the photo1 layer into the photo folder.

Notice how the bold line indicates the destination of your layer. When a layer is placed inside a folder, the layer name becomes indented.

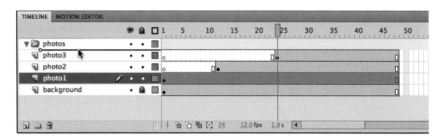

2   Drag the photo2 layer into the photo folder.

3   Drag the photo3 layer into the photo folder.

All three photo layers should be in the photo folder.

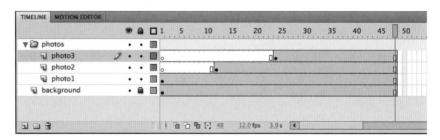

You can collapse the folder by clicking on the arrow. Expand the folder by clicking on the arrow again. Be aware that if you delete a layer folder, you delete all the layers inside that folder as well.

## Changing the Appearance of the Timeline

You can adjust the Timeline's appearance to accommodate your workflow. When you want to see more layers, select Short from the Frame View pop-up menu in the upper-right corner of the Timeline. The Short command decreases the height of frame cell rows.

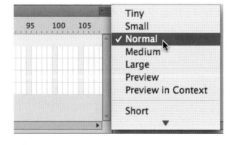

You can also change the width of the frame cells by selecting Tiny, Small, Normal, Medium, or Large.

# Using the Property Inspector

The Property inspector gives you quick access to the attributes you're most likely to need. What appears in the Property inspector depends on what you've selected. For example, if nothing is selected, the Property inspector includes options for the general Flash document including changing the Stage color or dimensions; if an object on the Stage is selected, the Property inspector shows its $x$ and $y$ coordinates. You'll use the Property inspector to move your photos on the Stage.

## Positioning an Object on the Stage

You'll begin by moving the photos with the Property inspector. You'll also use the Transform panel to rotate the photos.

1  In frame 1 of the Timeline, select the photo1.jpg that you dragged onto the Stage in the photo1 layer. A blue outline indicates that the object is selected.

2  In the Property inspector, type **30** for the X value and **0** for the Y value. Press Enter/Return to apply the values. You can also simply click and drag your mouse cursor over the X and Y values to change their positions. The photo moves to the left side of the Stage.

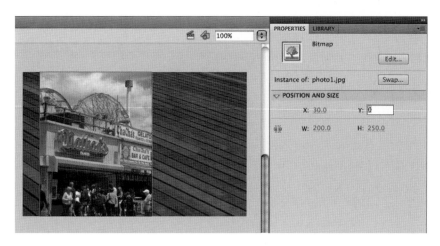

The X and Y values are measured on the Stage from the top-left corner. X begins at 0 and increases to the right, and Y begins at 0 and increases going down. The registration point for imported photos is at the top-left corner.

3  Choose Window > Transform to open the Transform panel.

● **Note:** If the Property inspector is not open, choose Window > Properties > Properties, or press Ctrl/Command+F3.

**4** In the Transform panel, select Rotate, and type **-12** in the Rotate box, or click and drag over the value to change the rotation. Press Enter/Return to apply the value.

**5** Select frame 12 of the photo2 layer. Now click on the photo2.jpg on the Stage.

**6** Use the Property inspector and Transform panel to position and rotate the second photo in an interesting way. Use X=40, Y=0, and a Rotate of 8 to give it some contrast with the first photo.

**7** Select frame 24 in the photo3 layer. Now click on the photo3.jpg on the Stage.

**8** Use the Property inspector and Transform panel to position and rotate the third photo in an interesting way. Use X=20, Y=25, and a Rotate of -2 to give it some contrast with the other photos.

# Working with Panels

Just about everything you do in Flash involves a panel. In this lesson, you use the Library panel, Tools panel, Property inspector, Transform panel, History panel, and the Timeline. In later lessons, you'll use the Actions panel, the Color panel, the Motion panel, and other panels that let you control various aspects of your project. Because panels are such an integral part of the Flash workspace, it pays to know how to manage them.

To open any panel in Flash, choose its name from the Window menu. In a few cases, you may need to choose the panel from a submenu, such as Window > Other Panels > History.

By default, the Property inspector, Library panel, and Tools panel appear together at the right of the screen, the Timeline and Motion Editor are at the bottom, and the Stage is on the top. However, you can move a panel to any position that is convenient for you.

- To undock a panel from the right side of the screen, drag it by its tab to a new location.

- To dock a panel, drag it by its tab into the dock at a new position on the screen. You can drag it to the top, bottom, or in between other panels. A blue highlight indicates where you can dock a panel.

- To group a panel with another, drag its tab onto the other panel's tab.

- To move a panel group, drag the group by its dark gray top bar.

You also have the option of displaying most of the panels as icons to save space but still maintain quick access. Click the upper-right arrows to collapse the panels to icons. Click the arrows again to expand the panels.

# Using the Tools Panel

The Tools panel—the long, narrow panel on the far right side of the work area—contains selection tools, drawing and type tools, painting and editing tools, navigation tools, and tool options. You'll use the Tools panels frequently to switch from the Selection tool to the Text tool to a drawing tool. When you select a tool, check the options area at the bottom of the panel for more options and other settings appropriate for your task.

## Selecting and Using a Tool

When you select a tool, the options available at the bottom of the Tools panel and the Property inspector change. For example, when you select a drawing tool, the Object Drawing mode and Snap To Object options appear. When you select the Zoom tool, the Enlarge and Reduce options appear.

The Tools panel contains too many tools to display all at once. Some tools are arranged in groups in the Tools panel; only the tool you last selected from a group is displayed. A small triangle in the lower-right corner of the tool's button indicates there are other tools in the group. Click and hold the icon for the visible tool to see the other tools available, and then select one from the pop-up menu.

You'll use the Text tool to add a title to your animation.

1  Select the top layer in the Timeline, and then click the Insert Layer button.

2  Name the new layer **text**.

3  Lock the other layers below it so you don't accidentally move anything into them.

4  In the Timeline, move the playhead to frame 36 and select frame 36 in the text layer.

5  Choose Insert > Timeline > Keyframe (F6) to insert a new keyframe at frame 36 in the text layer.

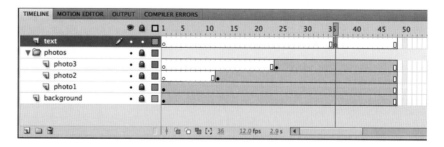

You will create text to appear at frame 36 in this layer.

**6** In the Tools panel, select the Text tool, which is indicated by the large capital letter T.

**7** In the Property inspector, choose Static Text from the pull-down menu.

Static Text is the option for any text that is used for display purposes. Dynamic and Input Text are special text options for more interactive purposes and can be controlled with ActionScript.

**8** Select a font and size in the Property inspector. Your computer may not have the exact same fonts as those shown in this lesson, but choose one that is close in appearance.

**9** Click on the colored square in the Property inspector to choose a text color. You can click on the color wheel at the upper right to access the Adobe Color Picker, or you can change the Alpha percentage at the upper right, which determines the level of transparency.

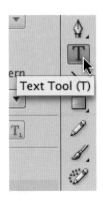

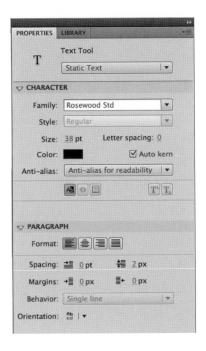
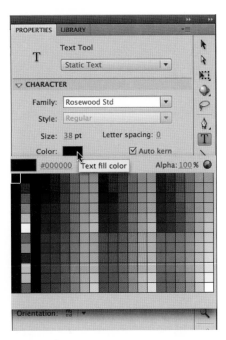

**10** Make sure that the empty keyframe in frame 36 of the title layer is selected, and then click on the Stage where you want to begin adding text.

**11** Type in a title that describes the photos that are being displayed on the Stage.

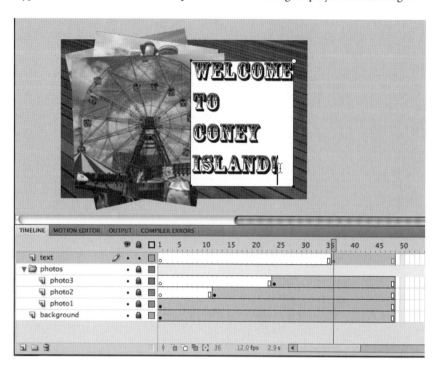

**12** Exit the Text tool by selecting the Selection tool ( ).

**13** Use the Property inspector or the Transform panel to reposition or rotate your text on the Stage, if you wish.

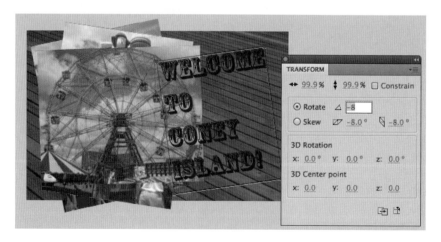

**14** Your animation for this lesson is finished! Compare your file with the final file, 01End.fla.

# Tools Panel Overview

The Tools panel contains selection tools, drawing and painting tools, and navigation tools. The options area in the Tools panel lets you modify the selected tool. The expanded menu on the right shows the hidden tools. The black squares on the expanded menu to the right indicate the default tool that appears in the Tools panel. The single capital letters in parentheses indicate the keyboard shortcuts to select those tools. Notice how the tools are grouped together by similar function.

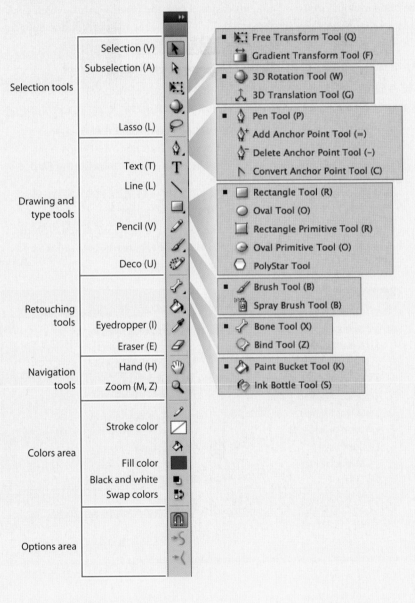

# Undoing Steps in Flash

In a perfect world, everything would go according to plan. But sometimes you need to move back a step or two and start over. You can undo steps in Flash using the Undo command or the History panel.

To undo a single step in Flash, choose Edit > Undo or press Ctrl/Command+Z. To redo a step you've undone, choose Edit > Redo.

To undo multiple steps in Flash, it's easiest to use the History panel, which displays a list of all the steps you've performed since you opened the current document. Closing a document clears its history.

To open the History panel, choose Window > Other Panels > History.

For example, if you aren't satisfied with the newly added text, you can undo your work and return your Flash document to a previous state.

1 Choose Edit > Undo to undo the last action you made. You can choose the Undo command multiple times to move backward up to 100 steps. You can change the maximum number of Undo commands by selecting Flash > Preferences.

2 Choose Window > Other Panels > History to open the History panel.

● **Note:** If you remove steps in the History panel and then perform additional steps, the removed steps will no longer be available.

3 Drag the History panel slider up to the step just before your mistake. Steps below that point are dimmed in the History panel and are removed from the project. To add a step back, move the slider back down.

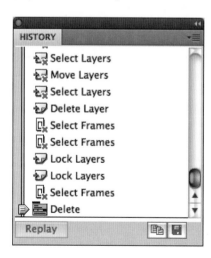 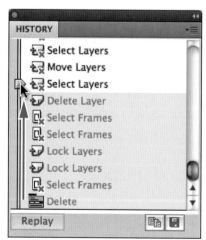

# Previewing Your Movie

As you work on a project, it's a good idea to preview it frequently to ensure that you're achieving the desired effect. To quickly see how an animation or movie will appear to a viewer, choose Control > Test Movie. You can also press Ctrl+Enter or Command+Return to preview your movie.

1   Choose Control > Test Movie. Flash opens and plays the movie in a separate window.

Flash automatically loops your movie in this preview mode. If you don't want the movie to loop, choose Control > Loop to deselect the option.

2   Close the preview window.

# Publishing Your Movie

● **Note:** You'll learn more about publishing options in Lesson 10.

When you're ready to share your movie with others, publish it from Flash. For most projects, Flash will create an HTML file and an SWF file. The SWF file is your final Flash movie, and the HTML file tells your Web browser how to display the SWF file. You'll need to upload both files to the same folder on your Web server. Always test your movie after uploading it to be certain that it's working properly.

1  Choose File > Publish Settings.

2  Click the Formats tab.

3  Select Flash (.swf) and HTML (.html).

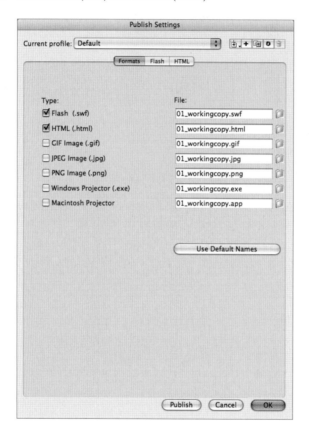

**4** Click the HTML tab.

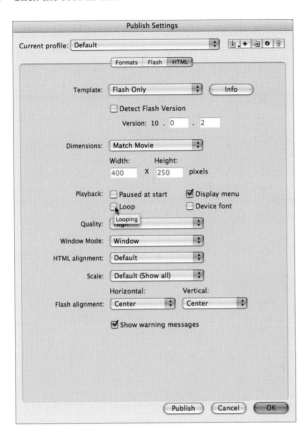

**5** Deselect the Loop option.

**6** Click Publish.

**7** Click OK to close the dialog box.

**8** Navigate to the Lesson01/01Start folder to see the files Flash created.

# Finding Resources for Using Flash

**Note:** If Flash detects that you are not connected to the Internet when you start the application, choosing Help > Flash Help opens the Help HTML pages installed with Flash. For more up-to-date information, view the Help files online or download the current PDF for reference.

For complete and up-to-date information about using Flash panels, tools, and other application features, visit the Adobe Web site. Choose Help > Flash Help. You'll be connected to the Adobe Community Help Web site, where you can search Flash Help and support documents, as well as other Web sites relevant to Flash users. You can narrow your search results to view only Adobe help and support documents as well.

If you plan to work in Flash when you're not connected to the Internet, download the most current PDF version of Flash Help from www.adobe.com/go/documentation.

For additional resources, such as tips and techniques and the latest product information, check out the Adobe Community Help page at community.adobe.com/help/main.

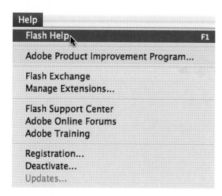

# Checking for Updates

Adobe periodically provides updates to software. You can easily obtain these updates through Adobe Updater, as long as you have an active Internet connection.

1  In Flash, choose Help > Updates. The Adobe Updater automatically checks for updates available for your Adobe software.

2  In the Adobe Updater dialog box, select the updates you want to install, and then click Download And Install Updates to install them.

● **Note:** To set your preferences for future updates, click Preferences. Select how often you want Adobe Updater to check for updates, for which applications, and whether to download them automatically. Click OK to accept the new settings.

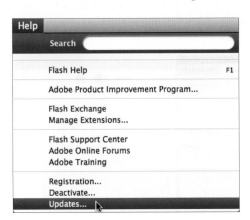

z

# Review Questions

1  What is the Stage?

2  What's the difference between a frame and a keyframe?

3  What's a hidden tool, and how can you access it?

4  Name two methods to undo steps in Flash and describe them.

5  How can you find answers to questions you have about Flash?

# Review Answers

1  The Stage is the area viewers see when a movie is playing in Flash Player or a Web browser. It contains the text, images, and video that appear on the screen. Objects that you store on the Pasteboard outside of the Stage do not appear in the movie.

2  A frame is a measure of time on the Timeline. A keyframe is represented on the Timeline with a circle and indicates a change in content on the Stage.

3  Because there are too many tools to display at once in the Tools panel, some tools are grouped, and only one tool in the group is displayed. (The tool you most recently used is the one shown.) Small triangles appear on tool icons to indicate that hidden tools are available. To select a hidden tool, click and hold the tool icon for the tool that is shown, and then select the hidden tool from the menu.

4  You can undo steps in Flash using the Undo command or the History panel. To undo a single step at a time, choose Edit > Undo. To undo multiple steps at once, drag the slider up in the History panel.

5  Choose Help > Flash Help to browse or search Flash Help for information about using Flash CS4 and ActionScript 3.0. Choose Help > Flash Support Center or visit www. adobe.com to see tutorials, tips, and other resources for Flash users.

# 2 WORKING WITH GRAPHICS

## Lesson Overview

In this lesson, you'll learn how to do the following:

- Draw rectangles, ovals, and lines
- Understand the difference between drawing modes
- Modify the shape, color, and size of drawn objects
- Understand fill and stroke settings
- Make symmetrical patterns
- Create and edit curves
- Apply gradients and transparencies
- Group elements
- Create and edit text

 This lesson will take approximately 90 minutes to complete. If needed, remove the previous lesson folder from your hard drive and copy the Lesson02 folder onto it.

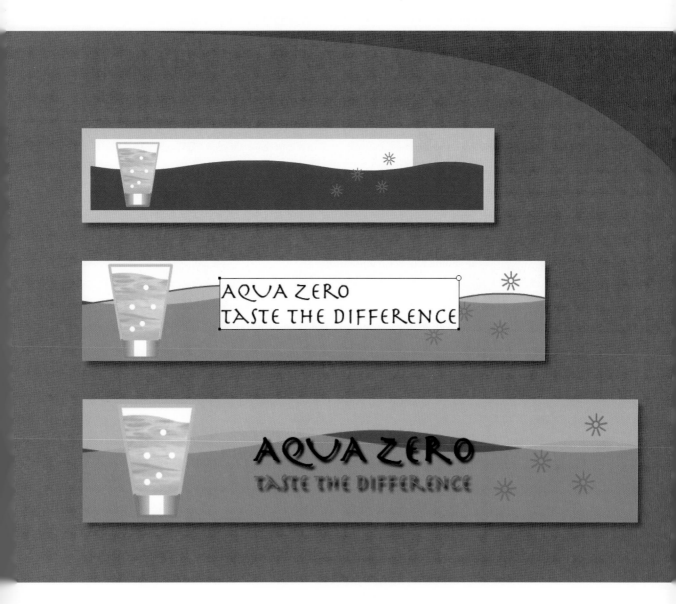

You can use rectangles, ovals, and lines to create interesting, complex graphics and illustrations in Flash. Combine them with gradients, transparencies, text, and filters for even greater possibilities.

# Getting Started

Start by viewing the finished movie to see the animation you'll be creating in this lesson.

1   Double-click the 02End.swf file in the Lesson02/02End folder to view the final project.

The project is a simple static illustration for a banner ad. This illustration is for Aqua Zero, a fictional company. In this lesson, you'll draw the shapes, modify them, and learn to combine simple elements to create more complex visuals. You won't create any animation just yet. After all, you must learn to walk before you can run! And learning to create and modify graphics is an important step before doing any Flash animation.

2   Choose File > New. In the New Document dialog box, choose Flash File (ActionScript 3.0).

3   In the Property inspector, make the Stage size 700 pixels by 150 pixels and make the color of the Stage a light blue.

4   Choose File > Save. Name the file **02_workingcopy.fla** and save it in the 02Start folder. Saving your file right away is a good working habit and ensures that your work won't be lost if the application or your computer crashes.

# Understanding Strokes and Fills

Every graphic in Flash starts with a shape. A shape is made of two components: the *fill*, or the insides of a shape, and the *stroke*, or the outline of the shape. If you can always keep these two components in mind, you're well on your way to creating beautiful and complicated visuals.

The fill and the stroke are independent of each other, so you can modify or delete either without affecting the other. For example, you can create a rectangle with a blue fill and a red stroke, and then later change the fill to purple and delete the red stroke entirely. All you'll be left with is a purple rectangle without an outline.

# Creating Rectangles

Flash includes several drawing tools, which work in different drawing modes. Many of your creations will begin with simple shapes such as rectangles and ovals, so it's important that you're comfortable drawing them, modifying their appearance, and applying fills and strokes.

You'll begin by drawing the glass of fizzy drink.

1 Select the Rectangle tool ▣ from the Tools panel. Make sure the Object Drawing mode icon ◯ is not selected.

2 Choose a stroke color and a fill color from the bottom of the Tools panel. The stroke and fill can be any color, but make sure a color is selected for each.

3 On the Stage, draw a rectangle that is about twice as tall as it is wide. You'll specify the exact size and position of the rectangle in step 6.

● **Note:** Flash applies the default fill and stroke to the rectangle, which is determined by the last fill and stroke you applied. You'll specify a different fill and stroke for the rectangle in the following sections.

4 Select the Selection tool.

5 Drag the Selection tool around the entire rectangle to select the stroke and the fill. When a shape is selected, Flash displays it with white dots. You can also double-click a shape, and Flash will select both the stroke and fill of the shape.

6 In the Property inspector, type **95** for the width and **135** for the height. Press Enter/Return to apply the values.

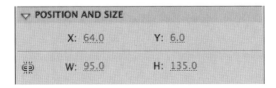

## Adding a Bitmap Fill

The *fill* is the interior of the drawn object. You can apply a solid color, a gradient, or a bitmap image (such as a TIFF, JPEG, or GIF file) as a fill in Flash, or you can specify that the object has no fill. For this lesson, to give the glass the appearance of holding liquid, you'll import an image of water to use as the fill. You can import a bitmap file in the Color panel.

**1** Make sure the entire rectangle is still selected. If necessary, drag the Selection tool around it again.

● **Note:** Be sure to click the Fill Color icon, not the Fill Color box. Clicking the Fill Color box opens the Adobe Color Picker, which you don't need when you're importing a bitmap.

**2** Open the Color panel (Window > Color). In the Color panel, click the Fill Color icon .

**3** Select Bitmap from the Type menu.

**4** In the Import to Library dialog box, navigate to the Water.tif file in the Lesson02/02Start folder.

**5** Select the Water.tif file and click Open.

The rectangle fills with the water image.

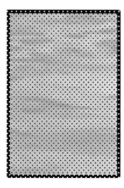

## Specifying Stroke Properties

The *stroke* is the outline of the object, in this case a rectangle. You can apply attributes to the stroke that are different from those of the fill; you can also specify that the object has no stroke. You'll give the rectangle a solid gray outline.

1   Select the rectangle on the Stage, if it isn't already selected.

2   In the Property inspector, click the Stroke Color box 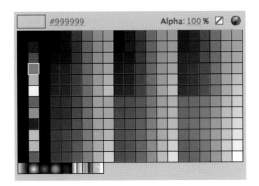.

3   In the Color Picker, select the fourth box down on the left, a gray color. Or, type **#999999** in the box.

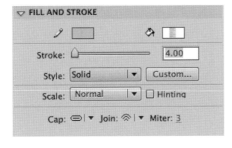

**Note:**  Each color has a hexadecimal value in Flash, HTML, and many other applications. Light gray is #999999; white is #FFFFFF; black is #000000. Appendix A lists the colors with their hexadecimal values. You may find it handy to memorize the values for the colors you use most often.

4   Type **4** in the Stroke Height box, and press Enter/Return to apply the value.

The rectangle should now have the water bitmap fill and a thick gray stroke.

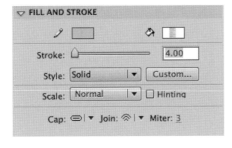

## Modifying Objects

Now you'll make the rectangle look more like a drinking glass. You'll use the Free Transform tool to nudge the bottom corners inward. With the Free Transform tool, you can adjust points on lines and shape outlines.

1 In the Tools panel, select the Free Transform tool ▓.

2 Drag the Free Transform tool around the rectangle on the Stage to select it.

Transformation handles appear on the rectangle.

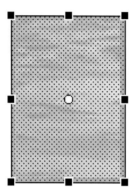

3 Press Ctrl/Command+Shift as you drag one of the corners inward. Pressing these keys lets you move both corners the same distance simultaneously.

4 Click outside the shape to deselect it.

The bottom of the rectangle is narrow, and the top is wide. It now looks more like a drinking glass.

# Flash Drawing Modes

Flash provides three drawing modes, which determine how objects interact with each other on the Stage and how you can edit them. By default, Flash uses merge drawing mode, but you can enable object drawing mode or use the Rectangle Primitive or Oval Primitive tool to use the primitive drawing mode.

**Merge drawing mode**

In this mode, Flash merges drawn shapes, such as rectangles and ovals, where they overlap, so that multiple shapes appear to be a single shape. If you move or delete a shape that has been merged with another, the overlapping portion is permanently removed.

## Object drawing mode

In this mode, Flash does not merge drawn objects; they remain distinct and separate, even when they overlap. To enable object drawing mode, select the tool you want to use, and then click the Object Drawing icon in the options area of the Tools panel.

To convert an object to shapes (merge drawing mode), select it and press Ctrl/Command+B. To convert a shape to an object (object drawing mode), select it and choose Modify > Combine Object > Union.

## Primitive drawing mode

When you use the Rectangle Primitive tool or the Oval Primitive tool, Flash draws the shapes as separate objects. Unlike regular objects, however, you can modify the corner radius of rectangle primitives, as well as the start and end angle and the inner radius of oval primitives using the Property inspector.

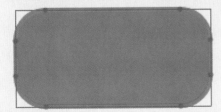

# Using a Gradient Fill

In a *gradient*, one color gradually changes into another. Flash can create *linear* gradients, which change color horizontally, vertically, or diagonally; or *radial* gradients, which change color moving outward from a central focal point. You'll use a linear gradient fill to add weight and depth to the base of the drinking glass.

**1**  Select the Selection tool.

**2**  Drag a rectangle around the bottom of the glass to select an area for its base.

**Note:** Be sure to click the Fill icon, not the Fill Color box.

**3**  In the Color panel (Window > Color), click the Fill icon, and then select Linear from the Type menu.

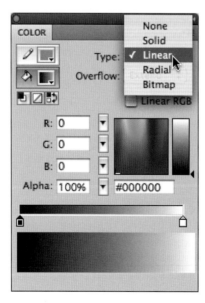

Flash applies a black and white linear gradient to the base of the glass.

## Customizing Gradient Transitions

By default, a linear gradient moves from one color to a second color, but you can use up to 15 color transitions in a gradient in Flash. A *color pointer* determines where the gradient changes from one color to the next. Add color pointers beneath the gradient definition bar to add color transitions.

You'll add a color pointer and adjust the existing pointers to create a gradient that moves from black to white to black in the base of the glass.

1   Click beneath the gradient definition bar to create a new color pointer.

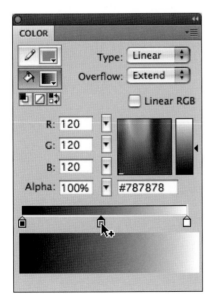

**2** Drag the new color pointer to the middle of the gradient.

**3** Select the new color pointer (the triangle above it turns black when selected), and then type **#FFFFFF** in the Hex value field to specify white for the pointer. Press Enter/Return to apply the color.

**4** Select the far-right color pointer, and then click the black area in the grayscale range above it, or type **#000000**.

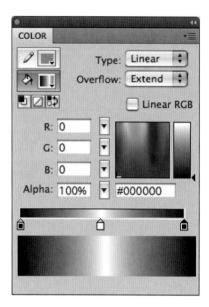

The gradient fill at the base of the glass changes from black to white to black.

## Using the Gradient Transform Tool

In addition to positioning the color pointers for a gradient, you can adjust the size, direction, or center of a gradient fill. To stretch the gradient in the glass, you'll use the Gradient Transform tool.

1 Select the Gradient Transform tool. (The Gradient Transform tool is grouped with the Free Transform tool.)

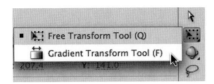

2 Click in the glass base. Transformation handles appear.

3 Drag the square handle on the side of the bounding box to stretch the gradient until the gradient color matches the stroke color of the glass. The gradient fill should blend into the edge of the glass.

● **Note:** Move the circle to change the center of the gradient; drag the arrow circle to rotate the gradient; or drag the arrow in the square to stretch the gradient.

# Making Selections

To modify an object, you must first select it. In Flash, you can make selections using the Selection, Subselection, or Lasso tool. Typically, you use the Selection tool to select an entire object or a section of an object. The Subselection tool lets you select a specific point or line in an object. With the Lasso tool, you can draw a freeform selection.

## Selecting Sections of a Fill and Grouping Objects

To give the base of the glass a stronger highlight, you'll select a section of it and apply a white fill. But first, to prevent accidentally selecting or modifying any part of the water fill, you'll make the glass base section into a group. A group holds together a collection of shapes and other graphics to preserve their integrity. Use groups to organize your drawing.

1   Select the Selection tool.

2   Double-click the gradient at the base of the glass to select the fill and the connected strokes.

3   Choose Modify > Group.

4   Double-click the newly created group to edit it.

Notice that all the other elements on the Stage dim, and the top horizontal bar above the Stage displays Scene 1 Group. This indicates that you are now in a particular group and can edit its contents.

**5** With the Selection tool, select the center area of the base shape. Start the selection area from outside the group—either above or below it—to prevent moving the entire base.

**6** Click the Fill Color icon in the Tools panel, and select white or type **#FFFFFF** in the Color Picker. The selected portion becomes white.

**7** Click the Scene 1 icon in the horizontal bar at the top of the Stage to return to the main scene.

## Using the Lasso Tool

To make the drink more believable, you'll curve or slope the top of the liquid in the glass. The Lasso tool is an ideal tool for this job because you can use it to make an irregular selection.

**Note:** When the Polygon Mode icon is selected, the Lasso tool is constrained to draw polygons.

1   Select the Lasso tool $\mathcal{P}$. Make sure the Polygon Mode icon $\bowtie$ is not selected.

2   Draw a closed shape around the top of the glass fill. Overlap the ends, and then release the mouse.

3   Click the Color Fill icon in the Tools panel, and select white in the Color Picker. The water bitmap is replaced with a solid white fill in the selected area.

The drink is complete! Rename the layer containing the drink **glass**. All that's left to do is to add bubbles and fizz.

# Drawing Ovals

The Oval tool is similar to the Rectangle tool, except, of course, it draws ovals. You'll use the Oval tool to draw a bubble in the drinking glass.

1   Select the Oval tool, which is grouped with the Rectangle tool.

2   In the Property inspector, set the Stroke color to No Color  and the Fill color to white (#FFFFFF).

3   While holding down the Shift key, click and drag the Oval tool on the Stage to draw a circle. Draw the circle outside of the glass so you can keep it intact. When you press the Shift key, the Oval tool draws a perfect circle.

4   You probably can't see your circle since it is white and you have a white Stage. Drag the Selection tool around the entire circle to select both the fill and the stroke.

5   Select the Free Transform tool to resize the bubble.

6   Hold down the Shift key to retain the bubble's proportions and drag a corner handle inward to make the bubble smaller. The resized circle should be about 8 pixels wide and 8 pixels tall. You may find it easier to resize the bubble if you zoom in on it with the Zoom tool. (The Property inspector displays the bubble's height and width.)

● **Note:** By default, the object is scaled relative to the upper-left corner. If you press Alt or Option, the object is scaled relative to its transformation point, represented by the circle icon. When in Free Transform mode, you can drag the transformation point anywhere in the object or even outside of the object.

7   While the bubble is still selected, choose Modify > Group to turn the bubble into a group. By grouping the bubble, you can move it over the glass and reposition it without clipping the shape of the glass or any shapes below it.

8   Move the bubble over the glass.

**9** Now choose Edit > Copy. The bubble is copied.

**10** Choose Edit > Paste in Center. Another bubble appears on the Stage. Move the second bubble over the glass. Repeat the copy and paste process until you have as many bubbles as you like.

# Making Patterns

You can make intricate patterns with the Deco tool 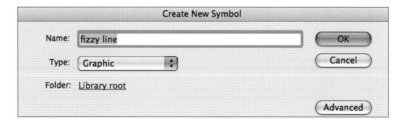, which is a new feature in Flash CS4. Several options allow you to quickly and easily build symmetrical designs, grids, or branching-type flourishes. In this lesson, you'll use the Deco tool to create a symmetrical starburst-like design for the fizzy shapes around the glass.

## Creating a Symbol for the Pattern

Before you can use the Deco tool, you must create a symbol to be used as the base shape that will repeat. You'll learn more about symbols in the next lesson.

**1** From the top menu, choose Insert > New Symbol.

**2** In the Create New Symbol dialog box that appears, enter **fizzy line** for the name and choose the Graphic type symbol. Click OK.

**3** Flash immediately takes you to Symbol-editing mode. Notice the top horizontal bar above the Stage, which indicates you are currently editing the symbol called fizzy line. You will now draw a line for this symbol.

**4** Select the Line tool.

**5** Select a blue color for the stroke and a stroke height of 2.

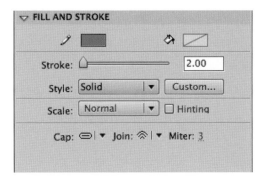

**6** Hold down the Shift key while you draw a line across the center of the Stage, where you see a crosshair representing the center point of your symbol. Make the line about 25 pixels high.

**7** Click on Scene 1 on the horizontal bar above the Stage to return to the main Timeline. Your new symbol called **fizzy line** has been created and is stored in your Library for later use.

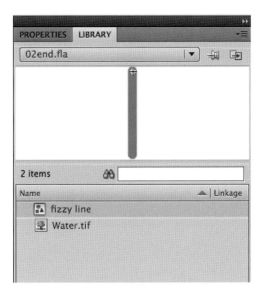

## Using the Deco Tool

You'll create a star shape with the Deco tool.

**1** On the Timeline, insert a new layer and name it **fizz**. You'll draw your fizzy shapes in this layer.

**2** In the toolbar, select the Deco tool 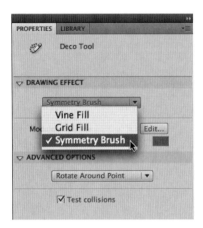.

**3** In the Property inspector, choose the Symmetry Brush option.

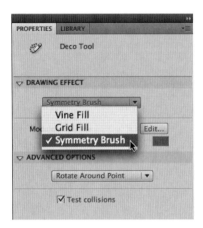

**4** Click the Edit button next to Module to change the shape that will repeat.

**5** In the Swap Symbol dialog box, choose the fizzy line symbol. Click OK.

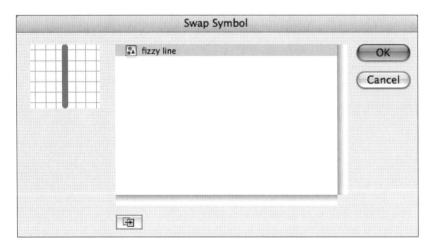

**6** Under the Advanced Options, choose Rotate Around Point.

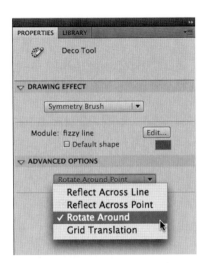

With these Deco tool options, you can create a repeating pattern of the fizzy line symbol that is symmetrical around a point. A green guide appears on the Stage that shows the center point, the main axis, and a secondary axis that determines how frequently the symbol is repeated.

7   Click on the Stage to place your symbol and move it around the green guides until you get the radial pattern you desire. The initial line should be vertical.

8   Drag the secondary green axis closer to the main axis to increase the repetitions.

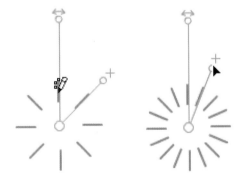

9   When you're done, select the Selection tool to exit the Deco tool.

The resulting pattern is a group consisting of a number of the fizzy line symbols.

## Aligning Objects

Now you'll create a center bubble for the fizzy radiating lines. The bubble should be located exactly in the center of the radiating lines, and for that, you can turn to the Align panel. The Align panel, as you might guess, aligns any number of selected objects horizontally or vertically. It can also distribute objects evenly.

1   Select the Oval tool.

2   Select a blue color for the stroke and no fill. Select a stroke thickness of 2.

3   Select the fizz layer. Hold down the Shift key while you draw a small  circle on the Stage.

4   Now select the Selection tool.

5   Drag the Selection tool over both the star-shaped group and the newly drawn oval. You might have to lock the lower layer so you don't accidentally select the shapes in the lower layers.

6   Open the Align panel (Window > Align).

7   Click on the Align horizontal center.

The star-shaped group and the oval become aligned horizontally.

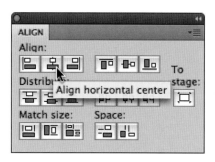

**8** Click on the Align vertical center.

The star-shaped group and the oval become aligned vertically.

 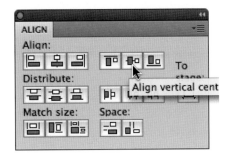

## Breaking Apart and Grouping Objects

You used the Deco tool to create the group of radiating lines and the Align panel to center the bubble with the lines. Now you'll group the fizzy shape into a single entity. To do so, you'll break apart the group of radiating lines and regroup them with the oval.

**1** With the Selection tool, drag a selection around the entire star so that all the lines and the circle are selected.

**2** Choose Modify > Break Apart.

The group of lines breaks into its component parts and becomes a collection of fizzy line symbols.

**3** Choose Modify > Break Apart one more time.

The collection of fizzy line symbols breaks into its component parts and becomes a collection of lines.

**4** Choose Modify > Group.

The lines and center circle become a group.

**5** Copy and paste the fizz group to create multiple sparkles around the Stage.

# Creating Curves

Ovals and rectangles are a good start, but to make more sophisticated graphics, you'll need to create and edit shapes with curves. You can use the Selection tool to pull and push on the edges of shapes to intuitively make curves, or you can use the Pen tool ✎ to have more precise control.

## Using the Pen Tool

Now you'll create a soothing, wave-like background graphic.

**1** Choose Insert > Timeline > Layer, and name the new layer **dark blue wave**.

**2** Drag the layer to the bottom of the layer stack.

**3** Lock all the other layers.

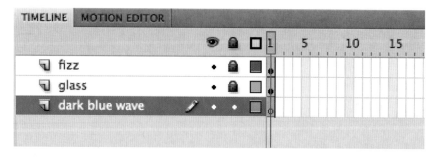

**4** In the Tools panel, select the Pen tool ✎.

**5** Set the Stroke color to blue.

**6** Begin your shape by clicking on the Stage to establish the first anchor point.

**7** Click on another part of the Stage to indicate the next anchor point in your shape. When you want to create a smooth curve, click and drag with the Pen tool.

A handle appears from the anchor point, indicating the curvature of the line.

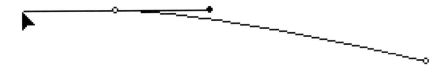

**8** Continue clicking and dragging to build the outline of the wave. Make the width of the wave wider than the Stage.

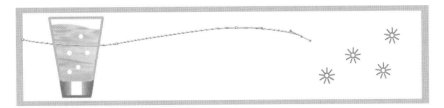

**9** Close your shape by clicking on the first anchor point. Don't worry about getting all the curves perfect. It takes practice to get used to the Pen tool. You'll also have a chance to refine your curves in the next part of the lesson.

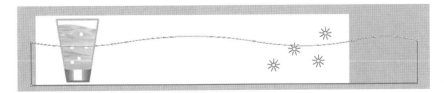

**10** Select the Paint bucket.

**11** Set the Fill color to a dark blue.

**12** Click inside the outline you just created to fill it with color.

## Editing Curves with the Selection and Subselection Tools

Your first try at creating smooth waves probably won't be very good. Use the Selection tool or the Subselection tool to refine your curves.

1   Choose the Selection tool.

2   Hover over a line segment and look at the curve that appears near your cursor. This indicates that you can edit the curve. If a corner appears near your cursor, this indicates that you can edit the vertex.

● **Note:** If you press Alt or Option as you click and drag a curve, you can create a new anchor point.

3   Drag the curve to edit its shape.

4   In the Tools panel, select the Subselection tool ![icon].

5   Click on the outline of the shape.

6   Drag the anchor points to new locations or move the handles to refine the overall shape.

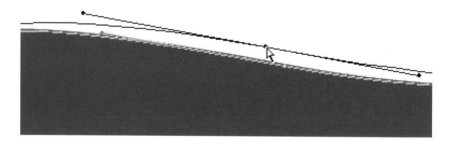

## Deleting or Adding Anchor Points

Use the hidden tools under the Pen tool to delete or add anchor points as needed.

1   Click and hold on the Pen tool to access the hidden tools under it.

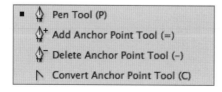

**2** Select the Delete Anchor Point tool 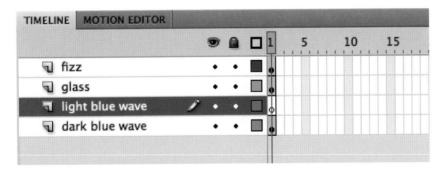.

**3** Click on an anchor point on the outline of the shape to delete it.

**4** Select the Add Anchor Point tool .

**5** Click on the curve to add an anchor point.

# Creating Transparencies

Next, you'll create a second wave to overlap the first wave. You'll make the second wave slightly transparent to create more overall depth. Transparency can be applied to either the stroke or the fill. Transparency is measured as a percentage and is referred to as alpha. An alpha of 100% indicates that a color is totally opaque, whereas an alpha of 0% indicates that a color is totally transparent.

## Modifying the Alpha Value of a Fill

**1** Select the shape in the dark blue wave layer.

**2** Choose Edit > Copy.

**3** Choose Insert > Timeline > Layer and name the new layer **light blue wave**.

**4** Choose Edit > Paste in Place.

The Paste in Place command puts the copied item in the exact same position from where it was copied.

**5** Choose the Selection tool and move the pasted shape slightly to the left or to the right so the crests of the waves are somewhat offset.

6  Select the fill of the shape in the light blue wave layer.

7  In the Color panel (Window > Color), set the fill color to a slightly different blue hue, and then change the Alpha value to **75%**.

● **Note:** You can also change the transparency of a shape from the Property inspector by clicking the Fill Color icon and changing the Alpha value in the pop-up color menu.

The color swatch at the bottom of the Color panel previews your newly selected color. Transparencies are indicated by the gray pattern that appears behind the color swatch.

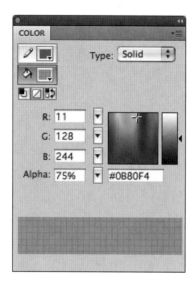

## Matching the Color of an Existing Object

If you want to match a color exactly, you can use the Eyedropper tool to sample a fill or a stroke. After you click on a shape with the Eyedropper tool, Flash automatically provides you with the Paint Bucket tool or the Ink Bottle tool with the selected color and associated properties that you can apply to another object.

1  In the Tools panel, choose the Eyedropper tool.

**2** Click on the blue fill of the shape in the dark blue wave layer.

Your tool automatically changes to the Paint Bucket with the sampled fill color.

**3** Click on the shape in the light blue wave layer.

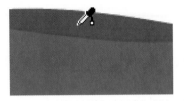 

The fill in the light blue wave layer changes to match that of the one in the dark blue wave layer.

# Creating and Editing Text

Finally, let's add text to complete this illustration. Flash has many text options. For display text that does not change, use Static Text. Two other options, Dynamic Text and Input Text, are reserved for text that can be controlled with ActionScript.

When you create static text on the Stage and publish your project, Flash automatically includes all the necessary fonts to display the text correctly. That means you don't have to worry about your audience having the required fonts to see the text as you intended it.

## Using the Text Tool

**1** Select the light blue wave layer.

**2** Choose Insert > Timeline > Layer and name the new layer **text**.

**3** Choose the Text tool **T**.

**4** In the Property inspector, select Static Text.

**5** Under the Paragraph options, you have additional choices for formatting the text such as justification, spacing, or orientation.

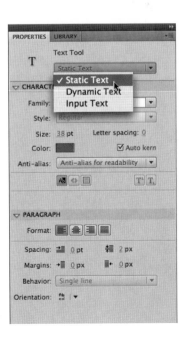

**6** Click on the Stage and begin typing. Enter **Aqua Zero Taste the Difference**. Alternately, you can click and drag out a text box to define the maximum width of your text.

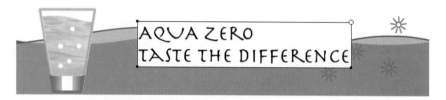

**7** Exit the Text tool by choosing the Selection tool.

## Editing Text

Text remains editable as long as you don't break it apart (Modify > Break Apart). If you break apart text, it results in a collection of individual characters. If you break those individual characters apart, they become simple shapes.

**1** Choose the Selection tool and double-click the text you want to edit. Or, choose the Text tool and click on the text you want to edit.

**2** Highlight the individual characters you want to edit.

**3** In the Property inspector, change the text options. In this lesson, change the first line of text to be 48 points and black and the second line of text to be 26 points and red.

## Hyperlinking Text

Flash makes it easy to create a hyperlink in static text. When a piece of text is hyperlinked, a user can click on it to go to a Web site. You'll link the title of this fictional company to its Web site so users can quickly get more information.

1   Choose the Text tool and click on the text.

2   Highlight the characters in the first line of text.

3   In the Property inspector, under the Options section, enter a URL in the Link field. Be sure to include **http://** before the Web site address.

4   In the Target field, choose _blank so that the Web site loads in a new browser window. Choose _self if you want the Web site to replace the contents of the current browser window.

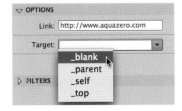

## Adding Special Effects with Filters

Filters are special effects that you can apply to text and to certain symbols. They can quickly help you add a little pizzazz to an otherwise ordinary title. For example, you can add bevels or a glow effect to your text. In this lesson, you'll add a drop shadow to the text to make it appear as if it is floating above the illustration.

1   Choose the Selection tool and click on your text.

2   In the Property inspector, expand the Filters section.

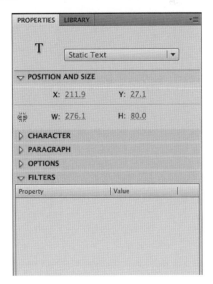

**3** From the bottom of the Filters section, click the Add Filter button and select Drop Shadow.

The Drop Shadow filter appears in the window with all the options to customize its appearance.

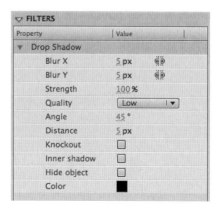

● **Note:** You can add more than one filter to text or to certain symbols. Simply click the Add Filter button and choose another filter. Delete a filter by selecting it and clicking the Delete icon.

Your selected text automatically displays a drop shadow. Move it around and continue to edit the text, and the filter will still apply.

# Review Questions

1  What are the three drawing modes in Flash, and how do they differ?

2  How can you draw a perfect circle using the Oval tool?

3  When would you use each of the selection tools in Flash?

4  What does the Align panel do?

# Review Answers

1  The three drawing modes are merge drawing mode, object drawing mode, and primitive drawing mode.

   - In merge drawing mode, shapes drawn on the Stage merge to become a single shape.

   - In object drawing mode, each object is distinct and remains separate, even when it overlaps another object.

   - In primitive drawing mode, you can modify the angles, radius, or corner radius of an object.

2  To draw a perfect circle, hold down the Shift key as you drag the Oval tool on the Stage.

3  Flash includes three selection tools: the Selection tool, the Subselection tool, and the Lasso tool.

   - Use the Selection tool to select an entire shape or object.

   - Use the Subselection tool to select a specific point or line in an object.

   - Use the Lasso tool to draw a freeform selection area.

4  The Align panel aligns any number of selected elements horizontally or vertically and can distribute elements evenly.

# 3 CREATING AND EDITING SYMBOLS

## Lesson Overview

In this lesson, you'll learn how to do the following:

- Import Illustrator and Photoshop files

- Create new symbols

- Edit symbols

- Understand the difference between symbol types

- Understand the difference between symbols and instances

- Adjust transparency and color

- Apply blending effects

- Apply special effects with filters

- Position objects in 3D space

 This lesson will take about an hour and a half to complete. If needed, remove the previous lesson folder from your hard drive and copy the Lesson03 folder onto it.

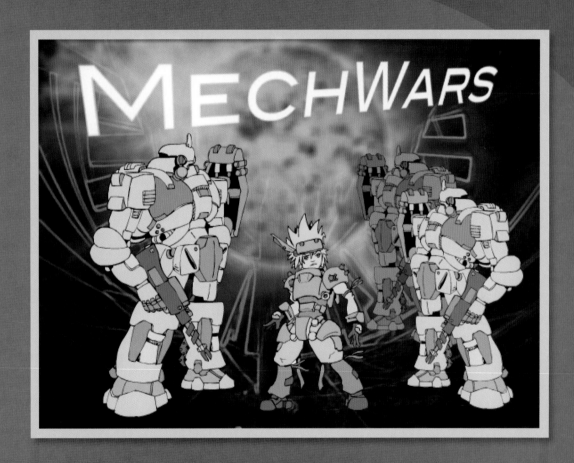

Symbols are reusable assets that are stored in your Library.
The movie clip, graphic, and button symbols are three
types of symbols that you will be creating and using often
for special effects, animation, and interactivity.

# Getting Started

Start by viewing the final project to see what you'll be creating as you learn to work with symbols.

1 Double-click the 03End.swf file in the Lesson03/03End folder to view the final project in Flash.

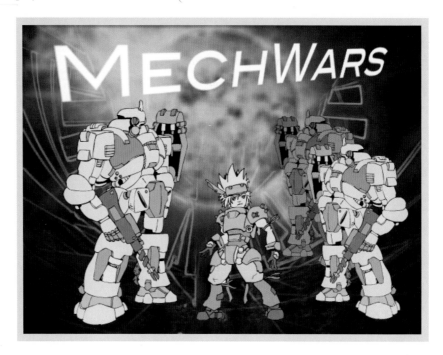

The project is a static illustration of a cartoon frame. In this lesson, you'll use Illustrator graphic files, imported Photoshop files, and symbols to create an attractive image with interesting effects. Learning how to work with symbols is an essential step to creating any animation or interactivity.

2 Close the 03End.swf file.

3 Choose File > New. In the New Document dialog box, choose Flash File (ActionScript 3.0).

4 In the Property inspector, click the Edit button next to the Size options to change the Stage to 600 pixels wide by 450 pixels high.

5 Choose File > Save. Name the file **03_workingcopy.fla** and save it in the 03Start folder.

# Importing Illustrator Files

As you learned in Lesson 2, you can draw objects in Flash using the Rectangle, Oval, and other tools. However, for complex drawings, you may prefer to create the artwork in another application. Adobe Flash CS4 supports native Adobe Illustrator files, so you can create original artwork in that application and then import it into Flash.

When you import an Illustrator file, you can choose which layers in the file to import and how Flash should treat those layers. You'll import an Illustrator file that contains all the characters for the cartoon frame.

1　Choose File > Import > Import to Stage.

2　Select the characters.ai file in the Lesson03/03Start folder.

3　Click Open (Windows) or Import (Mac OS).

4　In the Import to Stage dialog box, make sure all layers are selected. A check mark should appear in the check box next to each layer.

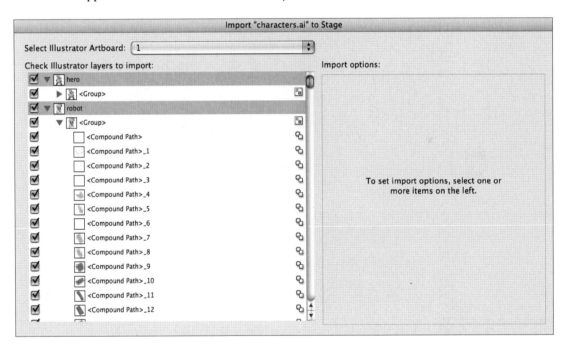

If you only want certain layers to be imported, you can deselect the layers you want to omit.

**5** Choose Flash Layers from the Convert layers to menu, and then select Place objects at original position. Click OK.

Flash imports the Illustrator graphics, and all the layers from the Illustrator file also appear in the Timeline.

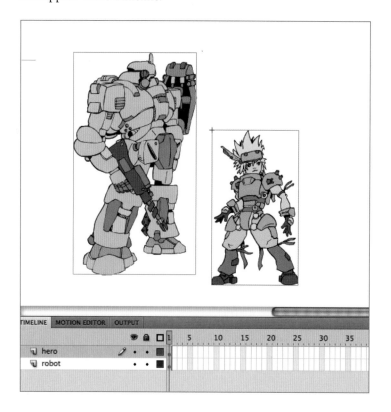

● **Note:** You can select any object displayed in your Illustrator file and choose to import it as a symbol or a bitmap image. In this lesson, you'll just import the Illustrator graphic and take the extra step of converting it to a symbol so you can see the entire process.

# Using Adobe Illustrator with Flash

Flash CS4 can import native Illustrator files and automatically recognize layers, frames, and symbols. If you're more familiar with Illustrator, you may find it easier to design layouts in Illustrator, and then import them into Flash to add animation and interactivity.

Save your Illustrator artwork in Illustrator AI format, and then choose File > Import To Stage or File > Import To Library to import the artwork into Flash. Alternatively, you can even copy artwork from Illustrator and paste it into a Flash document.

## Importing layers

When an imported Illustrator file contains layers, you can import them in any of the following ways:

- Convert Illustrator layers to Flash layers
- Convert Illustrator layers to Flash keyframes
- Convert each Illustrator layer to a Flash graphic symbol
- Convert all Illustrator layers to a single Flash layer

## Importing symbols

Working with symbols in Illustrator is similar to working with them in Flash. In fact, you can use many of the same symbol keyboard shortcuts in both Illustrator and Flash: Press F8 in either application to create a symbol. When you create a symbol in Illustrator, the Symbol Options dialog box lets you name the symbol and set options specific to Flash, including the symbol type (such as movie clip) and registration grid location.

If you want to edit a symbol in Illustrator without disturbing anything else, double-click the symbol to edit it in isolation mode. Illustrator dims all other objects on the artboard. When you exit isolation mode, the symbol in the Symbols panel—and all instances of the symbol—are updated accordingly.

Use the Symbols panel or the Control panel in Illustrator to assign names to symbol instances, break links between symbols and instances, swap a symbol instance with another symbol, or create a copy of the symbol.

For a video tutorial on using symbols between Illustrator and Flash, visit www.adobe.com/go/vid0198.

## Copying and pasting artwork

When you copy and paste (or drag and drop) artwork between Illustrator and Flash, the Paste dialog box appears. The Paste dialog box provides import settings for the Illustrator file you're copying. You can paste the file as a single bitmap object, or you can paste it using the current preferences for AI files. (To change the settings, choose Edit > Preferences in Windows or Flash > Preferences in Mac OS.) Just as when you import the file to the Stage or the Library panel, when you paste Illustrator artwork, you can convert Illustrator layers to Flash layers.

# About Symbols

A *symbol* is a reusable asset that you can use for special effects, animation, or interactivity. There are three kinds of symbols: the graphic, button, and movie clip. Symbols can reduce the file size and download time for many animations because they can be reused. You can use a symbol countless times in a project, but Flash includes its data only once.

Symbols are stored in the Library panel. When you drag a symbol to the Stage, Flash creates an *instance* of the symbol, leaving the original in the Library. An instance is a copy of a symbol located on the Stage. You can think of the symbol as an original photographic negative, and the instances on the Stage as prints of the negative. With just a single negative, you can create multiple prints.

Each of the three kinds of symbols in Flash is used for a specific purpose. You can tell whether a symbol is a graphic 🖼, button 👆, or movie clip 🎬 by looking at the icon next to it in the Library panel.

## Movie Clip Symbols

Movie clip symbols are one of the most common, powerful, and flexible of symbols. When you create animation, you will typically use movie clip symbols. You can apply filters, color settings, and blending modes to a movie clip instance to enhance its appearance with special effects.

Also notable is the fact that movie clip symbols contain their own independent Timeline. You can have an animation inside a movie clip symbol just as easily as you can have an animation on the main Timeline. This makes very complex animations possible; for example, a butterfly flying across the Stage can move from left to right as well as have its wings flapping independently of its movement.

Most important, you can control movie clips with ActionScript to make them respond to the user. For instance, a movie clip can have a drag-and-drop behavior.

## Button Symbols

Button symbols are used for interactivity. They contain four unique keyframes that describe how they appear when the mouse is interacting with them. However, buttons need ActionScript functionality to make them do something.

You can also apply filters, blending modes, and color settings to buttons. You'll learn more about buttons in Lesson 6 when you create a nonlinear navigation scheme to allow the user to choose what to see.

## Graphic Symbols

Graphic symbols are the most basic kind of symbol. Although you can use them for animation, you'll rely more heavily on movie clip symbols.

Graphic symbols are the least flexible symbols, because they don't support ActionScript and you can't apply filters or blending modes to a graphic symbol. However, in some cases when you want an animation inside a graphic symbol to be synchronized to the main Timeline, graphic symbols are useful.

# Creating Symbols

In the previous lesson, you learned how to create a symbol to be used for the Deco tool. In Flash, there are two ways to create a symbol. The first is to have nothing on the Stage selected, and then choose Insert > New Symbol. Flash brings you to symbol-editing mode, where you can begin drawing or importing graphics for your symbol.

The second way is to select existing graphics on the Stage, and then choose Modify > Convert to Symbol (F8). Whatever is selected will automatically be placed inside your new symbol.

Both methods are valid: Which you use depends on your particular workflow preferences. Most designers prefer to use Convert to Symbol because they can create all their graphics on the Stage and see them together before making the individual components into symbols.

For this lesson, you will select the different parts of the imported Illustrator graphic, and then convert the various pieces to symbols.

1   On the Stage, select the cartoon character in the hero layer.

● **Note:** When you use the command Convert to Symbol, you aren't actually "converting" anything, but rather you are placing whatever you've selected inside of a symbol.

2   Choose Modify > Convert to Symbol (F8).

3   Name the symbol **hero** and select Movie Clip for the Type.

4   Leave all other settings as they are. The Registration indicates the center point of your symbol. Leave the registration at the top-left corner.

5   Select Movie Clip for the Type.

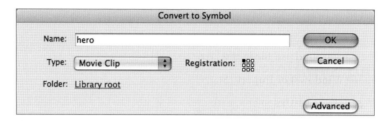

6   Click OK. The hero symbol appears in the Library.

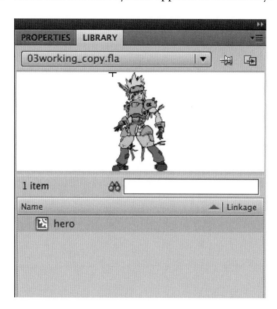

7   Select the other cartoon character in the robot layer and convert it to a movie clip symbol as well. Name it **robot**.

You now have two movie clip symbols in your Library and an instance of each on the Stage as well.

# Importing Photoshop Files

You'll import a Photoshop file for the background. The Photoshop file contains two layers with a blending effect. A blending effect can create special color mixes between different layers. You'll see that Flash can import a Photoshop file with all the layers intact and retain all the blending information as well.

1 Select the top layer in your Timeline.

2 From the top menu, choose File > Import > Import to Stage.

3 Select the background.psd file in the Lesson03/03Start folder.

4 Click Open (Windows) or Import (Mac OS).

5 In the Import to Stage dialog box, make sure all layers are selected. A check mark should appear in the check box next to each layer.

6 Choose the flare layer in the left window.

7 In the options on the right, choose Bitmap image with editable layers styles.

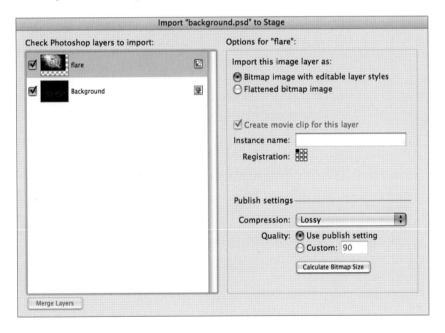

The movie clip symbol icon appears to the right of the Photoshop layer, indicating that the imported layer will be made into a movie clip symbol. The other option, Flatten bitmap image, will not preserve any layer effects such as transparencies or blending.

**8** Choose the Background layer in the left window.

**9** In the options on the right, choose Bitmap image with editable layers styles.

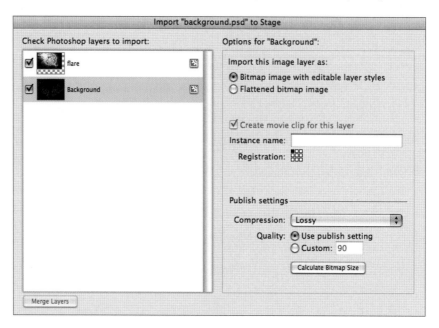

**10** At the bottom of the dialog box, set the Convert layers to Flash Layers option, and select Place layers at original position.

You also have the option of changing the Flash Stage size to match the Photoshop canvas. However, the current Stage is already set to the correct dimensions (600 pixels x 450 pixels).

**11** Click OK. The two Photoshop layers are imported into Flash and placed on separate layers on the Timeline.

The Photoshop images are automatically converted into movie clip symbols and saved in your Library. All the blending and transparency information is preserved. If you select the image in the flare layer, you'll see that the Blending option is set to Lighten in the Property inspector under the Display section.

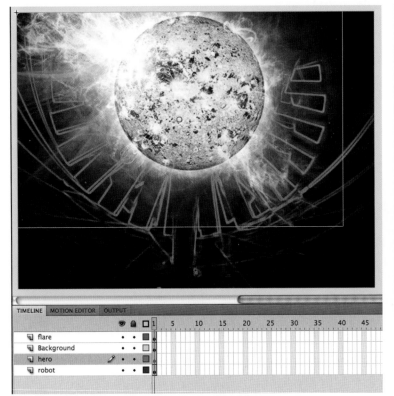
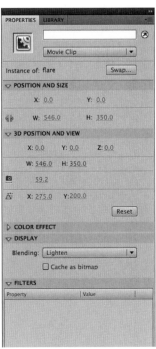

**12** Drag the robot and the hero layers to the top of the Timeline so they overlap the background layers.

## About Image Formats

Flash supports multiple image formats for import. Flash can handle JPEG, GIF, PNG, and PSD (Photoshop) files. Use JPEG files for images that include gradients and subtle variations, such as those that occur in photographs. GIF files are used for images with large solid blocks of color or black and white line drawings. Use PNG files for images that include transparency. Use PSD files if you want to retain all the layer, transparency, and blending information from a Photoshop file.

## Converting a Bitmap Image to a Vector Graphic

Sometimes you'll want to convert a bitmap image to a vector graphic. While Flash handles bitmap images as a series of colored dots (or pixels), vector graphics are handled as a series of lines and curves. This vector information is rendered on the fly, so that the resolution of vector graphics is not fixed like a bitmap image. That means you can zoom in on a vector graphic and your computer will always display it sharply and smoothly. Converting a bitmap image to a vector often has the effect of making it look "posterized" because subtle gradations are converted to editable, discrete blocks of color, which can be an interesting effect.

To convert a bitmap to a vector, import the bitmap image into Flash. Select the bitmap and choose Modify > Bitmap > Trace Bitmap. The options determine how faithful of a trace the vector image will be to the original bitmap.

Below, the left image is an original bitmap and the right image is a vector graphic.

Exercise caution when using the Trace Bitmap command, because a complicated vector graphic is often more memory and computer-processor intensive than the original bitmap image.

## Editing and Managing Symbols

You now have multiple movie clip symbols in your Library and several instances on the Stage. You can better manage the symbols in your Library by organizing them in folders. You can also edit any symbol at any time. If you decide you want to change the color of one of the robot's arms, for example, you can easily go into symbol-editing mode and make that change.

## Adding Folders and Organizing the Library

1   In the Library, right-click/Ctrl-click in an empty space and select New Folder. Alternatively, you can click the New Folder button ▭ at the bottom of the Library panel.

A new folder is created in your Library.

2   Name the folder **characters**.

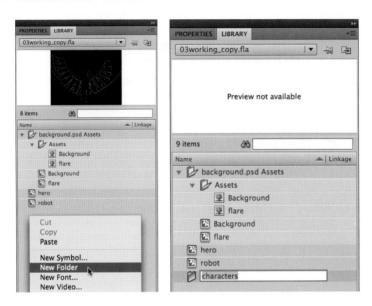

3   Drag the hero and the robot movie clip symbols into the characters folder.

4   You can collapse or expand folders to hide or view their contents and keep your Library organized.

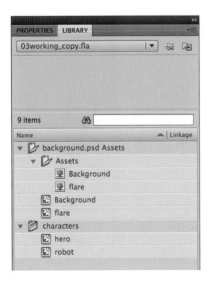

## Editing a Symbol from the Library

1 Double-click the robot movie clip symbol in the Library.

Flash takes you to symbol-editing mode. In this mode, you can see the contents of your symbol, in this case, the robot on the Stage. Notice on the top horizontal bar that you are no longer in Scene 1 but are inside the symbol called robot.

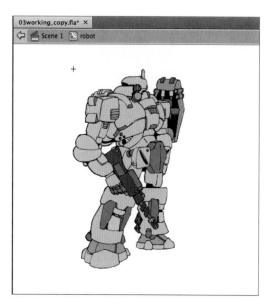

2 Double-click the drawing to edit it. You will need to double-click the drawing groups several times to drill down to the individual shape that you want to edit.

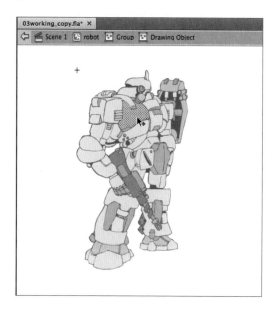

**3** Choose the Paint Bucket tool. Select a new fill color and apply it to the shape on the robot drawing.

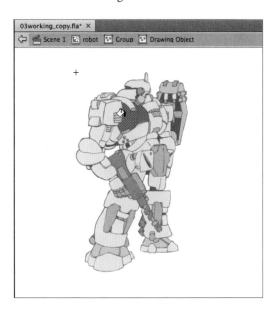

**4** Click on Scene 1 on the top horizontal bar above the Stage to return to the main Timeline.

The movie clip symbol in the Library reflects the changes you made. The instance on the Stage also reflects the changes you made to the symbol. All instances of the symbol on the Stage will change if you edit the symbol.

● **Note:** You can quickly and easily duplicate symbols in the Library. Select the Library symbol, right-click/Ctrl-click, and choose Duplicate. Or, from the top-right Options menu in the Library, choose Duplicate. An exact copy of the selected symbol will be created in your Library.

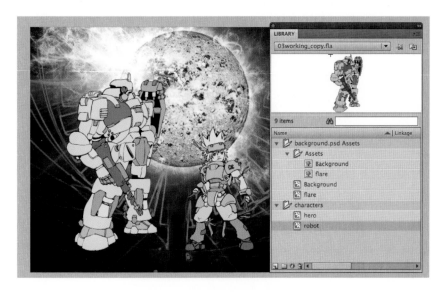

## Editing a Symbol in Place

You may want to edit a symbol in context with the other objects on the Stage. You can do so by double-clicking an instance on the Stage. You'll enter symbol-editing mode, but you'll also be able to see its surroundings. This editing mode is called editing in place.

1   Double-click the robot movie clip instance on the Stage.

Flash dims all other objects on the Stage and takes you to symbol-editing mode. Notice on the top horizontal bar that you are no longer in Scene 1 but are inside the symbol called robot.

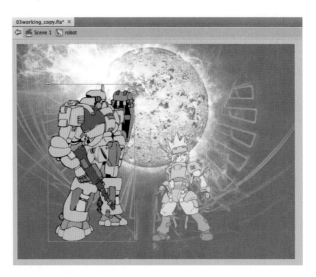

2   Double-click the drawing to edit it. You will need to double-click the drawing groups several times to drill down to the individual shape that you want to edit.

**3** Choose the Paint Bucket tool. Select a new fill color and apply it to the shape on the robot drawing.

**4** Click on Scene 1 on the top horizontal bar above the Stage to return to the main Timeline. You can also just double-click any part of the Stage outside the graphic to return to the next higher group level.

The movie clip symbol in the Library reflects the changes you made. The instance on the Stage also reflects the changes you made to the symbol. All instances of the symbol will change according to the edits you make to the symbol.

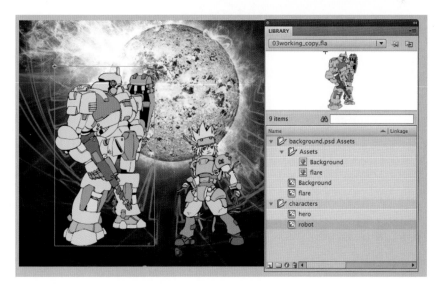

## Breaking Apart a Symbol Instance

If you no longer want an object on the Stage to be a symbol instance, you can use the Break Apart command to return it to its original form.

1 Select the robot instance on the Stage.

2 Choose Modify > Break Apart.

Flash breaks apart the robot movie clip instance. What's left on the Stage is a group, which you can break apart further to edit as you please.

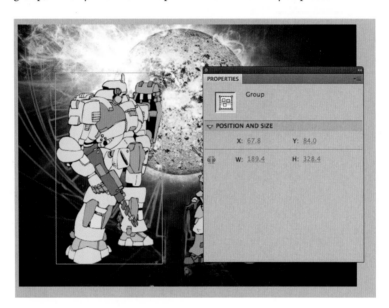

# Changing the Size and Position of Instances

You can have multiple instances of the same symbol on the Stage. Now you'll add a few more robots to create a small robot army. You'll learn how to change the size and position (and even rotation) of each instance individually.

1 Select the robot layer in the Timeline.

**2** Drag another robot symbol from the Library onto the Stage.

A new instance appears.

**3** Choose the Free Transform tool.

Control handles appear around the selected instance.

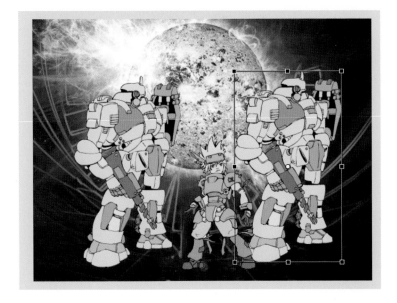

**4** Drag the control handles on the sides of the selection to flip the robot so it is facing in the other direction.

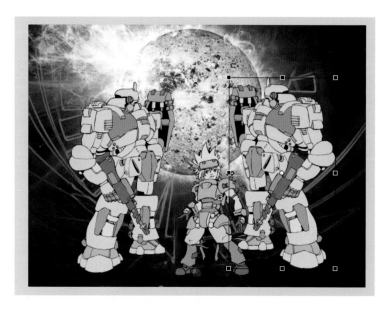

**5** Drag the control handles on the corner of the selection while holding down the Shift key to reduce the size of the robot.

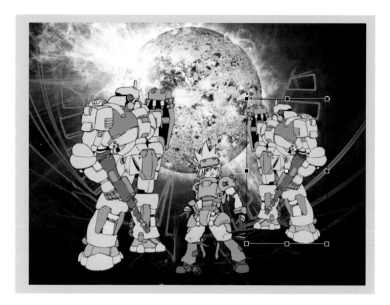

**6** Drag a third robot from the Library onto the Stage. With the Free Transform tool, flip the robot, resize it, and make it overlap the second robot.

The robot army is growing!

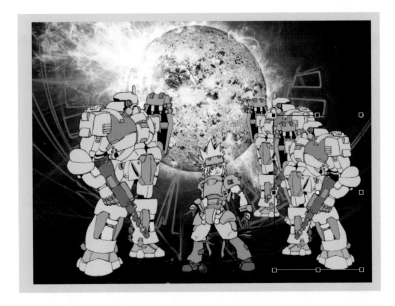

# Changing the Color Effect of Instances

The Color Effect option in the Property inspector allows you to change several properties of any instance: These properties include brightness, tint, or alpha.

Brightness controls how dark or light the instance appears, tint controls the overall coloring, and alpha controls the level of opacity. Decreasing the alpha value decreases the opacity and increases the amount of transparency.

## Changing the Brightness

**1** Using the Selection tool, click on the smallest robot on the Stage.

**2** In the Property inspector, choose Brightness from the Color Effect Style menu.

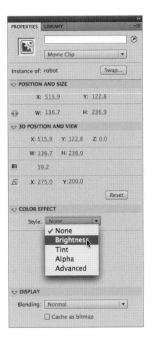

**3** Drag the Bright slider to **-40%**.

The robot instance on the Stage becomes darker and appears to recede into the distance.

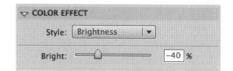

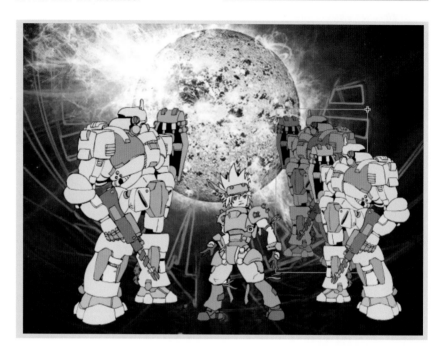

## Changing the Transparency

**1** Select the glowing orb in the flare layer.

**2** In the Property inspector, choose Alpha from the Color Effect Style menu.

**3** Drag the Alpha slider to a value of **75%**.

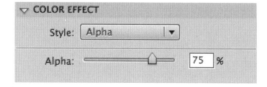

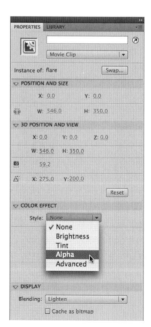

The orb in the flare layer on the Stage becomes more transparent.

**Note:** To reset the Color Effect of any instance, choose None from the Style menu.

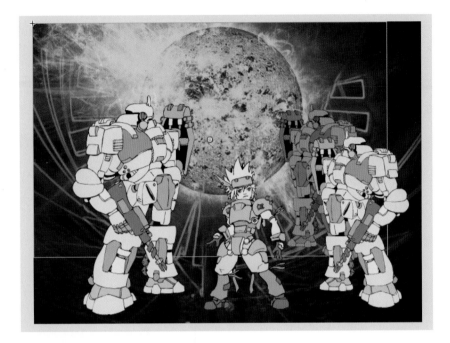

## Understanding Blend Effects

Blending refers to how the colors of an instance interact with the colors below it. You saw how the instance in the flare layer had the Lighten option applied to it (carried over from Photoshop), which integrated it more with the instance in the Background layer.

There are many kinds of Blending options. Some have surprising results, depending on the colors in the instance and the colors in the layers below it. Experiment with all the options to understand how they work. The following figure shows some of the Blending options and their effects on the robot instance over a blue-black gradient.

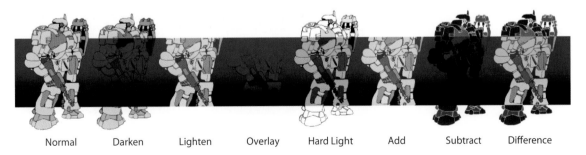

| Normal | Darken | Lighten | Overlay | Hard Light | Add | Subtract | Difference |

# Applying Filters for Special Effects

Filters are special effects that you can apply to movie clip instances. In the Chapter 2 lesson, you used a filter to apply a drop shadow effect to some text. Several filters are available in the Filters section of the Property inspector. Each filter has different options that can refine the effect.

## Applying a Blur Filter

You'll apply a blur filter to some of the instances to help give the scene a greater sense of depth.

1   Select the glowing orb in the flare layer.

2   In the Property inspector, expand the Filters section.

3   Click the Add Filters button at the bottom of the Filters section and select Blur.

The Blur filter appears in the Filters window with options for Blur X and Blur Y.

4   Click the link icon next to the Blur X and Blur Y options to link the blur effect in both directions.

5   Set the Blur X and Blur Y value to **10** pixels.

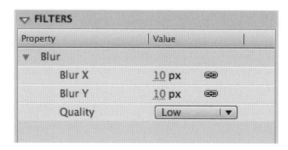

## More Filter Options

At the bottom of the Filters window is a row of options to help you manage and apply multiple filters.

The Presets button lets you save a particular filter and its settings so you can apply it to another instance. The Clipboard button lets you copy and paste any selected filter. The Enable or Disable Filter button lets you see your instance with or without the filter applied. The Reset button resets the filter parameters to their default values.

The instance on the Stage becomes blurry, helping to give an atmospheric perspective to this scene.

● **Note:** It's best to keep the Quality setting for filters on Low. Higher settings are processor-intensive and can bog down performance, especially if you have multiple filters.

## Positioning in 3D Space

New in Flash CS4 is the ability to position and animate objects in real three-dimensional space. However, objects need to be movie clip symbols to move them in 3D. Two tools allow you to position objects in 3D: the 3D Rotation tool and the 3D Translation tool. The Transform panel also provides information for position and rotation.

Understanding the 3D coordinate space is essential for successful 3D placement of objects. Flash divides space using three axes: the $x$, $y$, and $z$ axes. The $x$ axis runs horizontally across the Stage with $x=0$ at the left edge. The $y$ axis runs vertically with $y=0$ at the top edge. The $z$ axis runs into and out of the plane of the Stage (toward and away from the viewer) with $z=0$ at the plane of the Stage.

### Changing the 3D Rotation of an Object

You'll add some text to your image, but to add a little more interest, you'll tilt it to put it in perspective. Think about the beginning text introduction to the *Star Wars* movies and see if you can achieve the same effect.

1   Insert a new layer and rename it **text**.

2   Choose the Text tool from the Tools panel.

3   In the Property inspector, select a large-size font with an interesting color that will add some pizzazz.

4   Click on the Stage in your text layer and begin typing your title.

5   To exit the Text tool, select the Selection tool.

Your text is created, but now you must convert it to a movie clip symbol to rotate it and position it in 3D.

6   While the text on the Stage is still selected, chose Modify > Convert to Symbol.

**7** In the Convert to Symbol dialog box, enter a descriptive name, select Movie Clip type, and click OK.

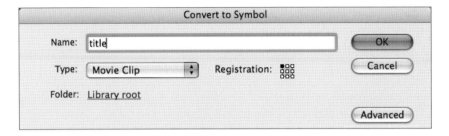

You now have a movie clip symbol in your Library with your text inside. An instance of the movie clip symbol appears on the Stage.

**8** Choose the 3D Rotation tool .

A circular multicolored target appears on the instance. This is a guide for the 3D rotation. It's useful to think of the guides as lines on a globe. The red longitudinal line rotates your instance around the $x$ axis. The green line along the equator rotates your instance around the $y$ axis. The circular blue guide rotates your instance around the $z$ axis.

**9** Click on one of the guides—red for $x$, green for $y$, or blue for $z$—and drag your mouse in either direction to rotate your instance in 3D space.

You can also click and drag the outer orange circular guide to freely rotate the instance in all three directions.

## Changing the 3D Position of an Object

In addition to changing an object's rotation in 3D space, you can move it to a specific point in 3D space. Use the 3D Translation tool, which is hidden under the 3D Rotation tool.

**1**  Choose the 3D Translation tool .

**2**  Click on your text.

A guide appears on the instance. This is a guide for the 3D translation. The red guide represents the *x* axis, the green is the *y* axis, and the blue is the *z* axis.

**3**  Click on one of the guide axes and drag your mouse in either direction to move your instance in 3D space. Notice that your text stays in perspective as you move it around the Stage.

## Resetting the Rotation and Position

If you've made a mistake in your 3D transformations and want to reset the position and rotation of your instance, you can use the Transform panel.

1 Choose the Selection tool and select the instance that you want to reset.

2 Open the Transform panel by choosing Window > Transform.

The Transform panel shows all the values for the *x*, *y*, and *z* angles and positions.

3 Click the Remove Transform button in the lower-right corner of the Transform panel.

The selected instance returns to its original settings.

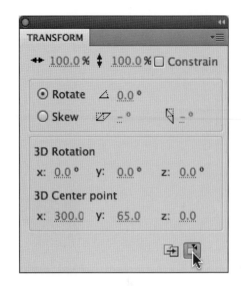

## Understanding the Vanishing Point and the Perspective Angle

Objects in 3D space represented on a 2D surface (such as the computer screen) are rendered with perspective to make them appear as they do in real life. Correct perspective depends on many factors, including the vanishing point and the perspective angle, both of which can be changed in Flash.

The vanishing point determines where on the horizon parallel lines of a perspective drawing converge. Think of railroad tracks and how the parallel tracks converge to a single point as they recede into the distance. The vanishing point is usually at eye level in the center of your field of view, so the default settings are exactly in the middle of the Stage. You can, however, change the vanishing point setting so it appears above or below eye level, or to the right or left.

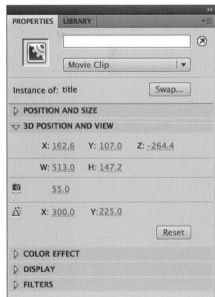

The perspective angle determines how quickly parallel lines converge to the vanishing point. The greater the angle, the quicker the convergence, and therefore, the more severe and distorted the illustration appears.

1 Select an object on the Stage that has been moved or rotated in 3D space.

2 In the Property inspector, expand the 3D Position and View section.

**3** Click and drag on the X and Y values of the Vanishing Point to change the vanishing point, which is indicated on the Stage by intersecting gray lines.

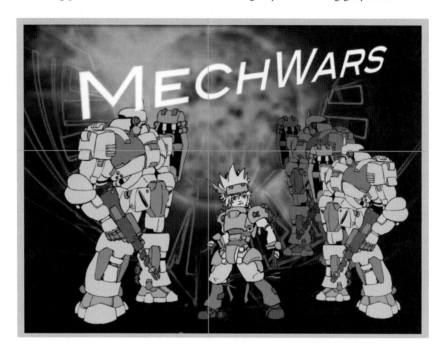

**4** To reset the Vanishing Point to the default values (to the center of the Stage), click the Reset button.

**5** Click and drag on the Perspective Angle value to change the amount of distortion. The greater the angle, the more the distortion.

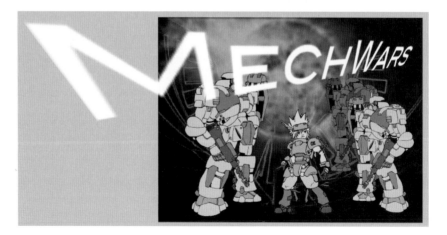

## Review Questions

1  What is a symbol, and how does it differ from an instance?

2  Name two ways that you can create a symbol.

3  When you import an Illustrator file, what happens if you choose to import layers as layers? As keyframes?

4  How can you change the transparency of an instance in Flash?

5  What are the two ways to edit symbols?

## Review Answers

1  A *symbol* is a graphic, button, or movie clip that you create once in Flash and can then reuse throughout your document or in other documents. All symbols are stored in your Library panel. An *instance* is a copy of a symbol located on the Stage.

2  You can create a symbol by choosing Insert > New Symbol, or you can select existing objects on the Stage and choose Modify > Convert to Symbol.

3  When you import layers in an Illustrator file as layers, Flash recognizes the layers in the Illustrator document and adds them as separate layers in the Timeline. When you import layers as keyframes, Flash adds each Illustrator layer to a separate frame in the Timeline and creates keyframes for them.

4  The transparency of an instance is determined by its alpha value. To change the transparency, select Alpha from the Color Effects menu in the Property inspector, and then change the alpha percentage.

5  The two ways to edit symbols are to either double-click the symbol in the Library to enter symbol-editing mode or to double-click the instance on the Stage to edit in place. Editing a symbol in place lets you see the other objects around the instance.

# 4 ADDING ANIMATION

## Lesson Overview

In this lesson, you'll learn how to do the following:

- Animate the position, scale, and rotation of objects

- Adjust the pacing and timing of your animation

- Animate transparency and special effects

- Change the path of the motion

- Create animation inside symbols

- Change the easing of the motion

- Animate in 3D space

 This lesson will take approximately two hours to complete. If needed, remove the previous lesson folder from your hard drive and copy the Lesson04 folder onto it.

Use Flash CS4 to change almost any aspect of an object—position, color, transparency, size, rotation, and more—over time. Motion tweening is the basic technique of creating animation with symbol instances.

# Getting Started

Start by viewing the finished movie file to see the animated title page that you'll create in this lesson.

1 Double-click the 04End.swf file in the Lesson04/04End folder to play the animation.

The project is an animated splash page for a soon-to-be-released fictional motion picture. In this lesson, you'll use motion tweens to animate several components on the page: the cityscape, the main actors, several old-fashioned cars, and the main title.

2 Close the 04End.swf file.

3 Double-click the 04Start.fla file in the Lesson04/04Start folder to open the initial project file in Flash. This file is partially completed and already contains many of the graphic elements imported into the Library for you to use.

4 Choose View > Magnification > Fit in Window, or Fit in Window from the view options above the Stage, so that you can see the entire Stage on your computer screen.

5 Choose File > Save As. Name the file **04_workingcopy.fla**, and save it in the 04Start folder. Saving a working copy ensures that the original start file will be available if you want to start over.

# About Animation

Animation is the movement, or change, of objects through time. Animation can be as simple as moving a box across the Stage from one frame to the next. It can also be much more complex. As you'll see in this lesson, you can animate many different aspects of a single object. You can move objects across the Stage, change their color or transparency, change their size or their rotation, and even animate the special filters that you saw in the previous lesson. You also have control over their path of motion, and even their easing, which is the way an object accelerates or decelerates.

The basic workflow for animation goes like this: To animate objects in Flash, you select the object on the Stage, right-click/Ctrl-click, and choose Create Motion Tween from the context menu. Move the red playhead to a different point in time and move the object to a new position. Flash takes care of the rest.

*Motion tweens* create animation for changes in position on the Stage and for changes in size, color, or other attributes. Motion tweens require you to use a symbol instance. If the object you've selected is not a symbol instance, Flash will automatically ask to convert the selection to a symbol. Flash also automatically separates motion tweens on their own layers, which are called Tween layers. There can only be one motion tween per layer without any other element in the layer. Tween layers allow you to change various attributes of your instance at different keypoints over time. For example, a spaceship could be on the left side of the Stage at the beginning keyframe and at the far-right side of the Stage at an ending key-frame, and the resulting tween would make the spaceship fly across the Stage.

The term "tween" comes from the world of classic animation. Senior animators would be responsible for drawing the beginning and ending poses for their characters. The beginning and ending poses were the keyframes of the animation. Junior animators would then come in and draw the "in-between" frames, or do the "in-betweening." Hence, "tweening" refers to the smooth transitions between keyframes.

# Understanding the Project File

The 04Start.fla file contains a few of the animated elements already or partially completed. Each of the six layers—man, woman, Middle_car, Right_car, footer, and ground—contains an animation. The man and woman layers are in a folder called actors, and the Middle_car and Right_car layers are in a folder called cars.

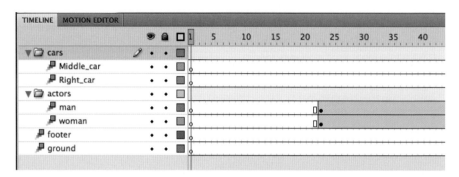

You'll be adding more layers to add an animated cityscape, refining the animation of one of the actors, as well as adding a third car and a 3D title. All the necessary graphic elements have been imported into the Library. The Stage is set at a generous 1280 pixels by 787 pixels to fill up a high-resolution monitor, and the Stage color is black. You might need to choose a different view option to see the entire Stage.

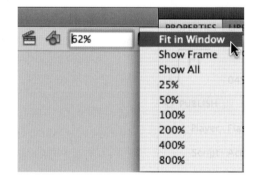

Choose View > Magnification > Fit in Window, or choose Fit in Window from the view options at the top-right corner of the Stage to view the Stage at a magnification percentage that fits your screen.

# Animating Position

You'll start this project by animating the cityscape. It will begin slightly lower than the top edge of the Stage, and then rise slowly until its top is aligned with the top of the Stage.

1 Lock all the existing layers so you don't accidentally modify them. Create a new layer above the footer layer and rename it **city**.

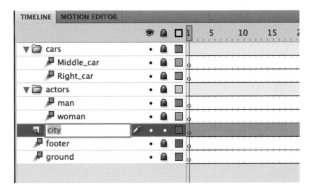

2 Drag the bitmap image called **cityBG.jpg** from the Bitmap folder in the Library to the Stage.

3 In the Property inspector, set the value of X to **0** and the value of Y to **90**.

This positions the cityscape image just slightly below the top edge of the Stage.

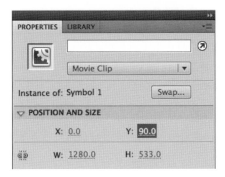

4  Right-click/Ctrl-click on the cityscape image and choose Create Motion Tween. From the top menu, you can also select Insert > Motion Tween.

5  A dialog box appears warning you that your selected object is not a symbol. Motion tweens require symbols. Flash asks if you want to convert the selection to a symbol so it can proceed with the motion tween. Click OK.

Flash automatically converts your selection to a symbol, which is saved in your Library. Flash also converts the current layer to a Tween layer so you can begin to animate the instance. Tween layers are distinguished by a special icon in front of the layer name, and the frames are tinted blue. Tween layers are reserved for motion tweens, and hence, no drawing is allowed on a Tween layer.

6  Move the red playhead to the end of the tween span at frame 190.

7  Select the instance of the cityscape on the Stage and while holding down the Shift key move the instance up the Stage.

Holding down the Shift key constrains the movement to right angles.

8  For more precision, set the value of Y to **0** in the Property inspector.

A small black triangle appears in frame 190 at the end of the tween span. This indicates a keyframe at the end of the tween. Flash smoothly interpolates the change in position from frame 1 to frame 190 and represents that motion with a motion path. Hide all the other layers to see the results of the motion tween on the cityscape.

9  Drag the red playhead back and forth at the top of the Timeline to see the smooth motion. You can also choose Control > Play (Enter) to make Flash play the animation.

Animating changes in position is simple, because Flash automatically creates keyframes at the points where you move your instance to new positions. If you want to have an object move to many different points, simply move the red playhead to the desired frame, and then move the object to its new position. Flash takes care of the rest.

● **Note:** Remove a motion tween by right-clicking/Ctrl-clicking the motion tween on the Timeline or the Stage and choosing Remove Tween.

# Changing the Pacing and Timing

You can change the duration of the entire tween span or change the timing of the animation by clicking and dragging keyframes on the Timeline.

## Changing the Animation Duration

If you want the animation to proceed at a slower pace, and hence take up a much longer period of time, you need to lengthen the entire tween span between the beginning and end keyframes. If you want to shorten the animation, you need to decrease the tween span. Lengthen or shorten a motion tween by dragging the ends on the Timeline.

1   Move your mouse cursor close to the end of the tween span.

    Your cursor changes to a double-headed arrow, indicating that you can lengthen or shorten the tween span.

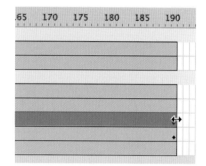

2   Click and drag the end of the tween span back toward frame 60.

    Your motion tween shortens to 60 frames, so now the cityscape takes a much shorter time to move.

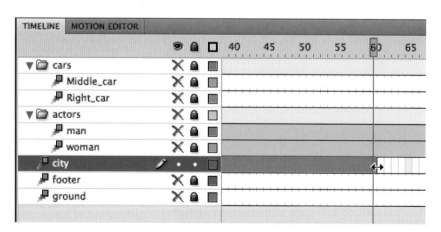

**3** Move your mouse cursor close to the beginning of the tween span (at frame 1).

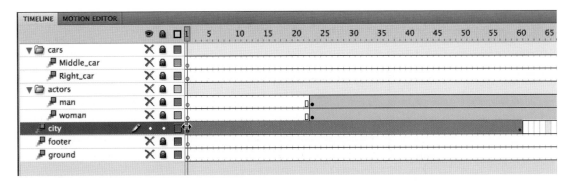

**4** Click and drag the beginning of the frame span forward to frame 10.

Your motion tween begins at an earlier time, so it now it only plays from frame 10 to frame 60.

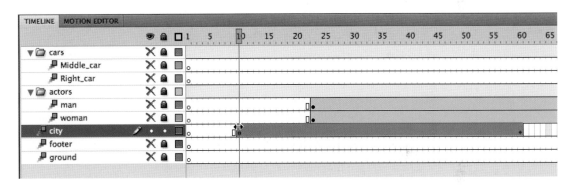

● **Note:** If you have multiple keyframes in a tween, dragging out your tween spans will distribute all your keyframes uniformly. The timing of your entire animation remains the same; just the length changes.

## Adding Frames

You'll want the last keyframe of your motion tween to hold for the entire duration of the animation, so you'll need to add frames so the animation lasts that long. Add frames by Shift-dragging the end of a tween span.

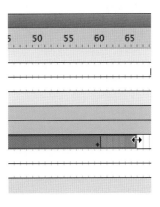

**1** Move your mouse cursor close to the end of the tween span.

**2** Hold down the Shift key and click and drag the end of the tween span forward to frame 190.

The last keyframe in the motion tween remains at frame 60, but additional frames are added to frame 190.

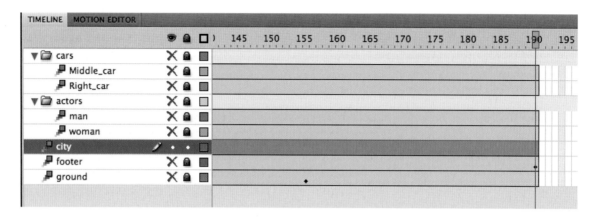

● **Note:** You can also add individual frames by choosing Insert > Timeline > Frame (F5) or remove individual frames by choosing Edit > Timeline > Remove Frames (Shift+F5).

## Moving Keyframes

When you click on a motion tween on the Timeline, the entire span is selected. This allows you to move the entire motion tween forward or backward in time as a single unit. However, if you want to move particular keyframes within a motion tween to change the pacing of the animation, you have to select individual frames. Holding down the Ctrl (Windows)/Command (Mac) key will let you select single frames or a span of frames within a motion tween.

1 Ctrl-click/Command-click on the keyframe at frame 60.

Just the keyframe at frame 60 is selected. A tiny box appears next to your mouse cursor indicating that you can move the keyframe.

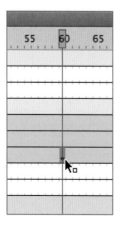

**2**  Click and drag the keyframe to frame 40.

The last keyframe in the motion tween moves to frame 40, so the motion of the cityscape proceeds quicker.

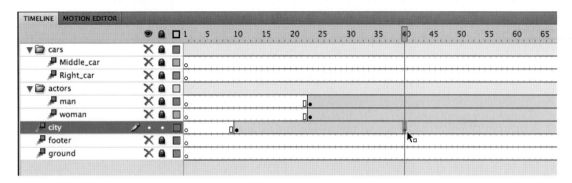

# Animating Transparency

In the previous lesson, you learned how to change the color effect of any symbol instance to change the transparency, tint, or brightness. You can change the color effect of an instance in one keyframe and change the value of the color effect in another keyframe, and Flash will automatically display a smooth change, just as it does with changes in position.

You'll change the cityscape in the beginning keyframe to be totally transparent but keep the cityscape in the ending keyframe opaque. Flash will create a smooth fade-in effect.

**1**  Move the red playhead to the first keyframe of the motion tween (frame 10).

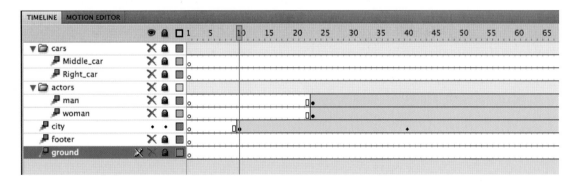

**2**  Select the cityscape instance on the Stage.

**3**  In the Property inspector, choose the Alpha option for Color Effect.

**4**  Set the Alpha value to **0%**.

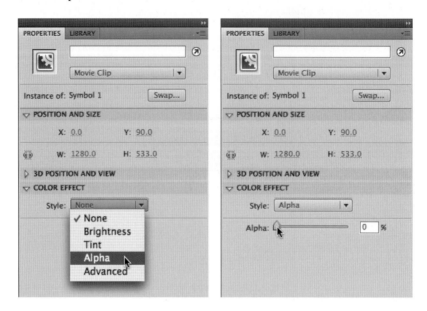

● **Note:** You can also apply a Color Effect through the Motion Editor, as explained later in this lesson. Click the Motion Editor tab next to the Timeline. Click the plus sign next to Color Effect and select Alpha.

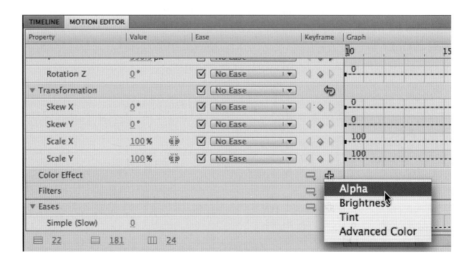

The cityscape instance on the Stage becomes totally transparent.

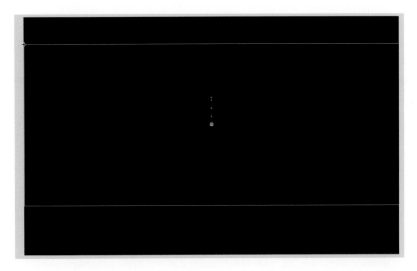

5  Move the red playhead to the last keyframe of the motion tween (frame 40).

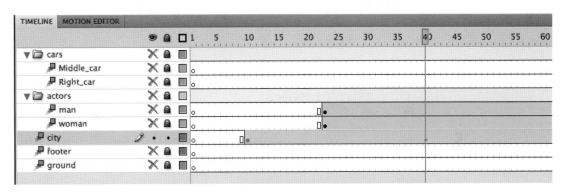

6  Select the cityscape instance on the Stage.

7  In the Property inspector, set the Alpha value to **100%**.

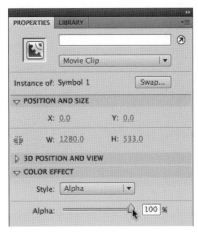

The cityscape instance on the Stage becomes totally opaque.

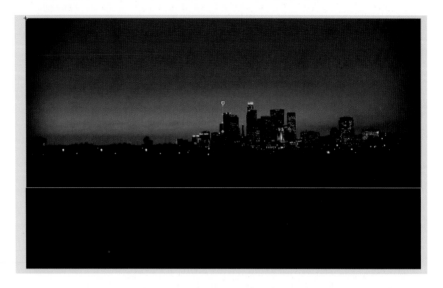

8  Preview the effect by choosing Control > Play (Enter).

Flash interpolates the changes in both position and transparency between the two keyframes.

## Animating Filters

Filters, which give instances special effects such as blurs and drop shadows, can also be animated. You'll refine the motion tween of the actors next by applying a blur filter to one of them to make it appear as if the camera changes focus. Animating filters is no different than animating changes in position or changes in color effect. You simply set the values for a filter at one keyframe and set different values for the filter at another keyframe, and Flash creates a smooth transition.

1  Make the actors layer folder on the Timeline visible.

2  Lock all the layers on the Timeline except the woman layer.

3  Move the red playhead to the beginning keyframe of the motion tween in the woman layer—at frame 23.

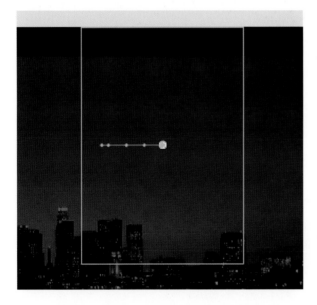

4   Select the instance of the woman on the Stage. You won't be able to see her
    because she has an alpha value of 0% (totally transparent), but if you click on the
    top-right side of the Stage, the transparent instance will be selected.

5   In the Property inspector, expand the Filters section.

6   Click the New Filters button at the bottom of the Filters
    section and select Blur.

    The Blur filter is applied to the instance.

● **Note:** You can also apply a Filter through the Motion Editor, as explained later in this lesson. Click the Motion Editor tab next to the Timeline. Click the plus sign next to Filters and select Blur.

7   In the Filters section of the Property inspector, click the link icon to constrain the blur values to both the *x* and *y* directions equally. Set the X and Y Blur values to **20** pixels.

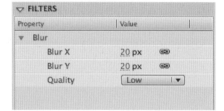

8   Move the red playhead on the Timeline to frame 160.

The 20-pixel Blur filter is applied to the woman instance throughout the motion tween.

**9** Right-click/Ctrl-click on the woman layer at frame 140 and choose Insert Keyframe > Filter.

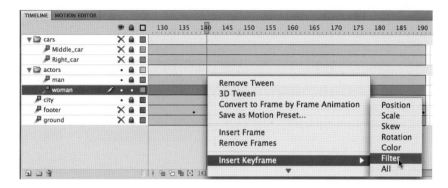

A keyframe for filters is established at frame 140.

**10** Move the red playhead to the end of the Timeline at frame 160.

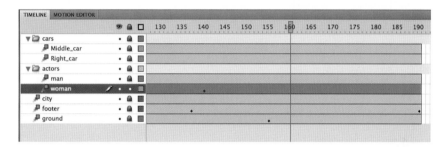

**11** Select the instance of the woman on the Stage.

**12** In the Property inspector, change the value of the Blur filter to X=**0** and Y=**0**.

The Blur filter changes from the keyframe at frame 140 to the keyframe at 160. Flash creates a smooth transition from a blurry instance to an in-focus instance.

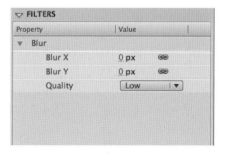

# Understanding Property Keyframes

Changes in properties are independent of each other and do not need to be tied to the same keyframes. That is, you can have a keyframe for position, a different keyframe for the color effect, and yet another keyframe for a filter. Managing many different kinds of keyframes can become overwhelming, especially if you want different properties to change at different times during the motion tween. Fortunately, Flash CS4 provides a few helpful tools.

When viewing the tween span, you can choose to view the keyframes of only certain properties. For example, you can choose to view only the position keyframes to see when your object moves. Or you can choose to view only the filter keyframes to see when there is a filter change. Right-click/Ctrl-click on a motion tween in the Timeline, choose View Keyframes, and then select the desired property among the list. You can also choose All or None to see all the properties or none of the properties.

When inserting a keyframe, you can also insert a keyframe specific to the property you want to change. Right-click/Ctrl-click on a motion tween in the Timeline, choose Insert Keyframes, and then select the desired property.

The Motion Editor is a special panel that displays all the properties of your motion tween visually as lines on a graph. The Motion Editor is helpful when multiple properties are changing at different times. For example, the Motion Editor for the woman is shown here and shows changes in the *x*-position and Alpha values in the first few frames, and changes in the Blur filter in the last few frames.

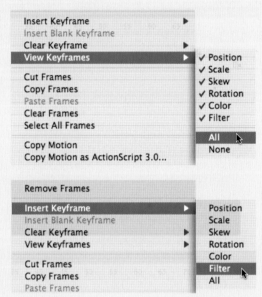

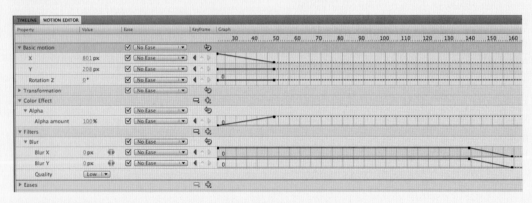

You'll learn more about how to use the Motion Editor later in this lesson.

# Animating Transformations

Now you'll learn how to animate changes in scale or rotation. These kinds of changes are made with the Free Transform tool or with the Transform panel. You'll add a third car to the project. The car will start small, and then become larger as it moves forward toward the viewer.

1  Lock all the layers on the Timeline.

2  Insert a new layer inside the Cars folder and rename it **Left_car**.

3  Insert a new keyframe at frame 75.

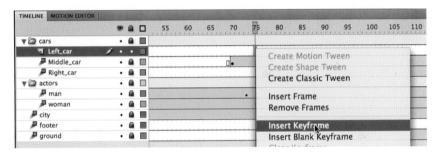

4  Drag the movie clip symbol called **carLeft** from the Library to the Stage at frame 75.

5  Select the Free Transform tool.

The transformation handles appear around the instance on the Stage.

**6** While holding down the Shift key, click and drag the corner handle inward to make the car smaller.

**7** In the Property inspector, make sure that the width of the car is about 400 pixels.

**8** Alternatively, you can use the Transform panel (Window > Transform) and change the scale of the car to about **29.4**%.

**9** Move the car to its starting position at about X=710 and Y=488.

**10** In the Property inspector, select Alpha for the Color Effect.

**11** Set the value of the Alpha to **0**%.

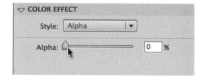

The car becomes totally transparent.

**12** Right-click/Ctrl-click on the car on the Stage and select Create Motion Tween.

The current layer becomes a Tween layer.

**13** Move the red playhead on the Timeline to frame 100.

**14** Select the transparent instance of the car, and in the Property inspector, change the Alpha value to **100**%.

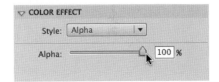

A new keyframe is automatically inserted at frame 100 to indicate the change in transparency.

**15** Select the Free Transform tool.

**16** While holding down the Shift key, click and drag the corner handle outward to make the car larger. For more precision, use the Property inspector and set the dimensions of the car to width=**1379.5** pixels and height=**467.8** pixels.

**17** Position the car at X=607 and Y=545.

**18** Move the Left_car layer in between the Middle_car and Right_car layers so that the car in the center overlaps the cars on the side.

Flash tweens the change in position and the change in scale from frame 75 to frame 100. Flash also tweens the change in transparency from frame 75 to frame 100.

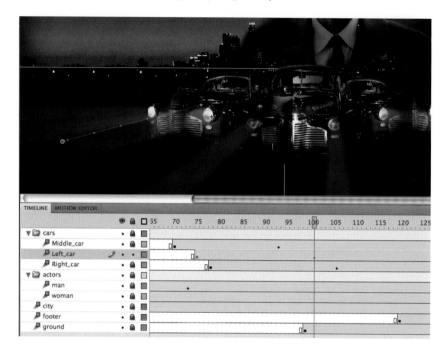

## Motion Presets

If your project involves creating identical motion tweens repeatedly, Flash provides a new panel called Motion Presets that can help. The Motion Presets panel (Window > Motion Presets) stores a particular motion tween so you can apply it to different instances on the Stage.

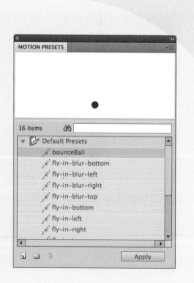

For example, if you want to build a slide show where each image fades out in the same manner, you can save that transition to the Motion Presets panel. Simply select the first motion tween on the Timeline or the instance on the Stage. In the Motion Presets panel, click the Save selection as preset button.

Name your motion preset, and it will be saved in the Motion Presets panel. Select a new instance on the Stage and choose the motion preset. Click Apply and your saved motion preset will be applied to the new instance.

Flash provides a number of motion presets that you can use to quickly build sophisticated animations without much effort.

# Changing the Path of the Motion

The motion tween of the left car that you just animated shows a colored line with dots indicating the path of the motion. The path of the motion can be edited easily so that the car travels in a curve, or the path can be moved, scaled, or even rotated just like any other object on the Stage.

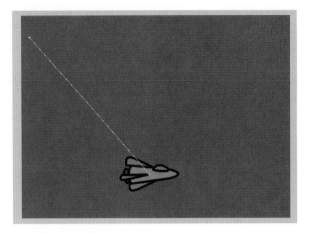

To better demonstrate how you can edit the path of the motion, open the sample file 04MotionPath.fla. The file contains a single Tween layer with a rocket ship moving from the top left of the Stage to the bottom right.

## Moving the Path of the Motion

You will move the path of the motion so the relative movement of the rocket ship remains the same but its starting and ending positions change.

1  Choose the Selection tool.

2  Click on the path of the motion to select it.

The path of the motion becomes highlighted when it is selected.

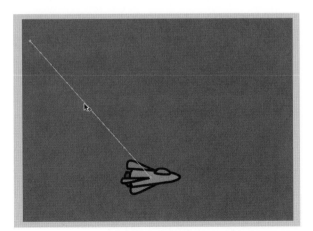

**3** Click and drag the motion path to move it to a different place on the Stage.

The relative motion and timing of the animation remain the same, but the starting and ending positions are relocated.

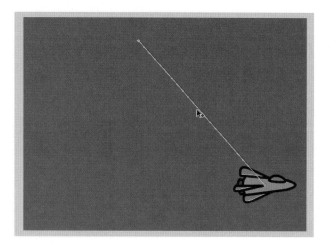

## Changing the Scale or Rotation of the Path

The path of the motion can also be manipulated with the Free Transform tool.

**1** Select the path of the motion.

**2** Choose the Free Transform tool.

Transformation handles appear around the path of the motion.

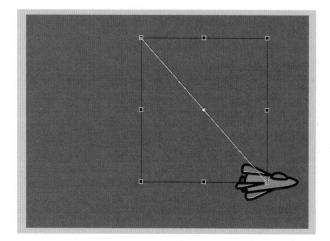

**3** Scale or rotate the path of the motion as desired. You can make the path smaller or larger, or rotate the path so the rocket ship starts from the bottom left of the Stage and ends at the top right.

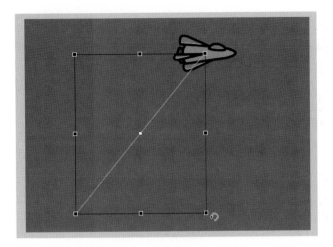

## Editing the Path of the Motion

Making your objects travel on a curved path is a simple matter. You can either edit the path with Bezier precision using anchor point handles, or you can edit the path in a more intuitive manner with the Selection tool.

**1** Choose the Convert Anchor Point Tool, which is hidden under the Pen Tool.

| | |
| --- | --- |
| ■ ◊ | Pen Tool (P) |
| ◊⁺ | Add Anchor Point Tool (=) |
| ◊⁻ | Delete Anchor Point Tool (-) |
| ⊼ | Convert Anchor Point Tool (C) |

**2** Click on the starting point or the ending point of the motion path on the Stage and drag the control handle out from the anchor point.

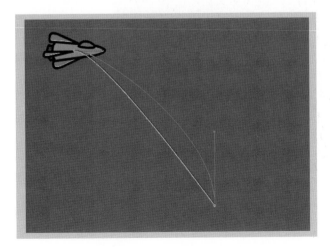

The handle on the anchor point controls the curvature of the path.

**3** Choose the Subselection tool.

**4** Click and drag the handle to edit the curve of the path. Make the rocket ship travel in a wide curve.

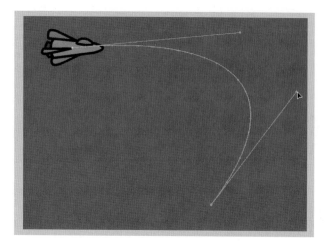

● **Note:** The path of the motion can also be directly manipulated with the Selection tool. Choose the Selection tool and move it close to the path of the motion. A curved icon appears next to your cursor indicating that you can edit the path. Click and drag the path of the motion to change its curvature.

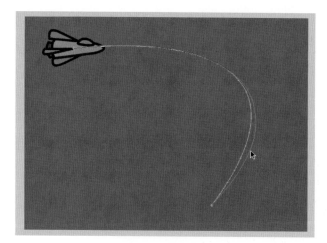

## Orienting Objects to the Path

Sometimes the orientation of the object traveling along the path is important. In the motion picture splash page project, the orientation of the car is constant as it rumbles forward. However, in the rocket ship example, the rocket ship should follow the path with its nose pointed in the direction in which it is heading. The Orient to path option in the Property inspector gives you this option.

1 Select the motion tween on the Timeline.

2 In the Property inspector, select the Orient to path option.

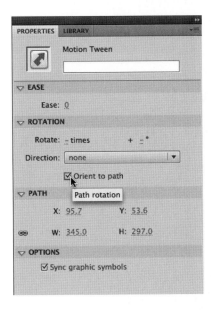

Flash inserts keyframes for rotation along the motion tween so that the nose of the rocket ship is oriented to the path of the motion.

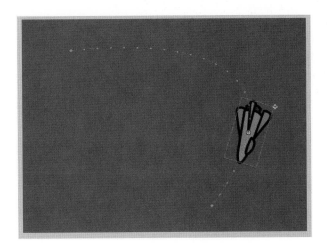

**Note:** To direct the nose of the rocket ship, or any other object, along the path of its motion, you must orient its initial position so that it is facing in the direction that you want it to travel. Use the Free Transform tool to rotate its initial position so that it is oriented correctly.

# Swapping Tween Targets

Unlike the previous versions of Flash, the motion tween model in Flash CS4 is object based. This means that you can easily swap out the target of a motion tween. If, for example, you'd rather see an alien moving around the Stage instead of a rocket ship, you can replace the target of the motion tween with an alien symbol from your Library and still preserve the animation.

**1** Select the rocket ship on the Stage to select the motion tween.

**2** Drag the movie clip symbol of the alien from the Library onto the rocket ship.

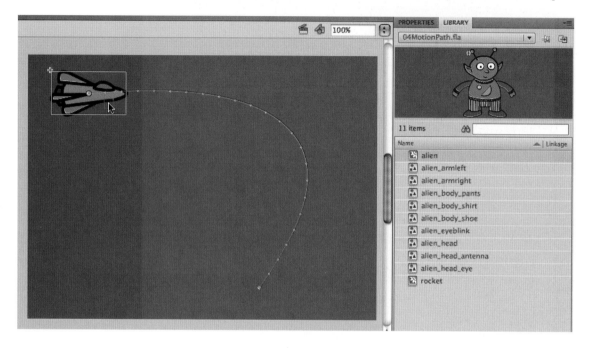

Flash asks you if you want to replace the existing object with a new object.

**3** Click OK.

**4**  The rocket ship is replaced with the alien.

The motion remains the same, but the target of the motion tween has been swapped.

**●Note:** You can also swap instances in the Property inspector. Select the object that you want to swap on the Stage. In the Property inspector, click the Swap button. In the dialog box that appears, choose a new symbol and click OK. Flash will swap the target of the motion tween.

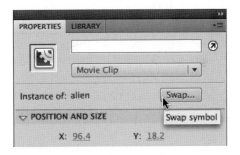

# Creating Nested Animations

Often, an object that is animated on the Stage will have its own animation. For example, a butterfly moving across the Stage will have an animation of its wings flapping as it moves. Or the alien that you swapped with the rocket ship could be waving his arms. These kinds of animations are nested animations, because they are contained inside the movie clip symbols. Movie clip symbols have their own Timeline that is independent of the main Timeline.

In this example, you'll make the alien wave his arms inside the movie clip symbol so he'll be waving as he moves across the Stage.

## Creating Animations Inside Movie Clip Symbols

**1** In the Library, double-click the alien movie clip symbol icon.

You are now in symbol-editing mode for the alien movie clip symbol. The alien is in the middle of the Stage. In the Timeline, the parts of the alien are separated in layers.

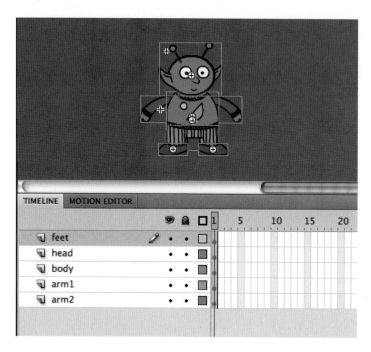

**2** Choose the Selection tool.

**3** Right-click/Ctrl-click on the alien's right arm and choose Create Motion Tween.

Flash converts the current layer to a Tween layer and inserts one second worth of frames so you can begin to animate the instance.

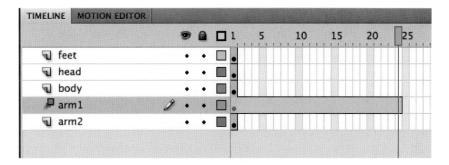

4 Choose the Free Transform Tool.

5 Drag the corner rotation control points to rotate the arm upward to the alien's shoulder height.

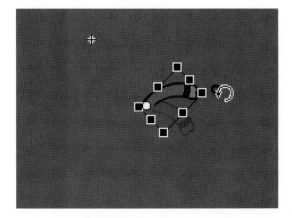

A keyframe is inserted at the end of the motion tween. The right arm rotates smoothly from the resting position to the outstretched position.

6 Move the red playhead back to frame 1.

7 Now create a motion tween for the alien's other arm. Right-click/Ctrl-click on the left arm and choose Create Motion Tween.

Flash converts the current layer to a Tween layer and inserts one second worth of frames so you can begin to animate the instance.

8 Choose the Free Transform Tool.

**9** Drag the corner rotation control points to rotate the arm upward to the alien's shoulder height.

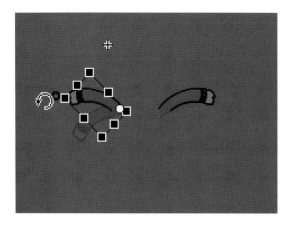

A keyframe is inserted at the end of the motion tween. The left arm rotates smoothly from the resting position to the outstretched position.

**10** Select the last frame in all the other layers and insert frames (F5) so that the head, body, and feet all remain on the Stage for the same amount of time as the moving arms.

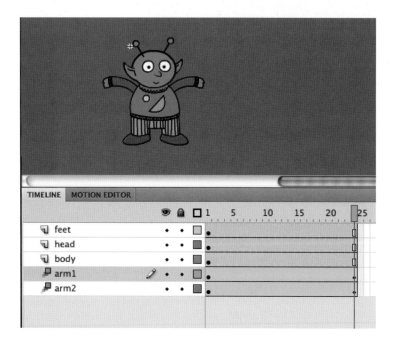

**11** Exit symbol-editing mode by clicking the Scene 1 button at the top-left of the Stage.

Your animation of the alien raising his arms is complete. Wherever you use the movie clip symbol, the alien will continue to play its nested animation.

**12** Preview the animation by choosing Control > Test Movie.

Flash opens a window showing the exported animation. The alien moves along the motion path while the nested animation of his arms moving plays and loops.

● **Note:** Animations inside movie clip symbols will loop automatically. To prevent the looping, you need to add ActionScript to tell the movie clip Timeline to stop on its last frame. You'll learn more about ActionScript in Chapter 6, "Creating Interactive Navigation."

## Using the Motion Editor

The Motion Editor is a panel that provides in-depth information and editing capabilities for all the properties of a motion tween. The Motion Editor is located behind the Timeline and can be accessed by clicking the top tab or by choosing Window > Motion Editor.

On the left side of the Motion Editor, an expandable list of properties is displayed along with their values and easing options. On the right side, a timeline shows various lines and curves representing how those properties change.

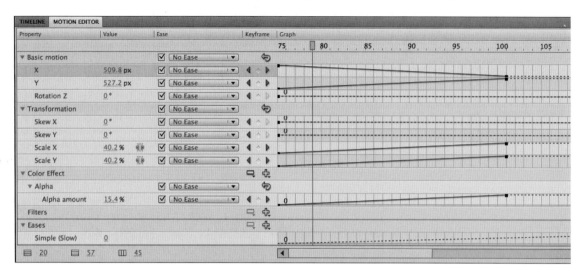

## Setting the Motion Editor Display Options

Options for displaying the Motion Editor are listed at the bottom of the panel.

1 Select the alien on the Stage.

2 Open the Motion Editor panel if it is not already showing.

3 Move your cursor over the gray horizontal bar separating the Motion Editor from the Stage.

   Your cursor changes to a double-headed arrow indicating that you can increase or decrease the height of the Motion Editor panel.

4 Click and drag the horizontal bar to increase the height of the Motion Editor panel.

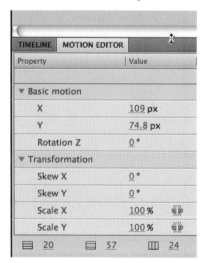

**5** Click the triangles to collapse all the properties categories on the left. You can expand or collapse the categories to see only those categories you are interested in.

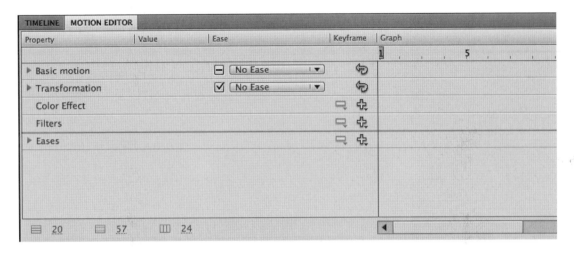

**6** Click and drag on the Viewable Frames icon at the bottom of the Motion Editor to change the number of frames that appear in the timeline. Set the Viewable Frames value to the maximum to see the entire motion tween.

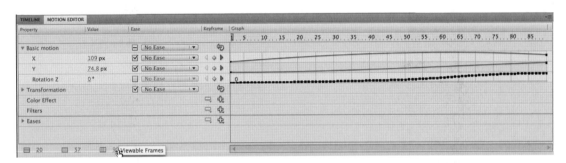

**7** Click and drag the Graph Size icon at the bottom of the Motion Editor to change the vertical height of each property that is listed on the left.

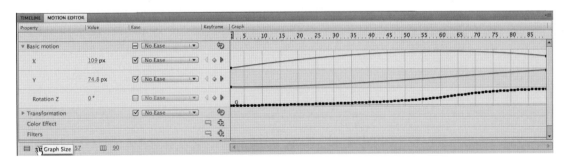

**8** Click and drag the Expanded Graph Size icon at the bottom of the Motion Editor to change the vertical height of each selected property.

To see how the Expanded Graph Size option affects the display, click the X property under Basic motion. The larger the Expanded Graph Size value, the more of the selected property you can view.

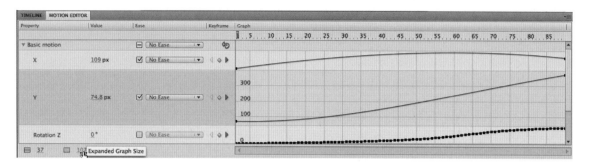

## Changing Property Values

You will change another property of your flapping alien with the Motion Editor and see how easy it is to animate multiple properties independently. For this example, you'll create a fade-in effect by changing the Alpha property.

**1** Next to the Color Effect property, click the Plus icon and choose Alpha.

The Alpha property appears in the Motion Editor under the Color Effect category.

**2** Select the Alpha amount.

The Alpha property expands, displaying a black-dotted horizontal line at 100% extending from frame 1 to the end of the timeline. This line represents the opacity of the alien throughout the motion tween.

**3** Click on the first keyframe, which is indicated by a black square, and drag it down to 0%. You can also change the Alpha value by clicking and dragging the value next to the Alpha amount.

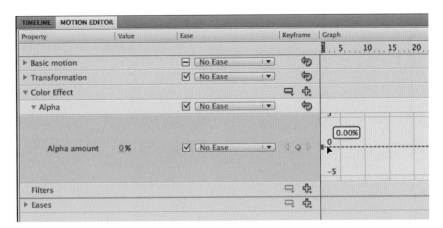

The alien becomes transparent beginning at frame 1.

## Inserting Keyframes

Inserting keyframes is easy.

**1** Move the red playhead to frame 20.

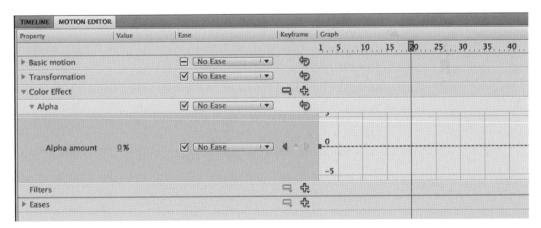

**2**  Click the diamond icon to add a keyframe at that point in time for the Alpha property. You can also right-click/Ctrl-click on the graph and choose Insert Keyframe.

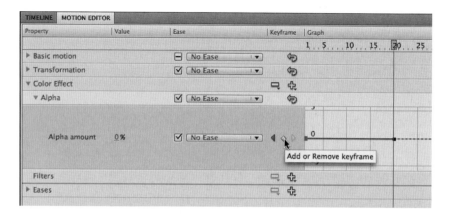

A new keyframe for the Alpha property is inserted at frame 20.

**3**  Click on the second keyframe.

The selected keyframe becomes highlighted.

**4**  Drag the second keyframe up to change the Alpha value to **100**%.

Flash animates the smooth transition of transparency from frame 1 to frame 20.

## Editing Keyframes

You can easily navigate keyframes and remove them, and you can move keyframes to control the precise timing of each of your transitions.

- Click the left or right arrow to move quickly between keyframes.

- Right-click/Ctrl-click on any keyframe and choose Remove Keyframe to delete a keyframe.

- Select a keyframe and click the yellow diamond to delete the keyframe.

- Shift-click to select multiple contiguous keyframes and move them together.

## Resetting Values and Deleting Properties

- Click the Reset Values button to reset the property to its default values.

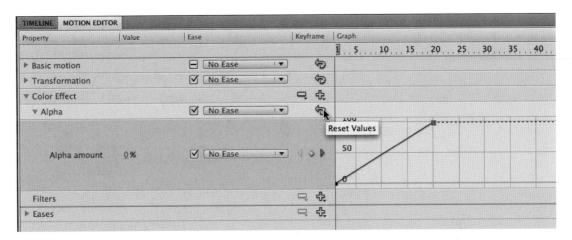

- Click the Minus button and select Alpha to delete the property from the Motion Editor.

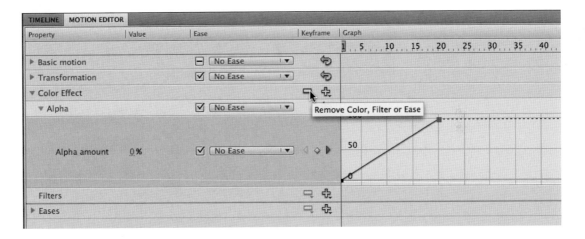

# Easing

Easing refers to the way in which a motion tween proceeds. In the most basic sense, it can be thought of as acceleration or deceleration. An object that moves from one side of the Stage to the other side can start off slowly, then build up momentum, and then stop suddenly. Or, the object can start off quickly, and then gradually come to a halt.

Easing is best visualized in the Motion Editor. The graphs that connect one keyframe to another are usually straight lines, which indicate that the change from one value to the next value proceeds linearly. However, if you want a more gradual change from the starting position (known as an ease-in), the line would be curved near the beginning keyframe, indicating a slower start. A gradual slowdown (known as an ease-out) would be represented by a curve near the ending keyframe.

## Setting Eases of a Motion Tween

1 In the Motion Editor, right-click/Ctrl-click the second keyframe in the Alpha property and choose Smooth point.

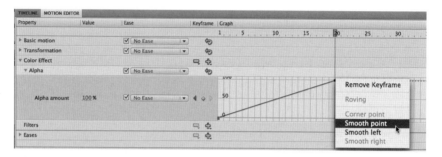

Control handles appear from the keyframe, which you can move to change the curvature of the line.

2 Click and drag the control handle to create a smooth curve approaching the 100% Alpha value.

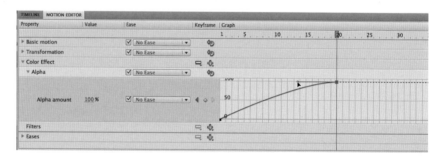

The transition from 0% to 100% Alpha slows down as it approaches 100% (ease-out).

3 Right-click/Ctrl-click the first keyframe in the Alpha property and choose Smooth point.

Control handles appear from the keyframe, which you can move to change the curvature of the line.

4  Click and drag the control handle to create a smooth curve as the line begins from 0%.

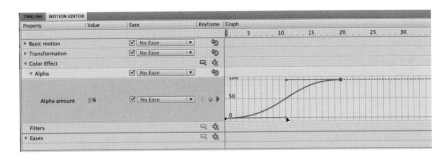

The transition from 0% to 100% Alpha begins gradually from 0% in addition to slowing down. The total effect of the S-shaped curve is both an ease-in and an ease-out effect.

● **Note:** You can also apply ease-in and ease-out effects from the Property inspector. In the Timeline (not the Motion Editor), select the motion tween. In the Property inspector, enter a value for the ease between -100 (ease-in) to 100 (ease-out).

Eases applied via the Property inspector, however, will be applied globally to all the properties throughout the entire motion tween. With the Motion Editor, you have precise control over individual properties and eases between keyframes.

## Using Preset Eases

Easing can be very powerful and can be used to create many specialized motions. For example, a bouncing motion can be created with just two positional keyframes and an ease that moves the object back and forth between the two positions.

For the next example, you'll return to the motion picture project and add a preset ease to the motion of the car. You'll make the car shudder up and down to mimic the motion of an idling car. The motion tween will be created inside the movie clip symbol of the car.

1   Continue with your Flash project in progress, 04_workingcopy.fla.

2   In the Library, double-click the movie clip symbol called carLeft.

  Flash takes you to symbol-editing mode for the movie clip symbol. Two layers are inside this symbol: the top layer called lights and the bottom layer called smallRumble.

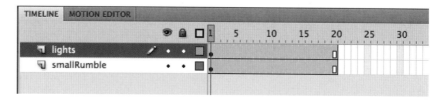

3   Lock the top lights layer.

4   Right-click/Ctrl-click on the car and choose Create Motion Tween.

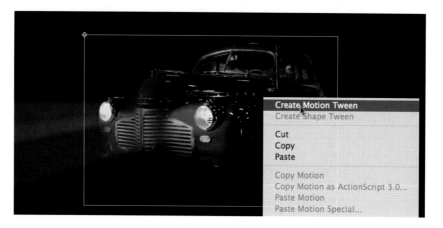

  Flash converts the current layer to a Tween layer so you can begin to animate the instance.

5   Move the red playhead to the end of the Timeline.

6   Choose the Selection tool.

**7** Move the car down about 5 pixels.

Flash creates a smooth animation of the car moving down slightly.

**8** Click on the motion tween in the Timeline and open the Motion Editor.

**9** Click the Plus button on the Eases category and choose Random.

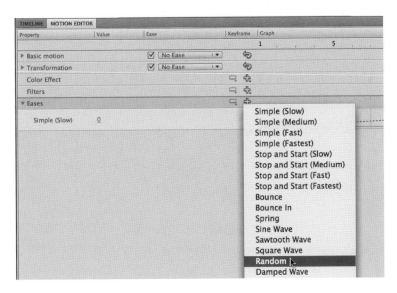

The Random preset ease appears.

**10** Select the Random ease.

The Random ease jumps from one value to the next in random intervals. This is shown graphically as a series of abrupt stair steps.

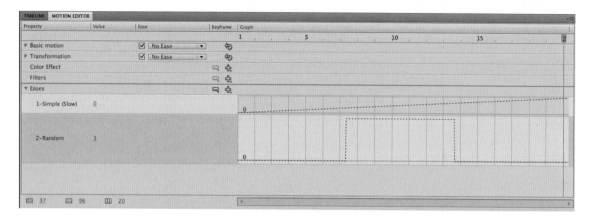

**11** Change the Random value to **15**.

The frequency of random jumps increases based on the Random value.

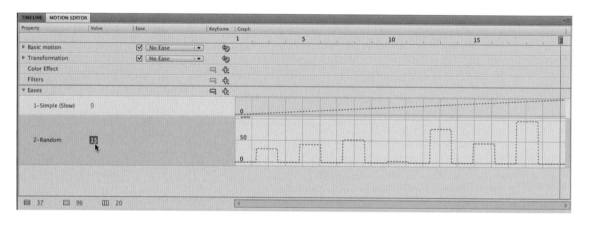

**12** Select the Basic motion category.

**13** In the Ease pull-down menu next to the Basic motion category, choose Random.

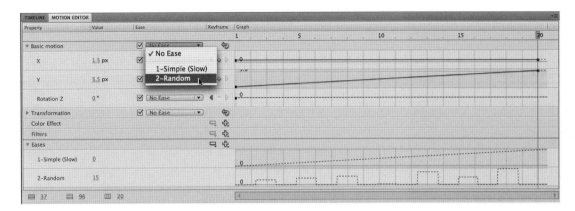

Flash applies the Random ease to the positional changes of the motion tween. Instead of a smooth change in the *y*-position, Flash makes the car jerk up and down randomly, simulating a rumbling, idling car.

## Classic Tween Model

For those animators who are used to previous versions of Flash, the new way of doing motion tweens may seem bewildering. In older versions of Flash, motion tweens were created by first establishing keyframes in the Timeline, then changing one or more of the properties of the instance, and then applying a motion tween between the two keyframes. The current model is much simpler, streamlined, and more powerful. However, if you are more comfortable working with the older way of animating, you can do so by relying on the Classic Tween option. Select the first keyframe containing your instance, and then choose Insert > Classic Tween. Flash applies a classic motion tween to your Timeline. The Motion Editor, however, is not available for classic tweens.

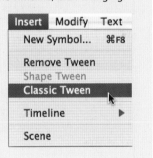

# Animating 3D Motion

Finally, you'll add a title and animate it in three-dimensional space. Animating in 3D presents the added complication of a third (z) axis. When you choose the 3D Rotation or 3D Translation tool, you need to be aware of the Global Transform option at the bottom of the Tools panel. The Global Transform option toggles between a global option (button depressed) and a local option (button raised). Moving an object with the global option on makes the transformations relative to the global coordinate system, whereas moving an object with the local option on makes the transformations relative to itself.

1 Insert a new layer at the top of the layer stack and rename it **title**.

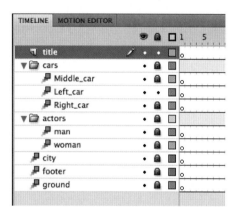

2 Lock all the other layers.

3 Insert a new keyframe at frame 120.

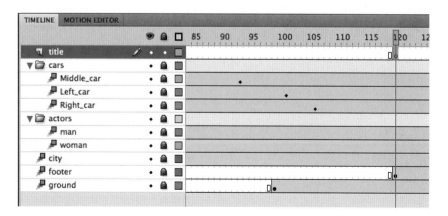

**4** Drag the movie clip symbol called movietitle from the Library onto the Stage.

The movie title instance appears in your new layer in the keyframe at frame 120.

**5** Position the title at x=180 and y=90.

**6** Right-click/Ctrl-click on the movie title and choose Create Motion Tween.

Flash converts the current layer to a Tween layer so you can begin to animate the instance.

**7** Move the red playhead to frame 140.

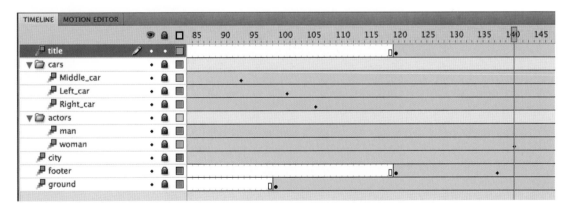

**8** Select the 3D Rotation tool.

**9** Deselect the Global Transform option at the bottom of the Tools panel.

**10** Click and drag the title to rotate it around the *y*-axis (green) so that its angle is at about -50 degrees. You can check the rotation values in the Transform panel (Window > Transform).

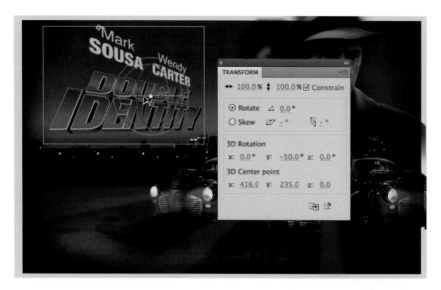

**11** Move the red playhead to the first keyframe at frame 120.

**12** Click and drag the title to rotate it around the *y*-axis in the opposite direction so that its angle is at about 25 degrees and the instance looks like just a sliver.

Flash motion tweens the change in the 3D rotation, so the title appears to swing in three dimensions.

# Previewing the Animation

You can quickly preview your animation by "scrubbing" the red playhead back and forth on the Timeline or by choosing Control > Play. You can also choose Window > Toolbars > Controller to display a controller panel with buttons to rewind and play your Timeline.

However, to preview your animation as your audience will see it and to preview any nested animations within movie clip symbols, you should test your movie. Choose Control > Test Movie.

Flash exports a SWF file and saves it in the same location as your FLA file. The SWF file is the compressed, final Flash media that you would embed in an HTML page. Flash displays the SWF file in a new window with the exact Stage dimensions and plays your animation.

**Note:** The exported SWF in Testing mode will loop automatically. To prevent the looping in Testing mode, choose Control > Loop to deselect the loop option.

To exit Testing mode, click the Close window button.

## Review Questions

1 What are two requirements of a motion tween?

2 What kinds of properties can a motion tween change?

3 What are property keyframes, and why are they important?

4 How can you edit the path of a motion?

5 What are three ways to add easing to a motion tween?

## Review Answers

1 A motion tween requires a symbol instance on the Stage and its own layer, which is called a Tween layer. No other tween or drawing object can exist on the Tween layer.

2 A motion tween creates smooth transitions between different keyframes of an object's location, scale, rotation, transparency, brightness, tint, filter values, or 3D rotation or translation.

3 A keyframe marks a change in one or more of an object's properties. Keyframes are specific to each property, so that a motion tween can have keyframes for position that are different from keyframes for transparency.

4 To edit the path of a motion, choose the Selection tool and click and drag directly on the path to bend it. You can also choose the Convert Anchor Point tool and Subselection tool to pull out handles at the anchor points. The handles control the curvature of the path.

5 The three ways to add easing to a motion tween include: First, you can select the motion tween on the Timeline and change the Ease value in the Property inspector. Second, in the Motion Editor, you can right-click/Ctrl-click on any keyframe to pull out control handles and change the curvature of the graph. Third, you can add a preset ease to the Ease category of the Motion Editor and apply it to a property.

# 5 ARTICULATED MOTION AND MORPHING

## Lesson Overview

In this lesson, you'll learn how to do the following:

- Animate armatures with multiple linked movie clips

- Constrain the joints

- Animate armatures with shapes

- Morph organic shapes with shape tweens

- Use shape hints to refine shape tweens

 This lesson will take approximately two hours to complete. If needed, remove the previous lesson folder from your hard drive and copy the Lesson05 folder onto it.

You can easily create complex motion with articulations—
joints between linked objects—with a new Flash CS4 feature
called inverse kinematics. You can also morph—create organic
changes in shapes—with shape tweens.

# Getting Started

You'll start the lesson by viewing the animated crane that you'll create as you learn about articulated motion and morphing in Flash. You'll also be animating a tentacle of an octopus.

1    Double-click the 05End.swf file in the Lesson05/05End folder to play the animation. Double-click the 05ShapeIK_End.swf to play that animation as well.

The first project is an animation depicting a crane working at the seaside dock. In this lesson, you'll animate the crane arm as well as the smooth motion of the waves. The other project is an animation showing an octopus curling one of its tentacles.

2    Double-click the 05Start.fla file in the Lesson05/05Start folder to open the initial project file in Flash.

3    Choose File > Save As. Name the file **05_workingcopy.fla**, and save it in the 05Start folder. Saving a working copy ensures that the original start file will be available if you want to start over.

# Articulated Motion with Inverse Kinematics

When you want to animate an articulated object (one that has multiple joints), such as a walking person, or as in this example, a moving crane, Flash CS4 makes it easy to do so with inverse kinematics. Inverse kinematics is a mathematical way to calculate the different angles of a jointed object to achieve a certain configuration. You can pose your object in a beginning keyframe, and then set a different pose at a later keyframe. Flash will use inverse kinematics to figure out the different angles for all the joints to get from the first pose to the next pose.

Inverse kinematics makes animating easy because you don't have to worry about animating each segment of an object or limb of a character. You just focus on the overall poses.

## Defining the Bones

The first step to create articulated motion is to define the bones of your object. You use the Bone tool ⚲ to do that. The Bone tool tells Flash how a series of movie clip instances are connected. The connected movie clips are called the *armature*, and each movie clip is called a *node*.

1   In your 05working_copy.fla file, select the crane layer.

2   Drag the cranearm1 movie clip symbol from the Library onto the Stage. Place the instance right above the rectangular crane base.

**3** Drag the cranearm2 movie clip symbol from the Library onto the Stage. Place the instance next to the tip of the cranearm1 movie clip instance.

**4** Drag another instance of the cranearm2 movie clip symbol from the Library onto the Stage. Place this instance next to the free tip of the first cranearm1 instance.

**5** Drag the cranerope movie clip symbol from the Library onto the Stage. Place the instance so it hangs down from the last cranearm2 instance.

Your movie clip instances are now in place and ready to be connected with bones.

**6** Select the Bone tool.

**7** Click on the base of the cranearm1 instance and drag the Bone tool to the base of the cranearm2 instance. Release the mouse button.

Your first bone is defined. Flash shows the bone as a skinny triangle with a round joint at its base and a round joint at its tip. Each bone is defined from the base of the first node to the base of the next node. For example, to build an arm, you would click on the shoulder side of the upper arm and drag it to the elbow side of the lower arm.

8  Click on the base of the cranearm2 instance and drag it to the base of the next cranearm2 instance. Release the mouse button.

Your second bone is defined.

9  Click on the base of the second cranearm2 instance and drag it to the base of the cranerope instance. Release the mouse button.

Your third bone is defined. Note that the four movie clip instances, which are now connected with bones, have been separated to a new layer with a new icon and name. The new layer is a Pose layer, which keeps your armatures separate from other objects on the Timeline such as graphics or motion tweens.

**10** Rename the Pose layer **cranearmature** and delete the empty crane layer that contained the initial movie clip instances.

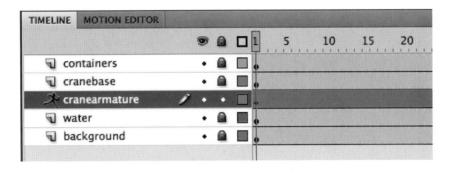

## Armature Hierarchy

The first bone of an armature is referred to as the parent, and the bone that is linked to it is called the child. A bone can actually have more than one child attached to it as well. For example, an armature of a puppet would have a pelvis connected to two thighs, which in turn are attached to two lower legs of their own. The pelvis is the parent, each thigh is a child, and the thighs are siblings to each other. As your armature becomes more complicated, you can use the Property inspector to navigate up and down the hierarchy using these relationships.

When you select a bone in an armature, the top of the Property inspector displays a series of arrows.

You can click the arrows to move through the hierarchy and quickly select and view the properties of each node. If the parent bone is selected, you can click the down arrow to select the child. If a child bone is selected, you can click the up arrow to select its parent, or click the down arrow to select its own child if it has one. The sideways arrows navigate between sibling nodes.

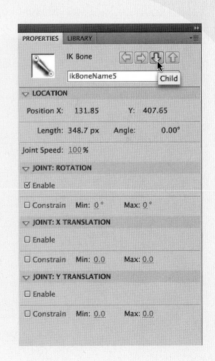

## Inserting Poses

Think of poses as keyframes for your armature. You have an initial pose for your crane in frame 1. You will insert two additional poses for the crane. The next pose will position the crane down as if it were picking something up from the ocean. The last pose will position the crane back up to lift up the object.

1   Move the red playhead to frame 25.

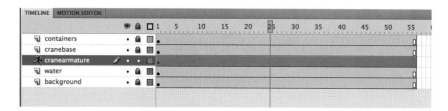

2   Click on the hook at the end of the cranerope instance and drag it down to the water.

A new pose is automatically inserted at frame 25. As you drag the cranerope instance, notice how the entire armature moves along with it. The bones keep all the different nodes connected.

**3** Move the red playhead to frame 56 (the last frame).

**4** Click on the hook at the end of the cranerope instance and drag it up out of the water.

A new pose is automatically inserted at frame 56.

**5** Preview the animation by choosing Control > Test Movie.

The crane animates, moving all its crane segments to move from one pose to the next.

● **Note:** You can edit poses on the Timeline just as you can with keyframes. Right-click/ Ctrl-click along the Timeline and choose Insert Pose to insert a new pose. Right-click/ Ctrl-click on any pose and select Clear Pose to remove the pose from the layer. Ctrl-click/ Command-click on a pose to select it. Click and drag the pose to move it to a different position along the Timeline.

## Isolating the Rotation of Individual Nodes

As you pull and push on the armature to create your pose, you may find it difficult to control the rotation of individual nodes because of their linkages. Holding down the Shift key as you move individual nodes will isolate their rotation.

**1**  Select the third pose at frame 56.

**2**  Holding down the Shift key, click and drag on the second node in the armature to rotate it so that it points downward.

The second node of the crane rotates, but the first node does not.

**3**  Holding down the Shift key, click and drag on the third node in the armature to rotate it so that it points upward.

The third node of the crane rotates, but the first and second nodes do not.

4   Holding down the Shift key, click and drag on the last node in the armature (the cranerope instance) so that it points straight down.

Holding down the Shift key helps you isolate the rotations of the individual nodes so that you can position your poses exactly as you want them. The crane now retracts by collapsing its different arm segments.

## Editing Armatures

You can easily edit the armature by repositioning the nodes or by deleting and adding new bones. If one of the nodes of your armature is slightly off, for example, you can use the Free Transform tool to rotate it or move it into a new position. This does not change the bones, however.

You can also move nodes into new positions by holding down the Alt/Option key while dragging the node to a different location.

If you want to remove bones, simply click on the bone that you want to delete and press the Delete key on the keyboard. The selected bone and all the bones connected to it down the chain will be removed. You can then add new bones if desired.

# Constraining Joints

The various joints of the crane can freely rotate, which isn't particularly realistic. Many armatures in real life are constrained to certain angles of rotation. For example, your forearm can rotate up toward your bicep, but it can't rotate in the other direction beyond your bicep. When working with armatures in Flash CS4, you can choose to constrain the rotation for various joints or even constrain the translation (movement) of the various joints.

Next, you'll constrain the rotation and translation of the various joints of the crane so they move more realistically.

## Constraining the Rotation of Joints

By default, the rotation of joints have no constraints, which means they can rotate in a full circle, or 360 degrees. If you only want a certain joint to rotate in a quarter circle arc, you would constrain the joint to 90 degrees.

1   Click the second pose at frame 25 in the cranearmature layer, right-click/Ctrl-click, and select Clear Pose.

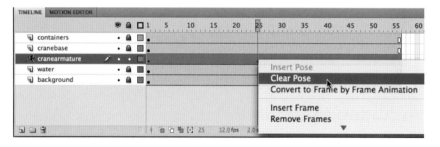

2   Click the third pose at frame 56 in the cranearmature layer, right-click/Ctrl-click, and select Clear Pose.

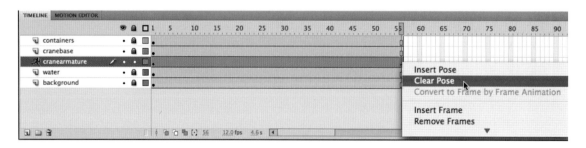

Your armature now has only a single pose at frame 1.

3   Move the red playhead to frame 1.

4   Choose the Selection tool.

**5** Click on the second bone in the crane armature.

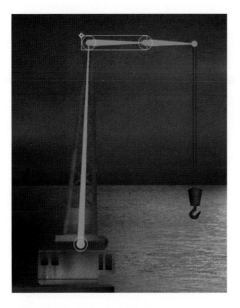

The bone becomes highlighted, indicating that it is selected.

**6** In the Property inspector, select the Constrain option in the Joint:Rotation section.

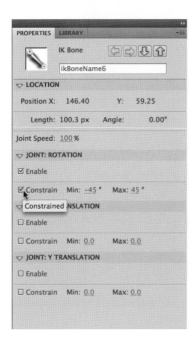

An angle indicator appears on the joint, showing the minimum and maximum allowable angles and the current position of the node.

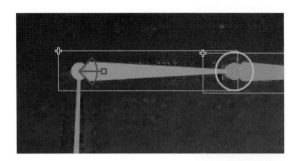

7  Set the minimum joint rotation angle to **0** degrees and the maximum joint rotation angle to **90** degrees.

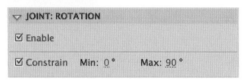

The angle indicator changes on the joint, showing the allowable angles. In this example, the second segment of the crane can only bend downward or raise up to be level with the horizon.

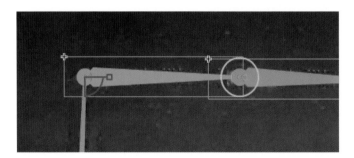

8  Click on the third bone in the crane armature.

The bone becomes highlighted, indicating that it is selected.

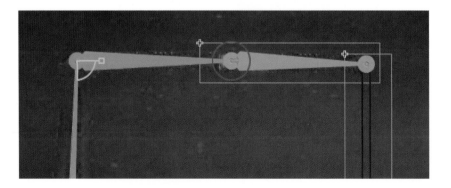

**9** In the Property inspector, select the Constrain option in the Joint:Rotation section.

An angle indicator appears on the joint, showing the minimum and maximum allowable angles and the current position of the node.

**10** Set the minimum joint rotation angle to **-90** degrees and the maximum joint rotation angle to **0** degrees.

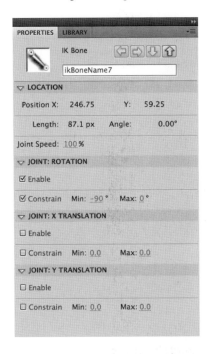

The angle indicator changes on the joint, showing the allowable angles. In this example, the third segment of the crane can only bend from a level position to a vertical position. Each joint in an armature can have its own rotation constraints.

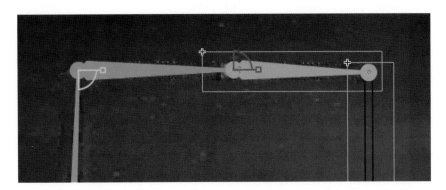

## Constraining the Translation of Joints

You don't normally think of joints that can move positions. However, in Flash CS4, you can allow joints to actually slide in either the $x$ or the $y$ direction, and set the limits on how far those joints can travel.

In the next example, you'll allow the first node (the tall first segment of the crane) to move back and forth as if it was on a track. This will give it the capability to pick up any sort of cargo from the ocean and place it on the dock.

1   Click on the first node in the crane armature.

2   Deselect the Enable option in the Joint:Rotation section of the Property inspector.

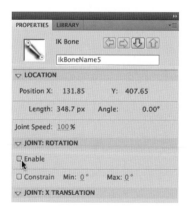

The circle around the joint disappears, indicating that it can no longer rotate.

3   Select the Enable option in the Joint:X Translation section of the Property inspector.

Arrows appear from the joint, indicating that the joint can travel in that direction.

**4**   Select the Constrain option in the Joint:X Translation section of the Property inspector.

The arrows turn into straight lines, indicating that the translation is limited.

**5**   Set the minimum X translation to **-50** and the maximum X translation to **50**.

The bars indicate how much translation in the *x* direction the first bone can do.

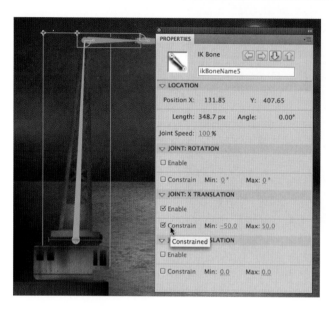

**6**   Grab the hook and pose the crane in the first keyframe so that the first node is close to the edge of the water and the hook is lowered.

**7** Move the red playhead to the last frame.

**8** Move the crane and hook back from the edge of the water, creating a new pose.

The constraints on joint rotation and joint translation impose limits on the poses that help you create more realistic animations.

**9** Watch your animation by choosing Control > Test Movie.

## Changing Joint Speed

Joint speed refers to the stickiness, or stiffness, of a joint. A joint with a low joint speed value will be sluggish. A joint with a high joint speed value will be more responsive. You can set the joint speed value for any selected joint in the Property inspector.

The joint speed is apparent when you drag the very end of an armature. If there are slow joints higher up on the armature chain, those particular joints will be less responsive and will rotate to a lesser degree than the others.

To change the joint speed, click on a bone to select it. In the Property inspector, set the Joint Speed value from 0% to 200%.

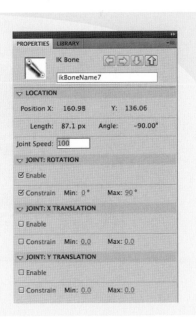

# Inverse Kinematics with Shapes

The crane is an armature made with various movie clip symbols. You can also create armatures with shapes, which are useful for animating objects without obvious joints and segments but can still have an articulated motion. For example, the arms of an octopus have no actual joints, but you can add bones to a smooth tentacle to animate its undulating motion.

## Defining Bones Inside a Shape

You'll add bones to an octopus—perhaps one that was picked up by the crane from the ocean depths—and animate one of its tentacles.

1   Open the file 05ShapeIK_Start.fla.

    The file contains an illustration of an octopus. One arm is separated on its own layer called arm1.

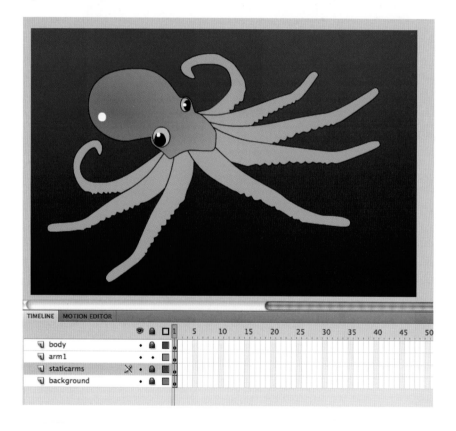

**2** Lock all the layers except for the arm1 layer and select the contents of the arm1 layer.

**3** Choose the Bone tool.

**4** Click on the base of the tentacle in the arm1 layer and drag out the first bone a little ways down toward the tip of the tentacle.

The first bone is defined. The contents of the arm1 layer are separated to a new Pose layer.

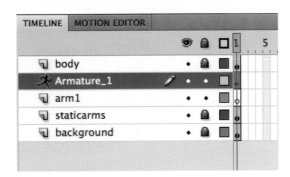

**5** Click on the end of the first bone and drag out the next bone a little farther down toward the tip of the tentacle.

The second bone is defined.

**6** Continue building the armature with a total of four bones.

**7** When the armature is complete, use the Selection tool to click and drag the last bone to see how the deformation of the tentacle follows the bones of the armature.

## Editing the Shape

You don't need any special tools to edit the shape that contains bones. Many of the same drawing and editing tools in the Tools panel, such as the Paint Bucket, the Ink Bottle, and the Subselection tools, are available to you to edit the fill, the stroke, or the contours.

**1** Choose the Paint Bucket tool.

**2** Choose a dark peach color for the Fill.

**3** Click on the shape in the Pose layer.

The fill color of the tentacle changes.

4 Choose the Ink Bottle tool.

5 Choose a dark red color for the stroke.

6 Click on the shape in the Pose layer.

The outline of the tentacle changes color.

7 Choose the Subselection tool.

8 Click on the contour of the shape.

The anchor points and the control handles appear around the contour of the shape.

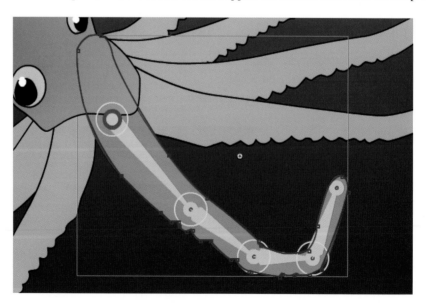

**9** Drag the anchor points to new locations or click and drag the handles to make edits to the tentacle shape.

● **Note:** Add new points on the contour of the shape with the Add Anchor Point tool. Delete points on the contour of the shape with the Delete Anchor Point tool.

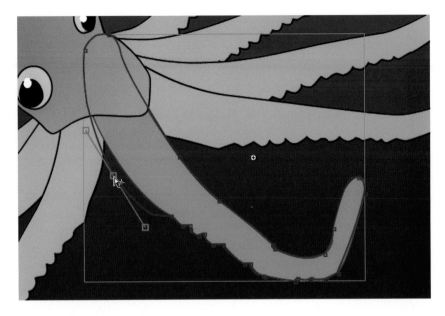

## Editing the Bones and Armature

The Subselection tool can move the joints within a shape and the Free Transform tool can move or rotate the entire armature.

**1** Choose the Subselection tool.

**2** Click on a joint.

**3** Click and drag the joint within the shape to a new location.

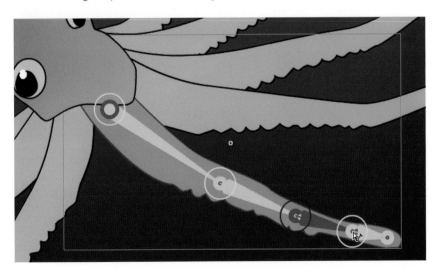

**Note:** You can easily remove bones or add additional bones to your armature. Choose the Selection tool and click on the bone you want to delete. Press the Delete key, and the selected bone and all the child bones will be removed. Add new bones by choosing the Bone tool and clicking on the armature to add new bones.

4  Hold down the Alt/Option key and drag the entire armature to a new location. Or, you can choose the Free Transform tool and rotate or move the entire armature.

# Refining the Shape Behavior with the Bind Tool

The organic control of a shape by its armature is a result of a mapping between the anchor points along the shape and its bones. The points along the tip of the tentacle, for example, are mapped to the very last bone, whereas the points farther up the tentacle are mapped to the bones farther up the tentacle. Hence, where the bones rotate, the shape follows.

You can edit the connections between the bones and their control points with the Bind tool 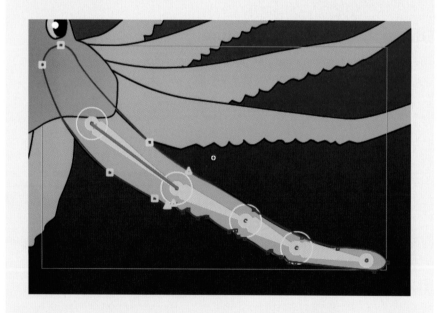. The Bind tool is hidden under the Bone tool. The Bind tool displays which control points are connected to which bones and lets you break those connections and make new ones.

Choose the Bind tool and click on any bone in the shape. The selected bone is highlighted in red, and all the connected control points on the shape are highlighted in yellow.

If you want to redefine which control points are connected to the selected bone, you can do the following:

- Shift-click to add additional control points.
- Ctrl-click/Command-click to remove control points.
- Drag a connection line between the bone and the control point. In the following figure, a line is being dragged from the selected bone to a point on the left to make the association.

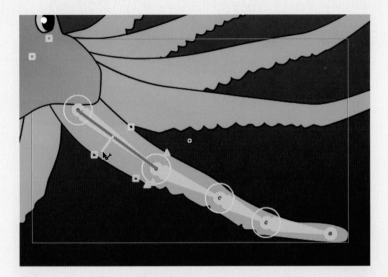

Click on any control point on the shape. The selected control point is highlighted in red, and all the connected bones are highlighted in yellow. In this figure, the red highlighted point is associated with the first bone.

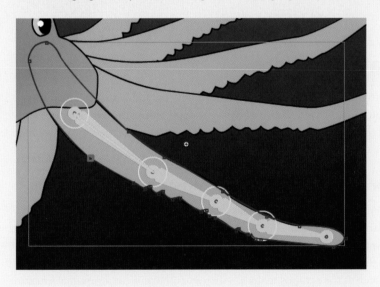

*continues on next page*

If you want to redefine which bones are connected to the selected control point, you can do the following:

- Shift-click to add additional bones.

- Ctrl-click/Command-click to remove bones.

- Drag a connection line between the control point and the bone. In the following figure, another control point farther down the tentacle is being associated with the first bone.

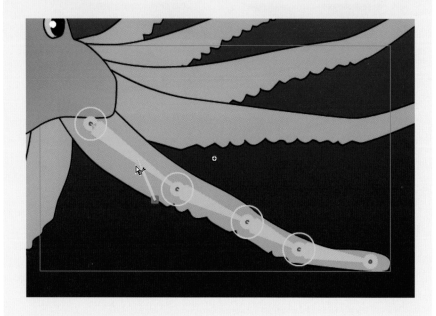

# Armature Options

Many settings are available through the Property inspector that can help you make your armature interactive or help you apply easing to your armature motion. You can also choose different viewing options for your armature to suit your working style.

## Authortime and Runtime Armatures

Authortime armatures are those that you pose along the Timeline and play as straightforward animations. Runtime armatures refer to armatures that are interactive and allow the user to move your armature. You can make any of your armatures— whether they are made with a series of movie clips such as the crane or made with a shape such as the octopus tentacle—into an authortime or a runtime armature. Runtime armatures, however, are restricted to armatures that only have a single pose.

1 Continue with the file 05ShapeIK_Start.fla.

2 Select the layer containing the tentacle armature.

3 In the Property inspector, select Runtime from the Type option.

The armature becomes a runtime armature, allowing the user to directly manipulate the octopus tentacle. The first frame of the Pose layer displays the armature icon to indicate that the runtime option is selected and no additional poses can be added.

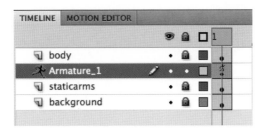

4 Test your movie by choosing Control > Test Movie.

The user can click and drag the tentacle and interactively move it on the Stage.

## Controlling Easing

The Motion Editor and its sophisticated controls for easing cannot be used with armatures. However, there are a few standard eases available from the Property inspector that you can apply to your armatures. Easing can make your armature move with a sense of gravity due to acceleration or deceleration of its motion.

1   Select the layer containing the tentacle armature.

2   In the Property inspector, deselect Runtime from the Type option.

The armature becomes an authortime armature again.

3   Select frame 40 for all the layers and choose Insert > Timeline > Frame.

Frames are inserted in all the layers, giving you room on the Timeline to create additional poses for the tentacle.

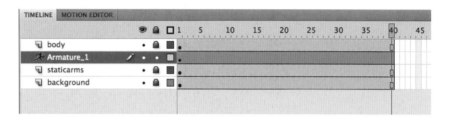

4   Move the red playhead to frame 40.

5   With the Selection tool, grab the tip of the tentacle, curl it upward, and move it to one side.

A new pose is inserted in frame 40 for the tentacle armature.

**6**  Select the first pose in frame 1.

**7**  In the Property inspector, select Simple (Medium) for the Type under the Ease section.

The variations of Simple eases (from Slow to Fastest) represent the severity of the ease. They represent the same curvatures provided in the Motion Editor for motion tweens.

**8**  Set the Strength to **-100**.

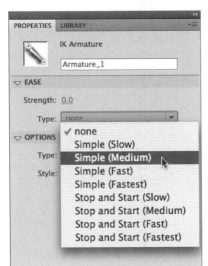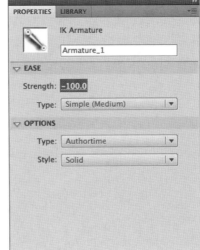

The Strength represents the direction of the ease. A negative value is an ease-in and a positive value is an ease-out.

**9**  Choose Control > Test Movie to preview your animation.

The tentacle curls up, easing into its motion gradually.

**10** Close the Test Movie window.

**11** Select the first pose in frame 1.

**12** Change the Strength setting to **100** and test your movie again.

The tentacle curls up, but the motion now eases out, gradually coming to a stop.

**13** Close the Test Movie window.

**14** Select the first pose in frame 1.

**15** In the Property inspector, select Start and Stop (Medium).

The variations of Stop and Start eases (from Slow to Fastest) represent the severity of the ease. The Stop and Start eases have curves on both ends of the motion, so the easing values affect the start of the motion and the end of the motion.

**16** Set the Strength to **-100**.

**17** Choose Control > Test Movie to preview your animation.

The tentacle curls up, easing into its motion gradually and also easing out of its motion gradually.

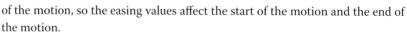

## Armature Viewing Options

You can view the bones of the armature in different ways, depending on how much of the bones you want to see superimposed on your graphics. Select the armature on the Timeline. In the Property inspector, you have three options for the Style:

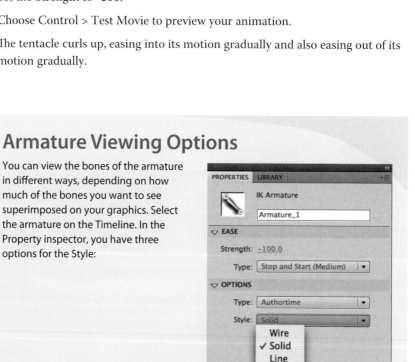

Wire shows the bones as an outline only.

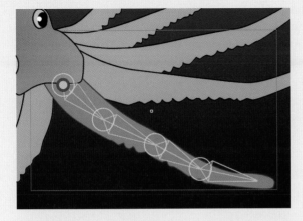

Solid shows the bones as a solid color.

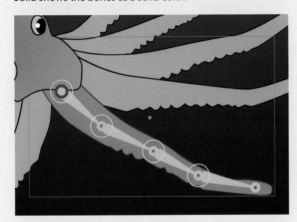

Line shows the bones as a straight line only.

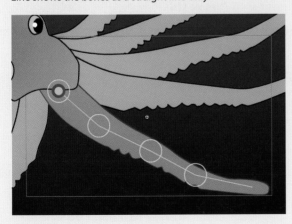

# Morphing with Shape Tweens

Shape tweening is a technique for interpolating amorphous changes between shapes in different keyframes. Shape tweens make it possible to smoothly morph one thing into another. Any kind of animation that requires that the contours of a shape change—for example, animation of clouds, water, or fire—is a perfect candidate for shape tweening.

Both the fill and the stroke of a shape can be smoothly animated. Because shape tweening only applies to shapes, you can't use groups, symbol instances, or bitmap images.

## Establish Keyframes Containing Different Shapes

In the following steps, you'll animate the gently undulating surface of the ocean beneath the crane with a shape tween.

1 Continue with the file of the crane animation called 05_workingcopy.fla.

2 Lock all the layers except for the water layer.

3 Move the red playhead to frame 27 in the water layer.

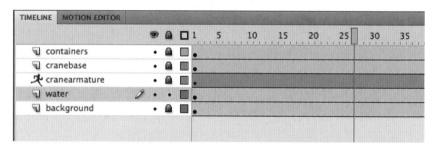

4 Right-click/Ctrl-click on frame 27 in the water layer and select Insert Keyframe. Or, choose Insert > Timeline > Keyframe (F6).

A new keyframe is inserted at frame 27. The contents of the previous keyframe are copied into the second keyframe.

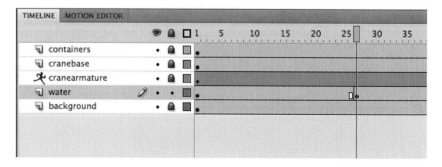

**5** Move the red playhead to frame 56.

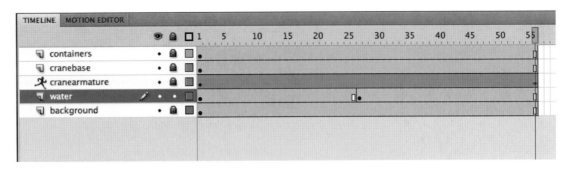

**6** Right-click/Ctrl-click on frame 56 in the water layer and select Insert Keyframe. Or, choose Insert > Timeline > Keyframe (F6).

A new keyframe is inserted at frame 56. The contents of the previous keyframe are copied into this keyframe. You now have three keyframes on the Timeline in the water layer: one at frame 1, a second at frame 27, and a third at frame 56.

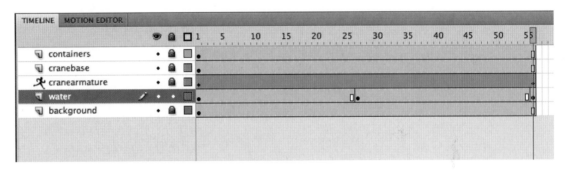

**7** Move the red playhead back to frame 27 and hide the top layers.

Next, you'll change the shape of the water in the second keyframe.

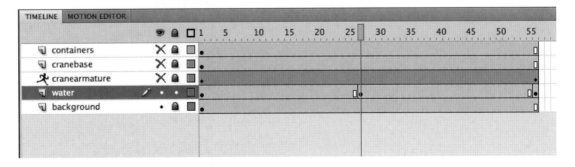

**8** Choose the Selection tool.

**9** Click and drag the contours of the water shape so that the crests become dips and the dips become crests.

Each keyframe in the water layer contains a different shape.

## Apply the Shape Tween

The next step is to apply a shape tween between the keyframes to create the smooth transitions.

**1** Click on any frame between the first keyframe and the second keyframe in the water layer.

**2** Right-click/Ctrl-click and select Create Shape Tween. Or, from the top menu choose Insert > Shape Tween.

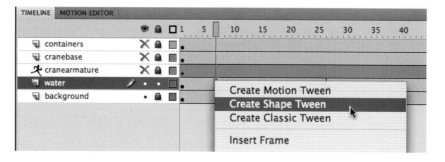

Flash applies a shape tween between the two keyframes, which is indicated by a black forward-pointing arrow.

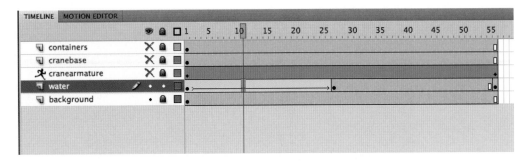

3  Click on any frame between the second keyframe and the last keyframe in the water layer.

4  Right-click/Ctrl-click and select Create Shape Tween. Or, choose Insert > Shape Tween.

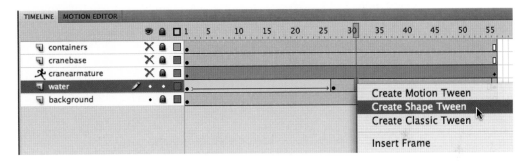

Flash applies a shape tween between the last two keyframes, which is indicated by a black forward-pointing arrow.

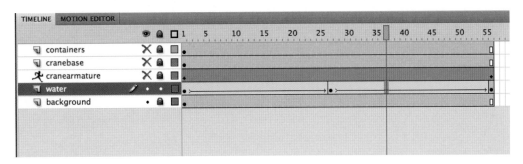

● **Note:** The Motion Editor is not available for shape tweens.

5 Watch your animation by choosing Control > Test Movie.

Flash creates a smooth animation between the keyframes in the water layer, morphing the shape of the ocean surface.

## Using Shape Hints

Shape hints force Flash to map points on the first shape to corresponding points on the second shape. By placing multiple shape hints, you can control more precisely how a shape tween appears.

### Adding Shape Hints

Now you'll add shape hints to the shape tween of the wave to modify the way it morphs from one shape to the next.

**1** Hide the top layers again and select the first keyframe of the shape tween in the water layer.

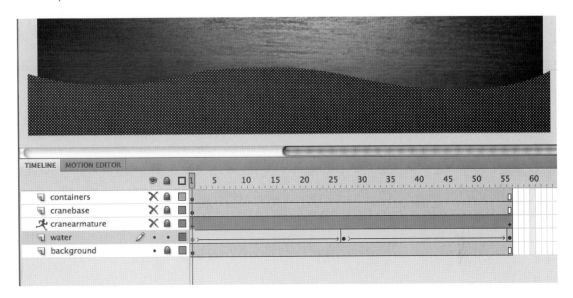

**2** Choose Modify > Shape > Add Shape Hint (Ctrl+Shift+H/Command+Shift+H).

A red circled letter "a" appears on the Stage. The circled letter represents the first shape hint.

**3** Drag the circled letter to the top-left corner of the ocean shape.

Shape hints should be placed on the contours of shapes.

**4** Choose Modify > Shape > Add Shape Hint again to create a second shape hint.

A red circled "b" appears on the Stage.

**5** Drag the "b" shape hint to the top edge of the ocean shape at the bottom of a dip of the wave.

**6** Add a third shape hint.

A red circled "c" appears on the Stage.

**7** Drag the "c" shape hint to the top-right corner of the ocean shape.

You have three shape hints mapped to different points on the shape in the first keyframe.

**8** Select the next keyframe of the water layer.

A corresponding red circled "c" appears on the Stage, although an "a" and a "b" shape hint are directly under it.

**9** Drag the circled letters to corresponding points on the shape in the second keyframe. The "a" hint goes on the top-left corner, the "b" hint goes on the bottom of the wave, and the "c" hint goes on the top-right corner.

The shape hints turn green, indicating that you've correctly placed the shape hint.

**10** Select the first keyframe.

Note that the initial shape hints have turned yellow, indicating that they are correctly placed.

**11** Choose Control > Test Movie to see the effects of the shape hints on the shape tween.

The shape hints force the crest of the first shape to map to the crest of the second shape, causing the shape tween to appear more like a traveling wave instead of an up-and-down bobbing motion.

## Removing Shape Hints

If you've added too many shape hints, you can easily delete the unnecessary ones. Removing a shape hint in one keyframe will remove its corresponding shape hint in the other keyframe.

- Drag an individual shape hint entirely off the Stage and Pasteboard.

- Choose Modify > Shape > Remove All Hints to delete all the shape hints.

# Review Questions

1 What are the two ways of using the Bone tool, and how are they different?

2 What is the Bind tool used for?

3 Define and differentiate these terms: a bone, a node, a joint, and an armature.

4 What is a shape tween, and how do you apply it?

5 What are shape hints, and how do you use them?

# Review Answers

1 The Bone tool can be used in two different ways: First, the Bone tool can connect movie clip instances together to form an articulated object that can be posed and animated with inverse kinematics. Second, the Bone tool can create an armature for a shape, which can also be posed and animated with inverse kinematics.

2 The Bind tool can redefine the connections between the control points of a shape and the bones of an armature. The connections between the control points and the bones determine how the shape reacts to the bending and rotations of the armature.

3 Bones are the objects that connect individual movie clips together or that make up the internal structure of a shape for motion with inverse kinematics. A node is one of the movie clip instances that have been linked with the Bone tool. A node can be described in terms of its relationship with other nodes, such as parent, child, or sibling. Joints are the articulations between bones. Joints can rotate as well as translate (slide in both the $x$ and $y$ directions). Armatures refer to the complete articulated object. Armatures are separated on a special Pose layer on the Timeline, where poses can be inserted for animation.

4 A shape tween creates smooth transitions between keyframes containing different shapes. To apply a shape tween, create different shapes in an initial keyframe and in a final keyframe. Then select any frame between the keyframes in the Timeline, right-click/Ctrl-click, and select Create Shape Tween.

5 Shape hints are labeled markers that indicate how one point on the initial shape of a shape tween will map to a corresponding point on the final shape. Shape hints help refine the way the shapes will morph. To use shape hints, first select the initial keyframe of a shape tween. Choose Modify > Shape > Add Shape Hint. Move the first shape hint to the edge of the shape. Move the playhead to the final keyframe and move the corresponding shape hint to a matching edge of the shape.

# 6 CREATING INTERACTIVE NAVIGATION

## Lesson Overview

In this lesson, you'll learn how to do the following:

- Create button symbols

- Add sound effects to buttons

- Duplicate symbols

- Swap symbols and bitmaps

- Name button instances

- Write ActionScript to create nonlinear navigation

- Create and use frame labels

- Create animated buttons

 This lesson will take approximately two and a half hours to complete. If needed, remove the previous lesson folder from your hard drive and copy the Lesson06 folder onto it.

Let your viewers explore your site and become active participants. Button symbols and ActionScript work together to create engaging, user-driven, interactive experiences.

# Getting Started

To begin, view the photography portfolio page that you'll create as you learn to make interactive projects in Flash.

1   Double-click the 06End.swf file in the Lesson06/06End folder to play the animation.

The project is an interactive Web page for a fictional photographer. Viewers can click a button to see an enlarged version of a photo. In this lesson, you'll create interactive buttons and structure the Timeline properly. You'll learn to write ActionScript to provide instructions for what each button will do.

2   Close the 06End.swf file.

3   Double-click the 06Start.fla file in the Lesson06/06Start folder to open the initial project file in Flash. The file includes several assets already in the Library and on the Stage.

4   Choose File > Save As. Name the file **06_workingcopy.fla** and save it in the 06Start folder. Saving a working copy ensures that the original start file will be available if you want to start over.

# About Interactive Movies

Interactive movies change based on the viewer's actions. For example, when the viewer clicks a button, a larger version of an image is displayed. Interactivity can be simple, such as a button click, or it can be complex, receiving inputs from a variety of sources, such as the movements of the mouse, key presses from the keyboard, or even data from databases.

In Flash, you use ActionScript to achieve most interactivity. ActionScript provides the instructions that tell each button what to do when the user clicks one of them. In this lesson, you'll learn to create a nonlinear navigation—one in which the movie doesn't have to play straight from the beginning to the end. ActionScript can tell the Flash playhead to jump around and to go to different frames of the Timeline based on which button the user clicks. Different frames on the Timeline contain different content. The user doesn't actually know that the playhead is jumping around the Timeline—all the user sees (or hears) is different content appearing as the buttons are clicked on the Stage.

# Designing a Layout

The first task when creating an interactive project like this is to design a layout that will accommodate the buttons and the content. The buttons are usually laid out in one section, called a navigation bar, or nav bar, for short. The nav bar remains constant while the content area changes, depending on which button is clicked. Space should also be allotted for a title and other global information. For this lesson, the Stage has already been set and a pleasant gradient shape has been added in a layer called Background.

## Adding a Simple Design Element

You'll create a black rectangle that will serve to visually separate the title and the nav bar from the main content.

1   Select the existing layer.

2   Click the Insert New Layer button and rename it **navbar**.

3   In the Tools panel, select the Rectangle tool.

**4** Select a black fill and black for a stroke color.

**5** Draw a rectangle on the Stage starting at the top corner of the Stage.

**6** In the Property inspector, set the width to **800**, the height to **130**, the X value to **0**, and the Y value to **0**.

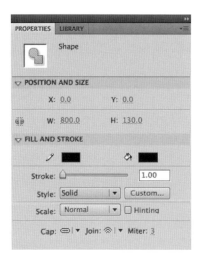

**7** Lock the navbar layer so you don't accidentally move it.

A horizontal black bar sits atop a large gradient.

## Adding a Title and Introductory Text

In this project, the title appears at the top of the Stage, no matter what else is displayed.

1 Select the topmost layer.

2 Click the Insert New Layer button and rename it **title**.

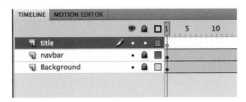

3 Select the Text tool and click an insertion point in the upper-left corner of the Stage.

4 Type **Leon Kritch Photography**.

5 Select all the text. In the Property inspector, select Static Text from the pop-up menu, select Arial for the typeface, and select 42 for the text size. Click the Left Align icon.

6 Select just *Leon Kritch* and change the text color to **#FFCC00**.

7 Select just *Photography* and change the text color to **#333333**.

8 Select the text with the Selection tool. In the Property inspector, set the X value to **30** and the Y value to **10**.

The finished title appears with gold and gray lettering at the top of the black rectangle.

9   Click the Insert New Layer button again and rename it **text**.

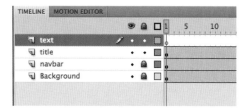

10  Select the Text tool again and drag out a text box on the Stage in the gradient area.

11  Enter some introductory text as in the 06End.swf file and as shown in the following figure. Make the title of the exhibition italic and a different color.

**12** Select the text with the Selection tool and use the Align panel (Window > Align) to position the introductory text in the middle of the Stage. Make sure the To Stage option is selected before aligning the text.

**13** Lock the title layer so you don't accidentally move it.

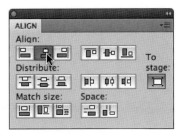

# Creating Buttons

A button is the visual indicator of what the user can interact with. The user usually clicks a button, but many other types of interactions are possible. For example, something can happen when the user rolls the mouse over a button.

Buttons are a kind of symbol that have four special keyframes that determine how the button appears. Buttons can look like virtually anything—they don't have to be those typical pill-shaped gray rectangles that you see on many Web sites.

## Creating a Button Symbol

In this lesson, you'll create buttons with small thumbnail images. A button symbol's four special keyframes include:

- Up keyframe. Shows the button as it appears when the mouse is not interacting with it.

- Over keyframe. Shows the button as it appears when the mouse is hovering over the button.

- Down keyframe. Shows the button as it appears when the mouse button is depressed.

- Hit keyframe. Indicates the clickable area of the button.

You'll understand the relationship between these keyframes and the button appearance as you work through this lesson.

**1** Choose Insert > New Symbol.

**2** In the Create New Symbol dialog box, select Button and name the symbol **button1**. Click OK.

**3**  Flash brings you to symbol-editing mode for your new button.

**4**  In the Up keyframe of the Timeline, drag the small image Photo1.bmp from the Library to the middle of the Stage.

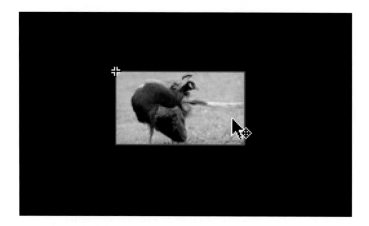

**5**  In the Property inspector, set the X value to **0** and the Y value to **0**.

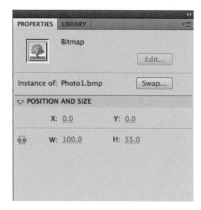

The upper-left corner of the small thumbnail image is now aligned to the center point of the symbol.

**6**  Select the Hit keyframe in the Timeline and choose Insert > Timeline > Frame to extend the Timeline.

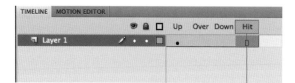

The peacock image now extends through the Up, Over, Down, and Hit keyframes.

7   Insert a new layer.

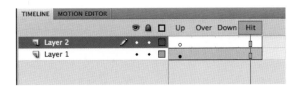

8   Select the Over keyframe and choose Insert > Timeline > Keyframe.

A new keyframe is inserted in the Over keyframe of the top layer.

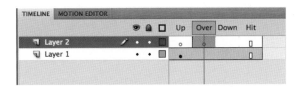

9   Drag the yellow line movie clip symbol from the Library to the Stage.

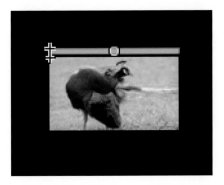

10  In the Property inspector, set the X value to **0** and the Y value to **-7**.

The yellow horizontal line appears over the thumbnail image whenever the mouse cursor rolls over the button.

11  Select the Down keyframe and choose Insert > Timeline > Keyframe.

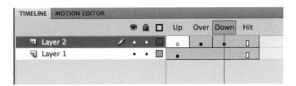

**12** Select the yellow horizontal line, and in the Property inspector, expand the Color Effect section.

**13** Choose Brightness from the Style pull-down menu and change the brightness value to **100%**.

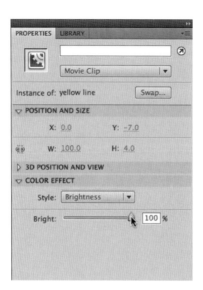

A bright, white, horizontal line appears whenever the mouse button is pressed over the button.

**14** Insert a third layer.

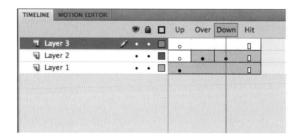

**15** Select the Down keyframe on the new layer and choose Insert > Timeline > Keyframe.

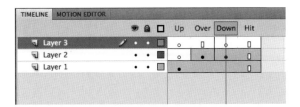

**16** Drag the sound file called Camera_shutter.wav from the Library to the Stage.

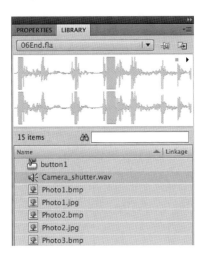

**17** Select the Down keyframe where the sound form appears, and in the Property inspector, make sure that the Sync is set to Event.

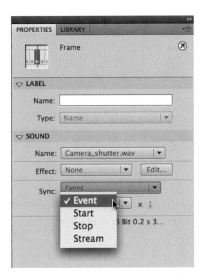

**18** Select the Hit keyframe and choose Insert > Timeline > Blank Keyframe.

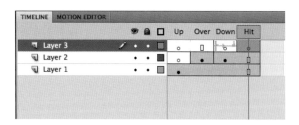

● **Note:** You'll learn more about sound in Chapter 7, "Working with Sound and Video."

The sound of a camera shutter will play only when a viewer clicks the button.

**19** Click Scene 1 above the Stage to exit symbol-editing mode and return to the main Timeline. Your first button symbol is complete! Look in your Library to see the new button symbol stored there.

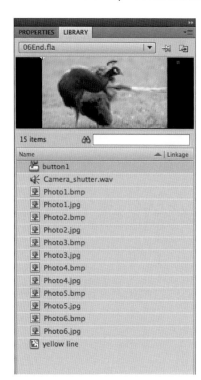

# Invisible Buttons and the Hit Keyframe

Your button symbol's Hit keyframe indicates the area that is "hot," or clickable, to the user. Normally, the Hit keyframe contains a shape that is the exact same size and location as the shape in your Up keyframe. In most cases, you want the graphics that users see to be the same area where they click. However, in certain advanced applications, you may want the Hit keyframe and the Up keyframe to be different. If your Up keyframe is empty, the resulting button is known as an invisible button.

Users can't see invisible buttons, but because the Hit keyframe still defines a clickable area, invisible buttons remain active. Hence, you can place invisible buttons over any part of the Stage and use ActionScript to program them to respond to users. Invisible buttons are useful for creating generic hotspots. For example, placing them on top of different photos can help you make each photo respond to a mouse click without having to make each photo a different button symbol.

## Duplicating Buttons

Now that you've created one button, the others will be easier to create. You'll duplicate the button and then modify each one to display a different thumbnail image.

1  In the Library panel, right-click/Ctrl-click the button1 symbol. Select Duplicate from the context menu. You can also click the options menu at the top-right corner of the Library and select Duplicate.

2  In the Duplicate Symbol dialog box, select Button, and name it **button2**. Click OK.

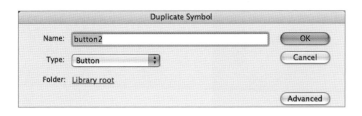

## Swapping Bitmaps

Bitmaps and symbols are easy to swap on the Stage and can significantly speed up your workflow.

1   In the Library panel, double-click the icon for the button2 symbol to edit it.

2   Select the thumbnail image of the peacock.

3   In the Property inspector, click Swap.

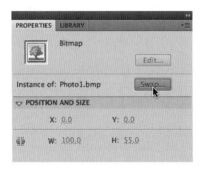

4   In the Swap Bitmap dialog box, select the next thumbnail image, called Photo2. bmp, and click OK.

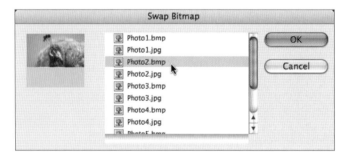

The original thumbnail is swapped for the one you selected. Because they are both the same size, the replacement is seamless.

5 Click Scene 1 to return to the main Timeline.

6 Continue duplicating your buttons and swapping the bitmaps until you have six different button symbols in your Library.

## Placing the Button Instances

The buttons need to be put on the Stage and given names in the Property inspector so that ActionScript can refer to them.

1 Insert a new layer and rename it **buttons**.

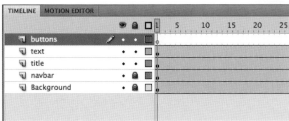

2 Drag each of your buttons from the Library to the Stage, placing them in a horizontal row. Don't worry about their exact position because you'll align them nicely in the next few steps.

**3** Select the first button, and in the Property inspector, set the X value to **35**.

**4** Select the last button, and in the Property inspector, set the X value to **664**.

**5** Select all six buttons. In the Align panel (Window > Align), deselect the To Stage option, click the Space Evenly Horizontally button, and then click the Align Top Edge button.

All six buttons are now evenly distributed.

**6** With all the buttons still selected, in the Property inspector, enter **72** for the Y value.

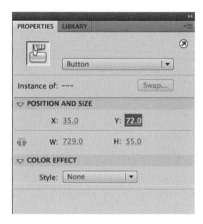

All six buttons are aligned horizontally.

**7** You can now test your movie to see how the buttons behave. Choose Control > Test Movie. Roll over and click each button to see how the Over and Down keyframes of each button appear. At this point, however, you haven't provided any instructions for the buttons to actually do anything. That part comes after you name the buttons and learn a little about ActionScript.

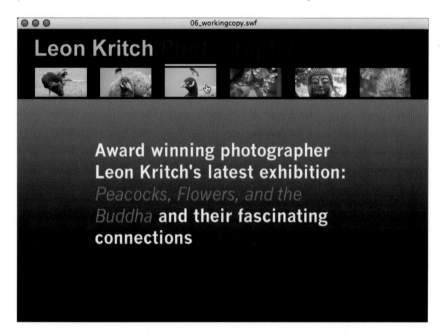

## Naming the Button Instances

Name each button instance so that it can be referenced by ActionScript. This is a crucial step that many beginners forget to do.

1   Select the first button on the Stage.

2   Type **btn1_btn** in the Instance Name field in the Property inspector.

3   Name each of the other buttons **btn2_btn**, **btn3_btn**, **btn4_btn**, **btn5_btn**, and **btn6_btn**.

4   Lock all the layers.

## Naming Rules

Naming instances is a critical step in creating interactive Flash projects. The most common mistake made by novices is not to name, or to incorrectly name, a button instance.

The instance names are important because ActionScript uses the names to reference those objects. Instance names are not the same as the symbol names in the Library. The names in the Library are simply organizational reminders.

Instance naming follows these simple rules:

1   Do not use spaces or special punctuation. Underscores are okay to use.

2   Do not begin a name with a number.

3   End your button name with _btn. Although it is not required, it helps identify those objects as buttons.

4   Do not use any word that is reserved for a Flash ActionScript command.

# Understanding ActionScript 3.0

Adobe Flash CS4 uses ActionScript 3.0, a robust scripting language, to extend the functionality of Flash. Although ActionScript 3.0 may seem intimidating to you if you're new to scripting, you can get great results with some very simple scripts. As with any language, it's best if you take the time to learn the syntax and some basic terminology.

## About ActionScript

ActionScript, which is similar to JavaScript, lets you add more interactivity to Flash animations. In this lesson, you'll use ActionScript to attach behaviors to buttons. You'll also learn how to use ActionScript for such simple tasks as stopping an animation.

You don't have to be a scripting expert to use ActionScript. In fact, for common tasks, you may be able to copy script that other Flash users have shared. However, you'll be able to accomplish much more in Flash—and feel more confident using the application—if you understand how ActionScript works.

This lesson isn't designed to make you an ActionScript expert. Instead, it introduces common terms and syntax, walks you through a simple script, and provides an introduction to the ActionScript language.

If you've used scripting languages before, the documentation included in the Flash Help menu may provide all the additional guidance you need to use ActionScript proficiently. If you're new to scripting and want to learn ActionScript, you may find an ActionScript 3.0 book for beginners helpful.

## Understanding Scripting Terminology

Many of the terms used in describing ActionScript are similar to terms used for other scripting languages. The following terms are used frequently in ActionScript documentation.

### Variable

A *variable* represents a specific piece of data that may or may not be constant. When you create, or *declare*, a variable, you also assign a data type, which determines what kind of data the variable can represent. For example, a String variable holds any string of alphanumeric characters, whereas a Number variable must contain a number.

● **Note:** Variable names must be unique, and they are case sensitive. The variable mypassword is not the same as the variable MyPassword. Variable names can contain only numbers, letters, and underscores; they cannot begin with a number. These are the same naming rules for instances. (In fact, they are conceptually the same.)

### Keyword

In ActionScript, a *keyword* is a reserved word that is used to perform a specific task. For example, *var* is a keyword that is used to create a variable.

You can find a complete list of keywords in Flash Help. Because these words are reserved, you can't use them as variable names or in other ways. ActionScript always uses them to perform their assigned tasks.

### Parameters

*Parameters* provide specific details for a particular command and are the values between parentheses () in a line of code. For example, in the code `gotoAnd-Play(3);` the parameter instructs the script to go to frame 3.

### Function

A *function* is a group of statements that you can refer to by name. Using a function makes it possible to run the same set of statements without having to type them repeatedly.

### Objects

In ActionScript 3.0, you work with objects, which are abstract types of data that help you do certain tasks. A Sound object, for example, helps you control sound, and a Date object can help you manipulate time-related data. The button symbols that you created earlier in this lesson are also objects—they are Button objects.

Every object should be named. An object that has a name can be referenced and controlled with ActionScript. Buttons on the Stage are referred to as instances, and in fact, *instances* and *objects* are synonymous.

### Methods

*Methods* are the keywords that result in action. Methods are the doers of ActionScript, and each kind of object has its own set of methods. Much of learning ActionScript is learning the methods for each kind of object. For example, two methods associated with a MovieClip object are `stop()` and `gotoAndPlay()`.

### Properties

*Properties* describe an object. For example, the properties of a movie clip include its height and width, *x* and *y* coordinates, and scale. Many properties can be changed, whereas other properties can only be "read," meaning they simply describe the object.

## Using Proper Scripting Syntax

If you're unfamiliar with program code or scripting, ActionScript code may be challenging to decipher. Once you understand the basic *syntax*, which is the grammar and punctuation of the language, you'll find it easier to follow a script.

- The **semicolon** at the end of the line tells ActionScript that it has reached the end of the code line and to go to the next line in the code.

- As in English, every open **parenthesis** must have a corresponding close parenthesis, and the same is true for **brackets** and **curly brackets**. If you open something, you must close it. Very often, the curly brackets in ActionScript code will be separated on different lines. This makes it easier to read what's inside the curly brackets.

- The **dot** operator (.) provides a way to access the properties and methods of an object. Type the instance name, followed by a dot, and then the name of the property or method. Think about the dot as a way to separate objects, methods, and properties.

- Whenever you're entering a string or the name of a file, use **quotation marks**.

- You can add **comments** that ActionScript will ignore to remind you or others what you are accomplishing with different parts of the script. To add a comment for a single line, start it with two slashes (//). To type a multiline comment, start it with /* and end it with */.

Flash provides assistance in the following ways as you write scripts in the Actions panel:

- Words that have specific meanings in ActionScript, such as keywords and statements, appear in blue as you type them in the Actions panel. Words that are not reserved in ActionScript, such as variable names, are in black. Strings are in green. Comments, which ActionScript ignores, are in gray.

- As you work in the Actions panel, Flash can detect the action you are entering and display a code hint. There are two types of code hints: a tooltip that contains the complete syntax for that action and a pop-up menu that lists possible ActionScript elements.

- To check the syntax of a script you're writing, click the AutoFormat icon ▤ (which will also format the script according to conventions so that it is easier for others to read) or click the Check Syntax icon ✔. Syntax errors are listed in the Compiler Errors panel.

## Navigating the Actions Panel

The Actions panel is where you write all your code. Open the Actions panel by choosing Window > Actions or select a keyframe on the Timeline and click the Actions panel icon 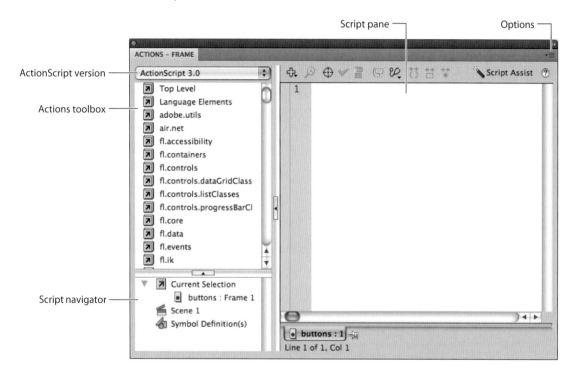 on the top right of the Property inspector. You can also right-click/Ctrl-click on any keyframe and select Actions from the context menu.

The Actions panel gives you quick access to the core elements of ActionScript as well as provides you with different options to help you write, debug, format, edit, and find your code.

The Actions panel is divided into several panes. At the top-left corner is the Actions toolbox. Several categories are listed in the Actions toolbox, which organizes all the ActionScript code. At the top of the Actions toolbox is a pull-down menu that displays only the code for the version of ActionScript you select. You should select ActionScript 3.0, the latest version. At the very bottom of the Actions toolbox categories is a yellow Index category that lists, in alphabetical order, all the language elements. You don't need to use the toolbox to add code to your script, but it can help to ensure that you're using the code correctly.

At the top right of the Actions panel is the Script pane—the blank slate in which all your code appears. You enter ActionScript in the Script pane just as you would in a text-editing application.

At the bottom left of the Actions panel is the Script navigator, which can help you find a particular piece of code. ActionScript is placed on keyframes on the Timeline, so the Script navigator can be particularly useful if you have lots of code scattered in different keyframes and on different Timelines.

All the panes in the Actions panel can be resized to suit your working style. They can even be collapsed completely to maximize the pane that you are working in. To resize a pane, click and drag the horizontal or vertical dividers.

# Adding a Stop Action

You've used stop actions in previous lessons. A stop action simply stops the movie from continuing by halting the playhead; in this case, you'll use it to stop the movie from showing any of the content along the Timeline until the user actually clicks a button.

1  Insert a new layer and rename it **actions**.

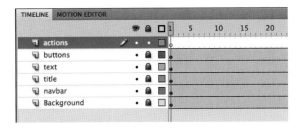

2  Select the first keyframe of the actions layer and open the Actions panel (Window > Actions).

3  In the Script pane, enter stop();

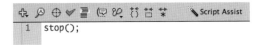

The code appears in the Script pane and a tiny lowercase "a" appears in the first keyframe of the actions layer to indicate it contains some ActionScript. The movie will now stop at frame 1.

## About Script Assist

Some actions are simple, such as stop actions. But others require parameters, and if you're unfamiliar with ActionScript, you may have difficulty remembering which options are available—or required—for each type of action. Script Assist mode prompts you to add the methods, parameters, or variables related to the action, and then it assembles the information using the correct syntax for you.

Script Assist won't write the script for you. You still have to know what you want to do and which variables, methods, or functions to use. However, it can help you put the pieces together coherently, so that you don't have to return to the script multiple times to troubleshoot syntax errors.

To use Script Assist, click Script Assist in the Actions panel.

Then double-click an item in the Actions toolbox to add it to the Script pane. The upper section of the Actions panel displays fields and options that are available for that item. Select options and enter values as appropriate for your script.

## Creating Event Handlers for Buttons

Events are occurrences that happen in the Flash environment that Flash can detect and respond to. For example, a mouse click, a mouse movement, and a key press on the keyboard are all events. These events are produced by the user, but some events can happen independently of the user, like the successful loading of a piece of data or the completion of a sound. With ActionScript, you can write code that detects events and respond to them with an event handler.

The first step in event handling is to create a listener that will detect the event. A listener looks something like this:

```
wheretolisten.addEventListener(whatevent, responsetoevent);
```

The actual command is addEventListener(). The other words are placeholders for objects and parameters for your situation. *Wheretolisten* is the object where the event occurs (usually a button), *whatevent* is the specific kind of event (such as a mouse click), and *responsetoevent* is a function that is triggered when the event happens. So if you want to listen for a mouse click over a button called btn1_btn, and the response is to trigger a function called showimage1, the code would look like this:

```
btn1_btn.addEventListener(MouseEvent.CLICK, showimage1);
```

The next step is to create the function that will respond to the event—in this case, the function called showimage1. A function simply groups a bunch of actions together; you can then trigger that function by referencing its name. A function looks something like this:

```
function showimage1 (myEvent:MouseEvent){ };
```

Function names, like button names, are arbitrary. You can name functions whatever makes sense to you. In this particular example, the name of the function is called showimage1. It receives one parameter (within the parentheses) called myEvent, which is an event that involves a mouse event. The colon describes what type of object it is. If this function is triggered, all the actions between the curly brackets are executed.

## Adding the Event Listener and Function

You'll add ActionScript code to listen for a mouse click on each button. The response will make Flash go to a particular frame on the Timeline to show different content.

1 Select the first frame of the actions layer.

2 Open the Actions panel.

3 In the Script pane of the Actions panel, beginning on the second line, type

```
btn1_btn.addEventListener(MouseEvent.CLICK, showimage1);
```

The listener listens for a mouse click over the btn1_btn object on the Stage. If the event happens, the function called showimage1 is triggered.

4 On the next line of the Script pane, type

```
function showimage1(event:MouseEvent):void {
    gotoAndStop(10);
}
```

**● Note:** Be sure to include the final curly bracket, or the function won't work.

The function called showimage1 contains instructions to go to frame 10 and stop there. The code for your button called btn1_btn is complete.

5  On the next line of the Script pane, enter additional code for the remaining five buttons. You can copy and paste lines 2 and 3, and simply change the names of the button, the name of the function (in two places), and the destination frame. The full script should be as follows:

```
stop();
btn1_btn.addEventListener(MouseEvent.CLICK, showimage1);
function showimage1(event:MouseEvent):void {
    gotoAndStop(10);
}
btn2_btn.addEventListener(MouseEvent.CLICK, showimage2);
function showimage2(event:MouseEvent):void {
    gotoAndStop(20);
}
btn3_btn.addEventListener(MouseEvent.CLICK, showimage3);
function showimage3(event:MouseEvent):void {
    gotoAndStop(30);
}
btn4_btn.addEventListener(MouseEvent.CLICK, showimage4);
function showimage4(event:MouseEvent):void {
    gotoAndStop(40);
}
btn5_btn.addEventListener(MouseEvent.CLICK, showimage5);
function showimage5(event:MouseEvent):void {
    gotoAndStop(50);
}
btn6_btn.addEventListener(MouseEvent.CLICK, showimage6);
function showimage6(event:MouseEvent):void {
    gotoAndStop(60);
}
```

## Mouse Events

The following list contains the ActionScript codes for common mouse events. Use these codes when you create your listener, and make sure that you pay attention to lowercase and uppercase letters. For most users, the first event (MouseEvent.CLICK) will be sufficient for all projects. That event happens when the user clicks the mouse button.

- MouseEvent.CLICK
- MouseEvent.DOUBLE_CLICK
- MouseEvent.MOUSE_MOVE
- MouseEvent.MOUSE_DOWN
- MouseEvent.MOUSE_UP
- MouseEvent.MOUSE_OVER
- MouseEvent.MOUSE_OUT

## ActionScript Commands for Navigation

The following list contains the ActionScript codes for common navigation commands. Use these codes when you create buttons to stop the playhead, start the playhead, or move the playhead to different frames. The gotoAndStop and gotoAndPlay commands require additional information, or parameters, within their parentheses as indicated.

- stop();
- play();
- gotoAndStop(framenumber or framelabel);
- gotoAndPlay(framenumber or framelabel);
- nextFrame();
- prevFrame();

## Checking Syntax and Formatting Code

ActionScript can be very picky, and a single misplaced period can cause your entire project to grind to a halt. Fortunately, the Actions panel provides a few tools to help you identify errors and help you fix them.

1 Select the first frame of your actions layer and open the Actions panel if it is not already open.

2 Click the Check Syntax button at the top of the Actions panel.

Flash checks the syntax of your ActionScript code. Flash notifies you if there are errors or if your code is error free.

3 Click the AutoFormat icon at the top of the Actions panel.

Flash formats your code so it conforms to standard spacing and line breaks.

● **Note:** Change the automatic formatting by selecting Preferences from the upper right options menu. Choose Auto Format from the left menu and select the various options for formatting your code.

# Creating Destination Keyframes

When the user clicks each button, Flash moves the playhead to a new spot on the Timeline. However, you haven't yet placed anything different at those particular frames. That's the next step.

## Inserting Keyframes with Different Content

You will create six keyframes in a new layer and place a different large photo in each of the keyframes.

1   Insert a new layer at the top of the layer stack but below the actions layer and rename it **images**.

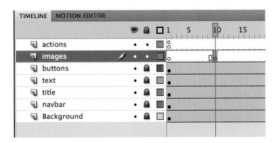

2   Select frame 10 of the images layer.

3   Insert a new keyframe at frame 10 (Insert > Timeline > Keyframe, or F6).

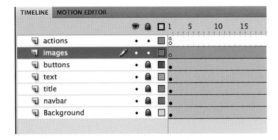

4   Insert new keyframes at frames 20, 30, 40, 50, and 60.

Your Timeline has seven empty keyframes in the images layer.

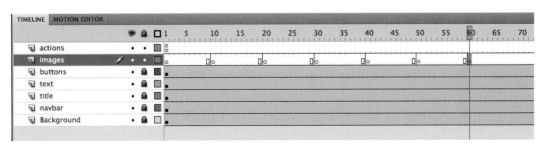

**5** Select the keyframe at frame 10.

**6** Drag the bitmap image called Photo1.jpg from the Library to the Stage. Photo1.jpg is a large photo of a peacock.

**7** In the Property inspector, set the X value to **35** and the Y value to **138**.

The keyframe at frame 10 contains a large photo of a peacock.

**8** Select the keyframe at frame 20.

**9** Drag the bitmap image called Photo2.jpg from the Library to the Stage.

**10** In the Property inspector, set the X value to **35** and the Y value to **138**.

The keyframe at frame 20 contains a large photo of the head of a peacock (see figure at top of next page).

**11** Place each of the large bitmaps from the Library in the corresponding keyframes in the images layer.

Each keyframe should contain a different photo from this photographer's portfolio.

**12** Choose Control > Test Movie and click any of the buttons.

Each button on the top row moves the playhead to a different frame on the Timeline, where a different photo is displayed. The user can choose to see any photo in any order.

## Using Labels on Keyframes

Your ActionScript code tells Flash to go to a different frame number when the user clicks each of the buttons. However, if you decide to edit your Timeline and add or delete a few frames, you'll need to go back into your ActionScript and change your code so the frame numbers match.

An easy way to avoid this problem is to use frame labels instead of fixed frame numbers. Frame labels are names that you give to keyframes. Instead of referring to keyframes by their frame number, you refer to them by their label. So, even if you move your destination keyframes as you edit, the labels remain with their keyframes. To reference frame labels in ActionScript, you must enclose them in quotation marks. The command `gotoAndStop("label1")` makes the playhead go to the keyframe with the label called label1.

1  Select frame 10 on the images layer.

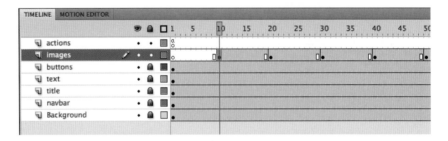

2  In the Property inspector, enter **label1** in the Label Name field.

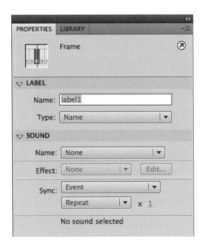

A tiny flag icon appears on each of the keyframes that have labels.

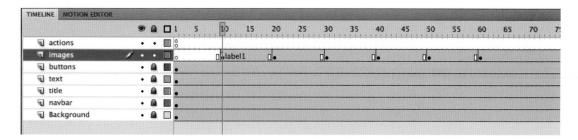

3   Select frame 20 on the images layer.

4   In the Property inspector, enter **label2** in the Label Name field.

5   Select frames 30, 40, 50, and 60, and in the Property inspector, enter
    corresponding names in the Label Name field: **label3**, **label4**, **label5**, and **label6**.

A tiny flag icon appears on each of the keyframes that have labels.

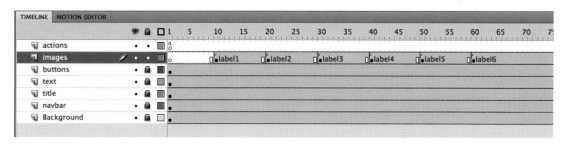

6   Select the first frame of the actions layer and open the Actions panel.

7   In your ActionScript code, change all the fixed frame numbers in each of the
    gotoAndStop() commands to the corresponding frame labels:

    •   gotoAndStop(10);  should be changed to gotoAndStop("label1");

    •   gotoAndStop(20);  should be changed to gotoAndStop("label2");

    •   gotoAndStop(30);  should be changed to gotoAndStop("label3");

    •   gotoAndStop(40);  should be changed to gotoAndStop("label4");

    •   gotoAndStop(50);  should be changed to gotoAndStop("label5");

    •   gotoAndStop(60);  should be changed to gotoAndStop("label6");

The ActionScript code now directs the playhead to a particular frame label instead of a particular frame number.

8  Test your movie by choosing Control > Test Movie.

The functionality of your interactive movie remains the same, but future edits to the Timeline will be easier to make.

## Playing Animation at the Destination

So far, this interactive portfolio works by using the `gotoAndStop()` command to show images in different keyframes along the Timeline. But how would you play an animation after a user clicks a button? The answer is to use the command `gotoAndPlay()`, which moves the playhead to the frame number or frame label specified by its parameter and plays from that point.

# Creating Transition Animations

Next, you will create a short transition animation for each of your photos. Then you'll change your ActionScript code to direct Flash to go to each of the keyframes and play the animation.

1   Move the playhead to the label1 frame label.

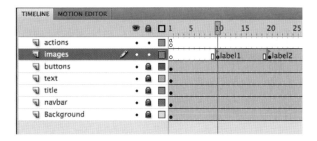

2   Right-click/Ctrl-click on the photo on the Stage and choose Create Motion Tween.

Flash asks to convert the photo to a symbol so that it can proceed with the motion tween. Click OK.

3   In the Property inspector, select Brightness from the Style pull-down menu in the Color Effect section.

**4** Set the Bright slider to **100%**.

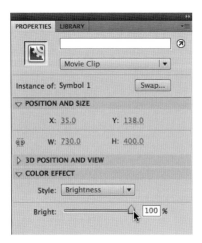

The instance on the Stage becomes bright white.

**5** Move the playhead to the end of the tween span at frame 19.

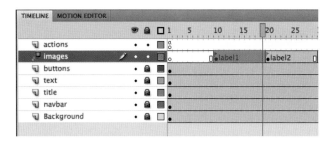

**6** Select the bright white instance on the Stage.

**7** In the Property inspector, set the Bright slider to **0%**.

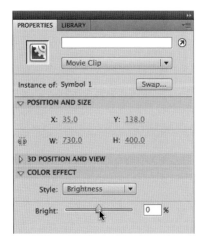

The instance is displayed at a normal brightness level. The motion tween from frame 10 to frame 19 shows a smooth transition from a bright white photo to a normal photo.

8   Create similar motion tweens for the remaining photos in the keyframes labeled label2, label3, label4, label5, and label6.

● **Note:** Recall that you can use the Motion Presets panel to save a motion tween and apply it to other objects to save you time and effort. Select the first motion tween on the Timeline and click Save selection as preset.

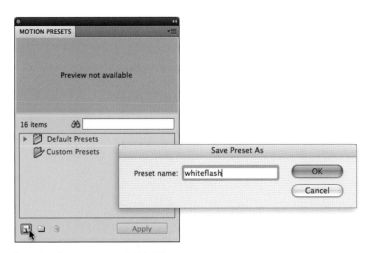

Provide a Preset name and click OK.

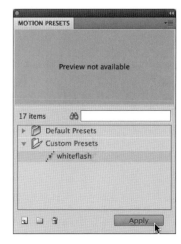

Click on the second photo, select the preset that you just saved, and click Apply.

## Using the gotoAndPlay Command

The gotoAndPlay command makes the Flash playhead move to a specific frame on the Timeline and begin playing from that point.

1   Select the first frame of the actions layer and open the Actions panel.

2   In your ActionScript code, change all the `gotoAndStop()` commands to `gotoAndPlay()` commands. Leave the parameter unchanged:

*   `gotoAndStop("label1");` should be changed to `gotoAndPlay("label1");`
*   `gotoAndStop("label2");` should be changed to `gotoAndPlay("label2");`
*   `gotoAndStop("label3");` should be changed to `gotoAndPlay("label3");`
*   `gotoAndStop("label4");` should be changed to `gotoAndPlay("label4");`
*   `gotoAndStop("label5");` should be changed to `gotoAndPlay("label5");`
*   `gotoAndStop("label6");` should be changed to `gotoAndPlay("label6");`

```
ACTIONS - FRAME
1   stop();
2   btn1_btn.addEventListener(MouseEvent.CLICK, showimage1);
3   function showimage1(event:MouseEvent):void {
4       gotoAndPlay("label1");
5   }
6   btn2_btn.addEventListener(MouseEvent.CLICK, showimage2);
7   function showimage2(event:MouseEvent):void {
8       gotoAndPlay("label2");
9   }
10  btn3_btn.addEventListener(MouseEvent.CLICK, showimage3);
11  function showimage3(event:MouseEvent):void {
12      gotoAndPlay("label3");
13  }
14  btn4_btn.addEventListener(MouseEvent.CLICK, showimage4);
15  function showimage4(event:MouseEvent):void {
16      gotoAndPlay("label4");
17  }
18  btn5_btn.addEventListener(MouseEvent.CLICK, showimage5);
19  function showimage5(event:MouseEvent):void {
20      gotoAndPlay("label5");
21  }
22  btn6_btn.addEventListener(MouseEvent.CLICK, showimage6);
23  function showimage6(event:MouseEvent):void {
24      gotoAndPlay("label6");
25  }
```

actions : 1
Line 25 of 25, Col 2

The ActionScript code now directs the playhead to a particular frame label and begins playing at that point.

● **Note:** A fast and easy way of doing multiple replacements is to use the Find and Replace command in the Actions panel. From the options menu in the upper-right corner, select Find and Replace.

In the Find field, enter **gotoAndStop**, and in the Replace field, enter **gotoAndPlay**.

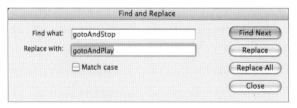

Click Replace All and Flash will make the substitutions in the code.

## Stopping the Animations

If you test your movie now (Control > Test Movie), you'll see that each button goes to its corresponding frame label and plays from that point, but it keeps playing, showing all the remaining animations in the Timeline. The next step is to tell Flash when to stop.

1   Select frame 19 of the actions layer, the frame just before the label2 keyframe on the image layer.

2   Right-click/Ctrl-click and choose Insert Keyframe.

A new keyframe is inserted in frame 19 of the actions layer.

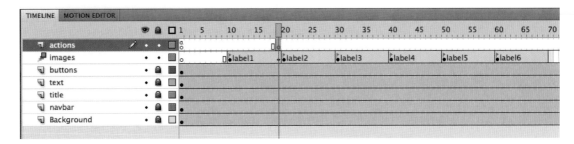

3   Open the Actions panel.

The Script pane in the Actions panel is blank. Don't panic! Your code has not disappeared. Your code for the event listeners is on the first keyframe of the actions layer. You have selected a new keyframe in which you will add a stop command.

4   In the Script pane, enter `stop();`

Flash will stop playing when it reaches frame 19.

```
1   stop();
```

5   Insert keyframes at frames 29, 39, 49, 59, and 69.

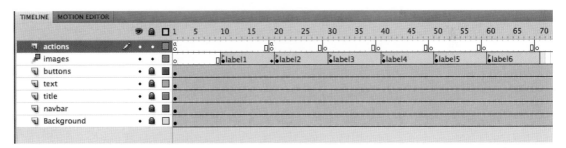

6   In each of those keyframes, add a stop command in the Actions panel.

7   Test your movie by choosing Control > Test Movie.

Each button takes you to a different keyframe and plays a short animation. At the end of the animation, the movie stops and waits for you to click another button.

**Note:** If you want a quick and easy way to duplicate the keyframe containing the stop command, hold down the Alt/Option key while you move it to a new location on the Timeline.

# Animated Buttons

Animated buttons display an animation in the Up, Over, or Down keyframes. When you hover your mouse cursor over one of the portfolio buttons, the yellow horizontal bar appears. But imagine if that yellow horizontal bar was animated. It would give more life and whimsy to the interaction between the user and the button.

The key to creating an animated button is to create an animation inside a movie clip symbol, and then place that movie clip symbol inside the Up, Over, or Down keyframes of a button symbol. When one of those button keyframes is displayed, the animation in the movie clip plays.

## Creating the Animation in a Movie Clip Symbol

Your button symbols in this portfolio project already contain the yellow line movie clip symbol. You will edit the movie clip symbol to add an animation inside it.

1 In the Library, double-click the yellow line movie clip symbol icon.

   Flash puts you in symbol-editing mode for the yellow line movie clip symbol.

2 Right-click/Ctrl-click on the yellow rectangular shape on the Stage and choose Create Motion Tween.

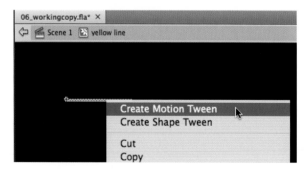

3 In the dialog box that appears asking for confirmation to convert the selection to a symbol, click OK.

Flash creates a Tween layer and adds one second worth of frames to the movie clip Timeline.

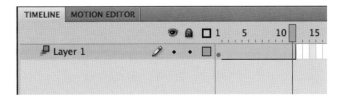

4 Select the Free Transform tool.

5 Click on the yellow rectangle on the Stage.

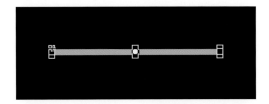

6 Drag the control handles on the side to reduce the width to about 10 pixels.

Flash creates a smooth transition between the long rectangle and the short rectangle.

7 Exit symbol-editing mode by clicking the Scene 1 button above the Stage.

8 Choose Control > Test Movie.

As your mouse cursor hovers over any of the buttons, the yellow rectangle pulses from wide to narrow. The motion tween inside the movie clip symbol plays continuously in a loop, and the movie clip symbol is placed inside the button symbol.

● **Note:** If you want your animated button to play its animation only once, you must add a stop command at the end of the movie clip's Timeline.

## Review Questions

1 How and where do you add ActionScript code?

2 How do you name an instance, and why is it necessary?

3 How can you label frames, and when is it useful?

4 What is a function?

5 What is an event? What is an event listener?

6 How do you create an animated button?

## Review Answers

1 ActionScript code resides in keyframes on the Timeline. Keyframes that contain ActionScript are indicated by a small lowercase "a". You add ActionScript through the Actions panel. Choose Window > Actions, or select a keyframe and click the Actions icon in the Property inspector, or right-click/Ctrl-click and select Actions. You enter code directly in the Script pane in the Actions panel, or you can select commands from the categories in the Actions toolbox.

2 To name an instance, select it on the Stage, and then type in the Instance Name field in the Property inspector. You need to name an instance to reference it in ActionScript.

3 To label a frame, select a keyframe on the Timeline, and then type a name in the Frame Label box in the Property inspector. You can label frames in Flash to make it easier to reference frames in ActionScript and to give you more flexibility. If you want to change the destination of a gotoAndStop or gotoAndPlay command, you can move the label rather than having to locate every reference to the frame number in the script.

4 A *function* is a group of statements that you can refer to by name. Using a function makes it possible to run the same set of statements without having to type them repeatedly into the same script. When an event is detected, a function is executed in response.

5 An event is an occurrence that is initiated by a button click, a key press, or any number of inputs that Flash can detect and respond to. An event listener, also called an event handler, is a function that is executed in response to specific events.

6 Animated buttons display an animation in the Up, Over, or Down keyframes. To create an animated button, make an animation inside a movie clip symbol, and then place that movie clip symbol inside the Up, Over, or Down keyframes of a button symbol. When one of those button keyframes is displayed, the animation in the movie clip plays.

# 7 WORKING WITH SOUND AND VIDEO

## Lesson Overview

In this lesson, you'll learn how to do the following:

- Import sound files

- Edit sound files

- Use the Adobe Media Encoder

- Understand video and audio encoding options

- Play external video from your Flash project

- Customize options on the playback component

- Work with video that contains alpha channels

- Embed video in your Flash project

 This lesson will take approximately two hours to complete. If needed, remove the previous lesson folder from your hard drive and copy the Lesson07 folder onto it.

Sound and video add new dimensions to your projects. Import sound files and edit them directly in Flash, and use the Adobe Media Encoder to compress and convert video files to use in Flash.

# Getting Started

Start the lesson by viewing the finished animated zoo kiosk. You'll create the kiosk by adding sound and video files to a project in Flash.

1   Double-click the 07End.swf file in the Lesson07/07End folder to play the animation.

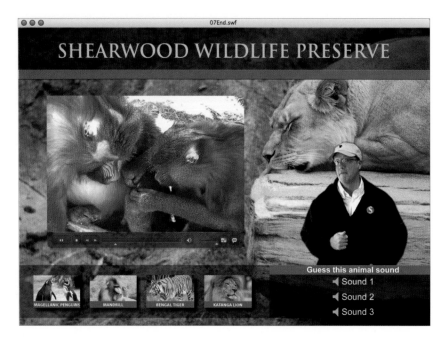

View the movie of the polar bear with a short soundtrack of an African beat. A zoo director appears on the screen, speaks, and then disappears.

2   Click a sound button to hear an animal sound.

3   Click a thumbnail button to view a short movie about the animal.

In this lesson, you'll import audio files and put them on the Timeline to provide the short audio flourish. You'll also learn how to embed sounds in each button. You'll use the Adobe Media Encoder to compress and convert the video files to the appropriate format for Flash. You'll also learn how to work with transparent backgrounds in video to create the silhouetted zoo director video.

1   Double-click the 07Start.fla file in the Lesson07/07Start folder to open the initial project file in Flash.

2   Choose File > Save As. Name the file **07_workingcopy.fla**, and save it in the 07Start folder. Saving a working copy ensures that the original start file will be available if you want to start over.

# Understanding the Project File

The initial setup of the project has been completed except for the audio and video portions. The Stage is 1000 x 700 pixels. A row of buttons of colorful animals is on the bottom row, another set of buttons on the right, a title at the top, and a background image of a resting lion.

The Timeline contains several layers that separate the different content.

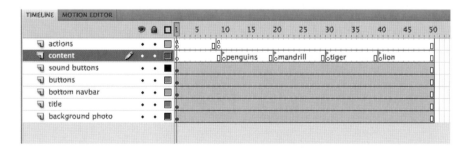

The bottom three layers, called background photo, title, and bottom navbar, contain design elements, text, and images. The next two layers above, called buttons and sound buttons, contain instances of button symbols. The content layer contains several labeled keyframes, and the actions layer contains ActionScript that provides the event handlers for the bottom row of buttons.

If you've completed the previous chapter, you should be familiar with the structure of this Timeline. The individual buttons on the bottom row are coded so that when the user clicks a button, the playhead moves to a corresponding labeled keyframe. You'll be inserting content into each of those keyframes. But first you'll learn to work with sound.

# Using Sounds

You can import several types of sound files into Flash. Flash supports MP3, WAV, and AIFF files, which are three common kinds of sound formats. When you import sound files into Flash, they are stored in your Library. You can then drag the sound files from the Library on to the Stage at different points along the Timeline to synchronize those sounds to whatever may be happening on the Stage.

## Importing Sound Files

You'll import several sound files in the Library to be used throughout this lesson.

1   Choose File > Import > Import To Library.

2   Select the Monkey.wav file in the Lesson07/07Start/Sounds folder, and click Open (Windows) or Import To Library (Mac OS).

The Monkey.wav file appears in your Library. The sound file is indicated by a unique icon, and the preview window shows a waveform—a series of peaks and valleys that represent the sound.

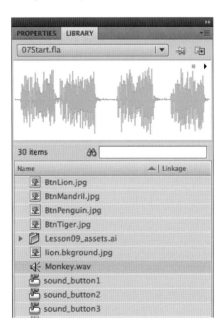

**3** Click the Play button on the far upper-right corner of the Library preview window.

The sound plays.

**4** Double-click the sound icon in front of your Monkey.wav file.

The Sound Properties dialog box appears, providing information on your sound file, including its original location, size, and other technical properties.

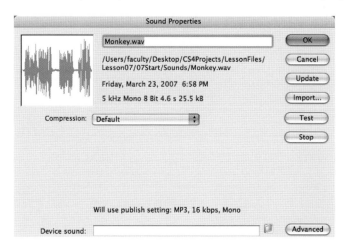

**5** Choose File > Import > Import To Library and select the other sound files to import into your Flash project. Import Elephant.wav, Lion.wav, Africanbeat. mp3, and Afrolatinbeat.mp3.

Your Library should contain all the sound files.

**6** Create a folder in your Library and place all the sound files inside it to organize your Library. Name the folder **sounds**.

## Where to Find Sound Clips

If you're looking for interesting sounds to use in your Flash movie, you can use the free sound files available from Adobe. Flash CS4 comes preloaded with dozens of useful sounds that you can access by choosing Window > Common Libraries > Sounds. An external library (a library that is not connected to the current project) appears.

Simply drag one of the sound files from the external library on to your Stage. The sound will appear in your own Library.

## Placing Sounds on the Timeline

You can place a sound at any point along the Timeline, and Flash will play that sound when the playhead reaches the keyframe. You'll place a sound on the very first keyframe to play as the movie starts to provide a pleasant audio introduction and set the mood.

1   Select the content layer on the Timeline.

2   Insert a new layer and rename it **sounds**.

3   Select the first keyframe of the sounds layer.

4   Drag the Afrolatinbeat.mp3 file from the sounds folder in your Library on to the Stage.

The waveform of your sound appears on the Timeline.

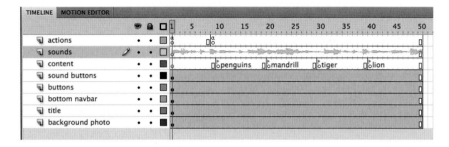

5  Select the first keyframe of the sounds layer.

In the Property inspector, note that your sound file is now listed on the pull-down menu under the Sound section.

6  Select Stream for the Sync option.

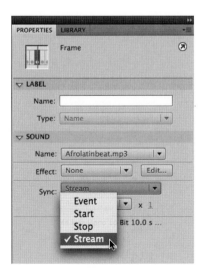

The Sync options determine how the sound plays on the Timeline. Use Stream sync for long passages of music or narration when you want to time the sound with the Timeline.

7   Move the playhead back and forth on the Timeline.

The sound plays as you scrub the Timeline.

8   Choose Control > Test Movie.

The sound plays only for a short while before getting cut off. Because the sound is set to Stream, it only plays when the playhead moves along the Timeline. There is a stop action at frame 9 that stops the playhead, and hence, stops the sound.

## Adding Frames to the Timeline

The next step is to extend the Timeline so that the entire sound (or at least the portions that you desire) plays before the stop action.

1   Click on the Stage to deselect the Timeline, and then place the playhead between frames 1 and 9 by clicking on the top frame numbers.

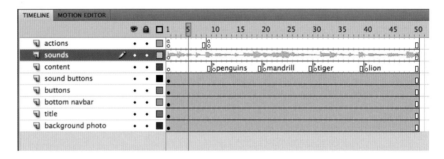

2   Choose Insert > Timeline > Frame, or press F5, to insert frames in all the layers between frames 1 and 9.

3   Insert enough frames so that the entire Timeline extends to frame 80.

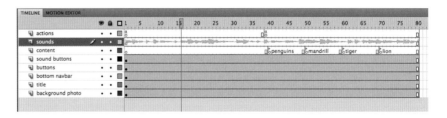

4   Choose Control > Test Movie.

The sound lasts longer because it has more frames to play before the playhead stops.

# Clipping the End of a Sound

The sound clip you imported is a bit longer than you need. You'll shorten the sound file by using the Edit Envelope dialog box. Then you'll apply a fade so that the sound gradually decreases as it ends.

1   Select the first keyframe of the sounds layer.

2   In the Property inspector, click the Pencil button.

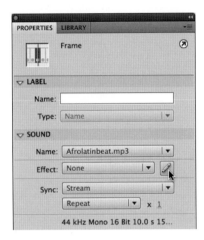

The Edit Envelope dialog box appears, showing you the waveform. The top and the bottom waveform are the left and right channels of the sound (stereo). A timeline is between the waveforms, a pull-down menu of preset effects at the left corner, and view options at the bottom.

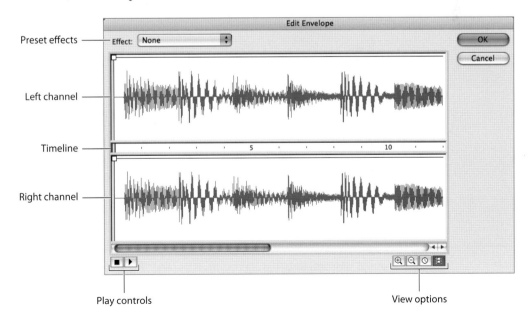

3  In the Edit Envelope dialog box, click the Seconds icon.

The timeline changes units to show seconds instead of frames. You can click the Frames icon to switch back, depending on how you want to view your sound.

4  Click the Zoom Out icon until you can see the entire waveform.

The waveform appears to end at around 120 frames, or about 10 seconds.

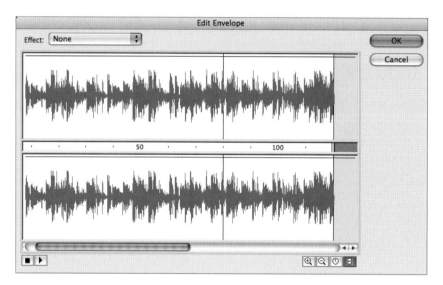

5  Drag the right end of the time slider inward to about frame 40.

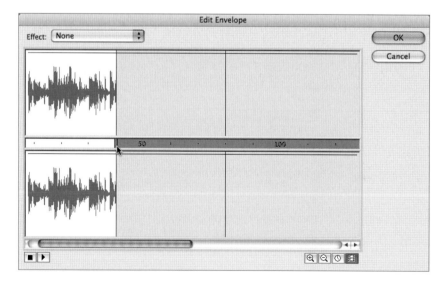

The sound shortens by being clipped from the end. The sound now only plays for about 40 frames.

**6** Click OK to accept the changes you've made.

The waveform on the main Timeline indicates the shortened sound.

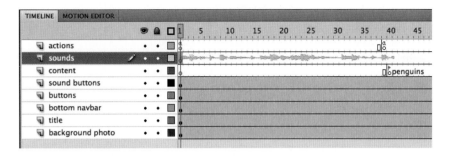

## Changing the Volume of a Sound

The sound will be more elegant if it slowly fades out instead of being abruptly cut off. You can change the volume levels through time in the Edit Envelope dialog box.

**1** Select the first keyframe of the sounds layer.

**2** In the Property inspector, click the Edit button.

The Edit Envelope dialog box appears.

**3** Select the Frames viewing option, and zoom in on the waveform to see its end near frame 40.

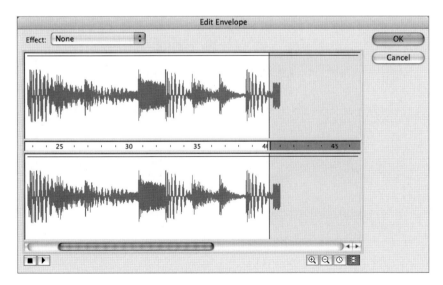

**4** Click on the top horizontal line of the top waveform above frame 35.

A box appears on the line, indicating a keyframe for the sound volume.

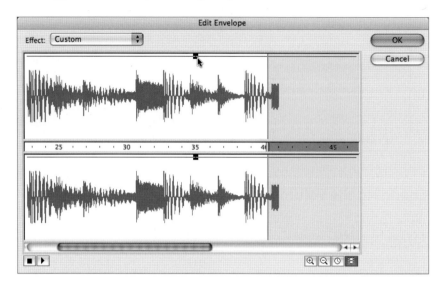

**5** Click on the top horizontal line of the upper waveform above frame 40 and drag it down to the bottom of the window.

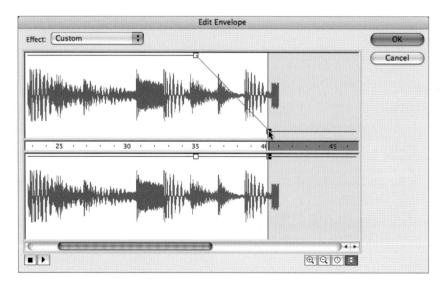

The downward diagonal line indicates the drop in volume from 100% to 0%.

**6** Click on the corresponding keyframe on the lower waveform and drag it down to the bottom of the window.

The volume levels for both the left and right channels slowly decrease starting at frame 35. By frame 40, the volume level is at 0%.

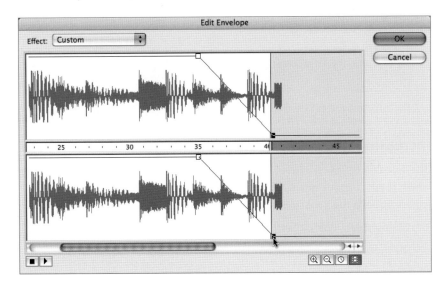

**7** Test the effects of your sound edits by clicking the Play button on the lower-left side of the dialog box. Click OK to accept the changes.

● **Note:** You can apply some of the preset effects from the pull-down menu in the Edit Envelope dialog box by just choosing them. Common effects like a fade in or a fade out are provided for your convenience.

## Deleting or Changing the Sound File

If you don't want the sound on your Timeline, or you want to change the sound to a different one, you can make those changes from the Property inspector.

**1** Select the first keyframe of the sounds layer.

**2** In the Property inspector, select None in the Name pull-down menu.

The sound is removed from the Timeline.

**3**  Select Africanbeat.mp3 for Name.

The Africanbeat.mp3 sound is added to the Timeline.

## Increasing the Quality of the Sounds

The default settings on a new Flash project use fairly high compression on sounds, which results in poor-quality audio. It's best to increase the quality of the sound export through the Publish Settings options.

**1**  Choose File > Publish Settings.

The Publish Settings dialog box appears.

**2**  Click the Flash tab and click the Set button for the Audio Stream options.

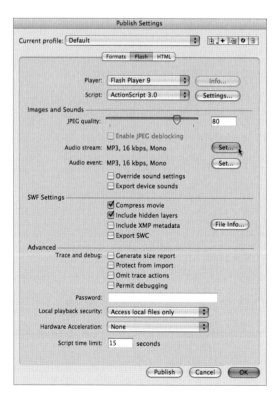

The Sound Settings dialog box appears.

3   Increase the Bit rate to 48 kbps.

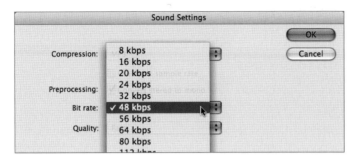

The Bit rate determines the quality of the sound in your final, exported Flash movie. The higher the bit rate, the better the quality. However, the higher the bit rate, the larger your file becomes. You must determine the balance of quality and file size based on the minimum acceptable level of quality.

4   Deselect the option to Convert stereo to mono.

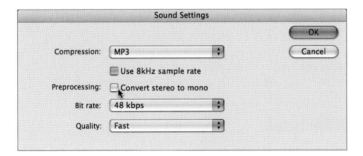

Stereo sounds will be preserved. The Africanbeat.mp3 file in particular relies on stereo effects, so keeping both the left and right channels is important. Click OK to accept the settings.

5   Click the Set button for the Audio Event options.

The Sound Settings dialog box appears.

6   Increase the Bit rate to 48 kbps and deselect the option to Convert stereo to mono. Click OK to accept the settings.

Both the Audio Stream and Audio Event settings should be at 48 kbps with Stereo.

7   Select Override sound settings.

The sound settings in the Publish Settings will determine how all your sounds are exported.

8  Choose Control > Test Movie.

The quality of the sound will be greatly increased in your exported SWF.

## Adding Sounds to Buttons

In the kiosk, the buttons appear in a column on the right. You'll add sounds to the buttons so that they play whenever the user clicks them.

1  In the Library, double-click the icon of the button symbol called sound_button1.

You enter symbol-editing mode for that button symbol.

2  There are three layers in the button symbol to help organize the content for the Up, Over, Down, and Hit keyframes.

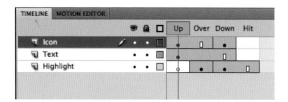

3  Insert a new layer and rename it **sounds**.

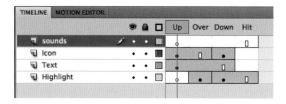

4  Select the Down frame in your sounds layer and insert a keyframe.

A new keyframe appears in the Down state of your button.

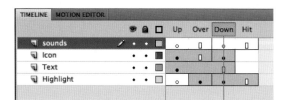

**5** Drag the Monkey.wav file from the sounds folder in your Library to the Stage.

A waveform for the Monkey.wav file appears in the Down keyframe of the sounds layer.

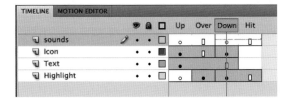

**6** Select the Down keyframe in the sounds layer.

**7** In the Property inspector, choose Start for the Sync option.

A Start sync option triggers the sound whenever the playhead enters that particular keyframe.

**8** Choose Control > Test Movie. Test the first button to hear the monkey, and then close the preview window.

**9** Edit the sound_button2 and the sound_button3 to add the Lion.wav and the Elephant.wav sounds to their Down frames.

## Understanding Sound Sync Options

Sound sync refers to the way the sound is triggered and played. There are several options: Event, Start, Stop, and Stream. Stream links the sound to the Timeline so you can easily synchronize animated elements to the sound. Event and Start are used to trigger a sound (usually a short sound) to a specific event, like a button click. Event and Start are similar except that the Start sync does not trigger the sound if it is already playing (so there are no overlapping sounds possible with Start sync). The Stop option is used to stop a sound, although you'll use it rarely, if ever. If you want to stop a sound with a Stream sync, simply insert a blank keyframe.

# Understanding Flash Video

Flash is fast becoming the de facto method of delivering video over the Web. In fact, more Internet users can view video with Flash than with any other technology including QuickTime, Windows Media Player, or RealPlayer. News sites such as the *New York Times* and content sharing sites such as *YouTube* all use Flash to present video.

Adding video to Flash is easy, whether you want to present straight video alone, or whether you want to incorporate it with other animated elements. There are two options to display video in Flash. The first option is to embed the video in your Flash file, and the second option is to keep the video separate from your Flash file and use a playback component from Flash to play the video.

Both methods require that the video be formatted correctly first. The appropriate video format for Flash is Flash Video, which uses the extension .flv or the extension .f4v. F4V is the latest Flash Video format that supports the H.264 standard, a state-of-the-art video codec that delivers high quality with remarkably efficient compression. A codec (*c*ompression-*de*compression) is a method computers use to compress a video file to save space, and then decompress it to play it back. FLV is the standard format for previous versions of Flash and uses the older codecs Sorenson Spark or On2VP6.

● **Note:** Flash can actually play back any video encoded in H.264, so your video file doesn't have to have the .f4v extension. For example, a video with a .mov extension encoded by QuickTime Pro with H.264 is compatible with Flash.

# Using the Adobe Media Encoder

You can convert your video files to the FLV or F4V format using the Adobe Media Encoder CS4, a stand-alone application that comes with Flash CS4. The Adobe Media Encoder can convert single files or multiple files (known as batch processing) to make your workflow easier.

## Adding a Video File to the Adobe Media Encoder

The first step to convert your video file to a compatible Flash format is to add the video to the Adobe Media Encoder for encoding.

1  Launch the Adobe Media Encoder, which comes installed with Adobe Flash CS4.

   The opening screen displays a window that lists any current video files that have been added for processing. The window should be empty.

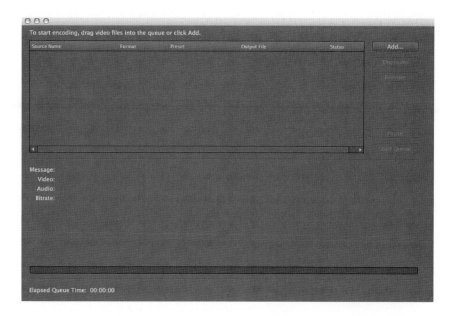

**2** Choose File > Add or click the Add button on the right.

A dialog box opens for you to select a video file.

**3** Navigate to the Lesson07/07Start folder, select the Penguins.mov file, and click OK.

The Penguins.mov file is added to the display list and is ready for conversion to an FLV or F4V format.

● **Note:** You can also drag the file directly to the queue from your Desktop.

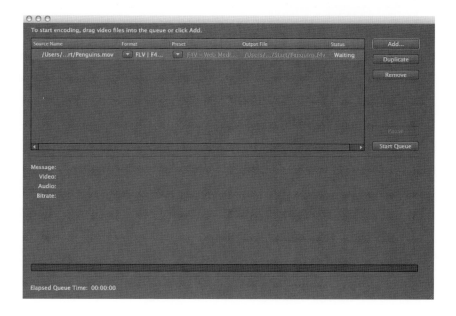

## Converting Video Files to Flash Video

1   In the options under Format, select the FLV/F4V (H.264) option.

2   Under the Preset options, choose F4V-Web Medium.

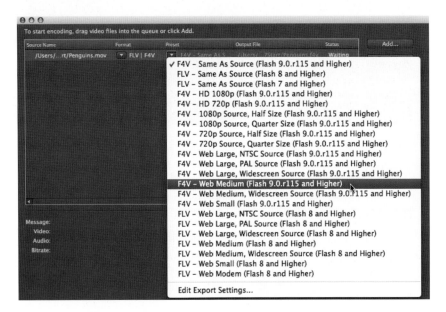

You can choose one of many of the standard preset options from the menu. The options determine the format (either the newer F4V or the older FLV) and the size of the video. The Web Medium option converts your original video to 360 pixels wide by 272 pixels high, which is an average size to display video in a Web browser. In parentheses, Flash indicates the minimum Flash Player version required to play the selected video format.

3   Click on the Output File.

You can choose to save the converted file in a different location on your computer and choose a different filename. Your original video will not be deleted or altered in any way.

4   Click Start Queue.

Flash begins the encoding process. Flash displays the settings for the encoded video and shows the progress and a preview of the video.

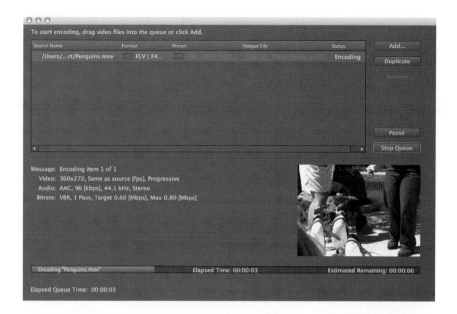

When the encoding process finishes, a green check in the display list indicates that the file has been converted successfully. You now have the file, Penguins.f4v in your Lesson07/07Start folder, along with the original Penguins.mov file.

● **Note:** If you have multiple video files to encode to F4V or FLV format, you can do so all at once and easily with the Adobe Media Encoder in a process known as batch processing. Each file can even have its own settings. Click the Add button to add videos to the display list. Choose a different format for each file, if desired. Click Start Queue to begin the batch processing. In the following figure, two additional files are in line to be encoded.

● **Note:** You can change the status of individual files in the queue by selecting the file in the display list and choosing Edit > Reset Selection or Edit > Skip Selection. Reset Selection removes the green check from a completed file so it can be encoded again, whereas Skip Selection makes Flash skip that particular file in the batch processing.

# Understanding Encoding Options

You can customize many settings when converting your original video to the Flash Video format. You can crop and resize your video to specific dimensions, just convert a snippet of the video, adjust the type of compression and the compression levels, and even apply filters to the video. To display the encoding options, click the Preset selection in the display list or choose Edit > Export Settings. The Export Settings dialog box appears.

## Cropping Your Video

If you only want to show a portion of your video, you can crop it. Choose Edit > Reset Status to reset the Penguins.mov file so you can experiment with the cropping settings.

1   Click the Crop button at the upper-left corner of the Export Settings dialog box.

The cropping box appears over the video preview window.

2   Drag the sides inward to crop from the top, bottom, left, or right.

The grayed-out portions outside the box will be discarded. Flash displays the new dimensions next to your cursor. You can also use the Left, Top, Right, and Bottom settings above the preview window to enter exact pixel values.

**3** If you want to keep the crop in a standard proportion, click the Crop Proportions menu and choose a desired ratio.

The cropping box will be constrained to the selected proportions.

**4** To see the effects of the crop, click the Output tab.

The preview window shows how your final video will appear.

**5** Exit the cropping mode by clicking the Crop button again under the Source tab. You will not need to crop the Penguins.mov video for this lesson.

## Adjusting Video Length

Your video may have unwanted segments at the beginning or the end. You can shave off footage from either end to adjust the overall length of your video.

**1** Click and drag the playhead (top marker) to scrub through your video to preview the footage. Place the playhead at the desired beginning point of your video.

Time markers indicate the number of seconds that have elapsed.

**2** Click the Set In Point icon.

The In point moves to the current position of the playhead.

**3** Drag the playhead to the desired ending point of your video.

**4** Click the Set Out Point icon.

The Out point moves to the current position of the playhead.

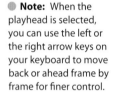**Note:** When the playhead is selected, you can use the left or the right arrow keys on your keyboard to move back or ahead frame by frame for finer control.

**5** You can also simply drag the In and Out point markers to bracket the desired video segment. Drag the In and Out points back to their original positions because you do not need to adjust the video length for this lesson.

## Cue Points

At the bottom left of the Export Settings dialog box is an area where you can set cue points for your video.

Cue points are an advanced feature that lets you add special markers at various points along the video. With ActionScript, you can program Flash to recognize when those cue points are encountered, or you can navigate to specific cue points. Cue points can transform an ordinary, linear video into a true interactive, immersive video experience.

## Setting Advanced Video and Audio Options

The right side of the Export Settings dialog box contains all the advanced video and audio options. You can toggle between Simple mode and Advanced mode using the Mode icon 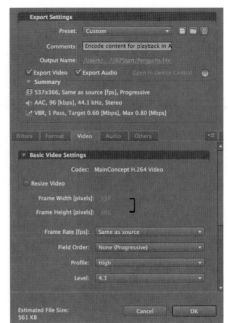.

The Advanced mode shows all the settings for audio and video at the top of the panel. You can choose one of the preset options from the top Preset menu. At the bottom, you can navigate to different encoding options using the tabs. At the very bottom, Flash displays the estimated final output size.

You will export the Penguins.mov again but at a larger size.

1   Make sure that the Export Video and Export Audio boxes are selected.

2   Click the Format tab and choose F4V.

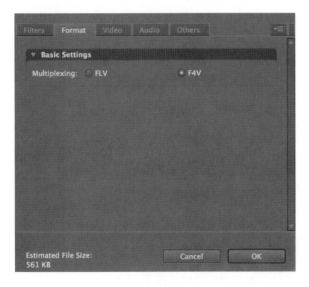

3   Click the Video tab.

4   Select Resize Video and click the Constrain option (the chain link icon). Enter **480** for the Width and click outside the field to accept the change.

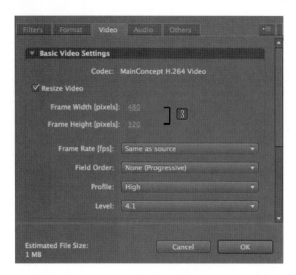

The Height automatically changes to keep the proportions of the video.

5   Click OK.

Flash closes the Export Settings dialog box and saves your advanced video and audio settings.

6   Click Start Queue to begin the encoding process with your custom resize settings.

Flash creates another F4V file of Penguins.mov. Delete the first one you created and rename the second one **Penguins.f4v**.

## Saving Advanced Video and Audio Options

If you want to process many videos similarly, it makes sense to save your advanced video and audio options. You can do that in the Adobe Media Encoder. Once saved, you can easily apply your settings to other videos in the queue.

1   In the Export Settings dialog box, click the Save Preset button.

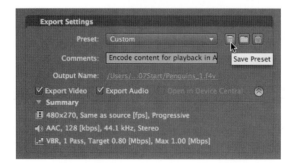

2   In the dialog box that opens, provide a descriptive name for the video and audio
    options. Click OK.

3   Return to the queue of videos. You can apply your custom settings to additional
    videos by simply choosing the preset from the Preset pull-down menu.

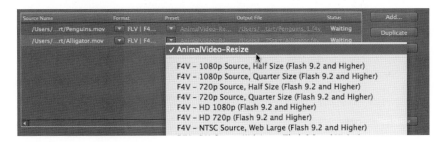

# Playback of External Video

Now that you have successfully converted your video to the correct Flash Video
format, you can use it in your Flash zoo kiosk project. You will have Flash play each
of the animal videos at the different labeled keyframes on the Timeline.

You will keep your videos external to the Flash project. By keeping videos external,
you keep your Flash project small, and the videos can maintain different frame rates
from your Flash project.

1   Open your 07_workingcopy.fla project in Flash CS4.

2   Select the keyframe labeled penguins in the content layer.

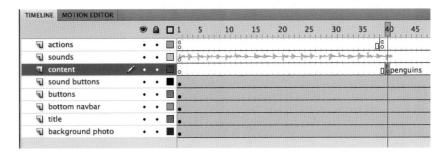

**3**  Choose File > Import > Import Video.

The Import Video wizard appears.

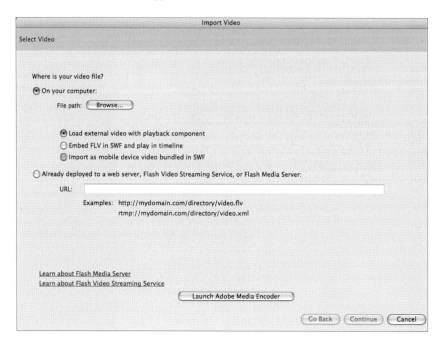

**4**  In the Import Video wizard, select On Your Computer and click Browse (Windows) or Choose (Mac).

**5**  In the dialog box, select Penguins.f4v from the Lesson07/07Start folder and click Open.

**6**  Select the Load external video with playback component option. Click Next or Continue.

● **Note:** The skin is a small SWF file that determines the functionality and appearance of the video's controls. You can use one of the skins provided with Flash, or you can customize your own. To preview a skin, select it from the Skin menu.

**7**  Select SkinUnderAllNoFullNoCaption.swf from the Skin menu and select color #333333 with a 75% Alpha. Click Next or Continue.

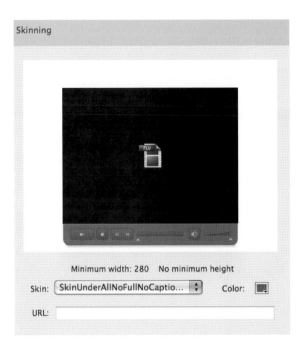

**Skinning**

Minimum width: 280    No minimum height

Skin: `SkinUnderAllNoFullNoCaptio...`    Color: ▣

URL:

8   On the next screen of the Import Video wizard, review the information for the video file, and then click Finish to encode the file.

9   A black box representing your video with the selected skin appears on the Stage. Place the video box on the left side of the Stage.

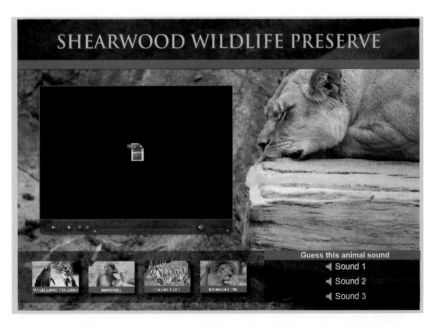

A playback component also appears in your Library. The component is a special widget that is used on the Stage to play your video.

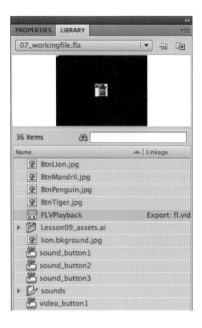

10 Choose Control > Test Movie. Click the Magellanic Penguins button.

The video begins streaming into your Flash file. Use the controls to play, stop, and change the volume for the movie. Close the preview window.

**11** The other animal videos have already been encoded (in FLV format) and provided in the 07Start folder. Import the Mandril.flv, Tiger.flv, and Lion.flv videos in each of their corresponding keyframes.

● **Note:** The FLV or F4V files, the 07_workingcopy.swf file, and the skin file are all required for your zoo kiosk project to work.

## Controlling the Video Playback

The playback component lets you control which video plays, whether the video plays automatically, and other aspects of playback. The options for playback can be accessed by selecting Window > Component Inspector (Shift-F7). Parameters are listed in the left column, and their corresponding values are listed in the right column.

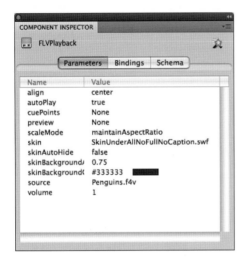

• To change the AutoPlay option, select true or false from the right column. True makes the video play automatically, and false pauses the video on the first frame.

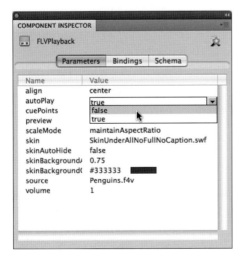

- To hide the controller and only display it when users roll their mouse cursor over the video, select true for the SkinAutoHide option.

- To choose a new controller (the skin), double-click the SkinUnderAllNoFullNoCaption.swf and select a new skin in the dialog box that appears.

- To change the transparency of the controller, enter a decimal value from 0 (totally transparent) to 1 (totally opaque) for the SkinBackgroundAlpha.

- To change the color of the controller, click on the color chip and choose a new color for the SkinBackgroundColor.

- To change the video file or the location of the video file that Flash looks for to play, click the Source option.

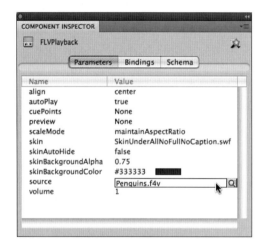

In the Content Path dialog box, enter a new filename or click on the Folder icon to choose a new file to play.

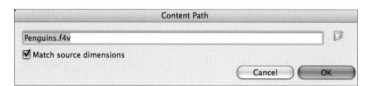

# Working with Video and Transparency

For the various animal videos, you want to show the entire frame with the animals in the foreground and the lush environment in the background. But sometimes you want to use a video file that doesn't include a background. For this project, the zoo director was filmed in front of a green screen, which was removed using Adobe After Effects. When you use the video in Flash, the zoo director appears to be in front of the Flash background. A similar effect is used for news weatherpersons, where the background of the video is totally transparent and can show weather graphics behind the person.

Transparencies in video (called alpha channels) are supported only in the FLV format using the On2VP6 codec. When encoding a video with an alpha channel, be sure to select the Encode Alpha Channel option in the Video tab of the Export Settings.

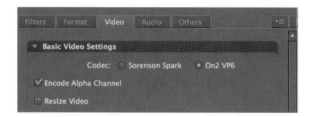

You'll import the video file, which is already in FLV format, into Flash for display with the playback component. However, you won't include a skin, so users will be unable to control the video. The zoo director will appear directly on the Stage.

## Importing the Video Clip

Now you'll use the Import Video wizard to import the Popup.flv file.

1 Insert a new layer called **popup video**.

2 Insert a keyframe at frame 35 and insert another keyframe at frame 40.

3 Select the keyframe at frame 35.

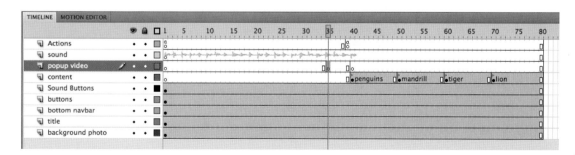

**4** Choose File > Import > Import Video.

**5** In the Import Video wizard, select On Your Computer and click Browse or Choose. Select the Popup.flv file in the Lesson07/07Start folder and click Open.

**6** Select Load external video with playback component. Click Next or Continue.

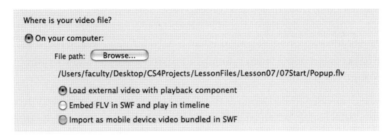

**7** Select None from the Skin menu and click Next or Continue.

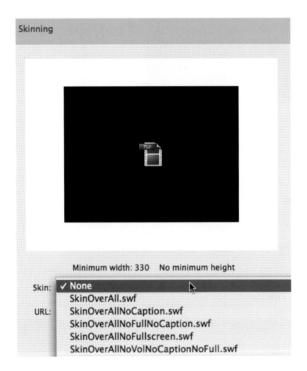

**8**  Click Finish to import the video.

A black box indicating the video appears on the Stage.

**9**  Use the Selection tool to position the new video just above the red bar and the sound buttons.

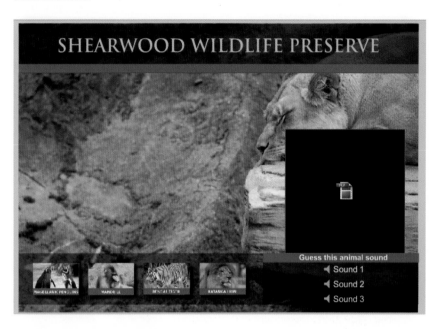

The video appears in the popup video layer in the keyframe at frame 35 as the sound begins to fade out. At frame 40, where the penguin video is placed, the popup video is removed from the Timeline.

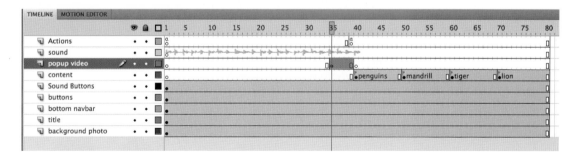

# Using a green screen

Professionals often film people in front of solid green or blue backgrounds, so that they can easily remove, or key, the background in a video-editing application such as Adobe After Effects. Then, the person is merged with a different background. The image of the zoo director was filmed in front of a green screen, which was removed in After Effects.

1 Shoot footage in front of a green screen.

- Use a green background that is flat, smooth, and free of shadows, so that the color is as pure as possible.

- Minimize the light that reflects off the green screen onto the subject.

- Keep movement to a minimum for Flash video; use a tripod if possible.

2 Remove the background in After Effects.

Import the file as footage into After Effects, create a new composition, and drag it onto the Composition Timeline.

Create a garbage mask to roughly outline the shape and remove most of the background. But be sure the subject never moves outside the mask!

Use the Color Range keying effect to delete the rest of the background. You may need to do some fine-tuning with the Matte Choker and Spill Suppressor effects. A spill suppressor removes the light that splashes onto the edges of the subject.

3 Export to FLV format.

Export the video file to Flash Video (FLV) format directly from After Effects. Be sure to select Encode Alpha Channel. The alpha channel is the selection around the subject. Encoding the alpha channel ensures that the video exports without a background.

**10** Choose Control > Test Movie to see the video file that uses alpha channels. Close the preview window.

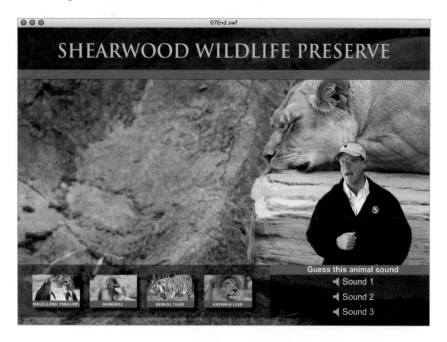

## Embedding Flash Video

Embedded video is best for short clips that you want to integrate with other Flash elements. Embedded video requires the FLV format. The FLV file is saved in the Library of your Flash file, where you can place it on the Timeline and synchronize it with other animations or graphics.

Embedding video in Flash is supported by Flash Player versions 6 and later. Keep in mind the following limitations of embedded video: Flash cannot maintain audio synchronization in embedded video that runs over 120 seconds. The maximum length of embedded movies is 16,000 frames. Another drawback of embedding your video is the increase in the size of your Flash project, making testing the movie (Control > Test Movie) a longer process and the authoring sessions more tedious.

Because the embedded FLV plays within your Flash project, it is critically important that your FLV have the same frame rate as your Flash file. If not, your embedded video will not play at its intended speed. To make sure your FLV has the same frame rate as your FLA, be sure to set the correct frame rate in the Video tab of the Adobe Media Encoder.

## Encoding the FLV for Embedding

You'll embed a short video of a polar bear in the beginning of your zoo kiosk project.

1 Open the Adobe Media Encoder.

2 Click the Add button and choose the polarbear.mov file in the Lesson07/ 07Start folder.

The polarbear.mov file is added to the queue.

3 Click Preset to open the Edit Export options. Click the Format tab and select FLV.

4 Click the Video tab and set the Frame Rate to 12. Make sure that the Resize Video checkbox is unchecked.

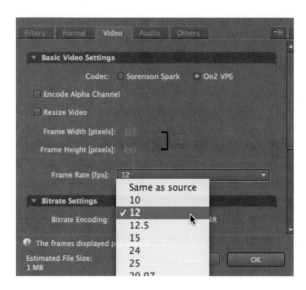

The Flash file 07_workingcopy.fla is set at 12 frames per second, so you want your FLV to also be at 12 frames per second.

5   Deselect Export Audio at the top of the dialog box. Click OK.

6   Click Start Queue to encode your video.

The polarbear.flv file is created.

## Embedding an FLV on the Timeline

Once you have an FLV, you can import it into Flash and embed it on the Timeline.

1   Open the file 07_workingcopy.fla.

2   Select the first frame of the popup video layer.

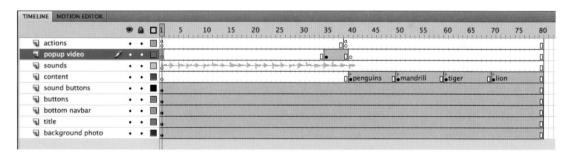

3   Choose File > Import > Import Video. In the Import Video wizard, select On Your Computer and click Browse or Choose. Select the polarbear.flv file in the Lesson07/07Start folder and click Open.

**4** In the Video Import wizard, select Embed FLV in SWF and play in timeline. Click Next or Continue.

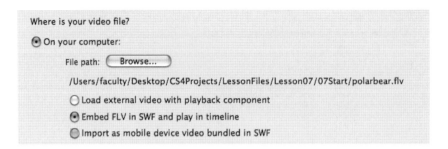

**5** Deselect Expand timeline if needed and deselect Include audio. Click Next or Continue.

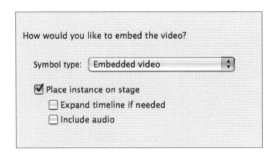

**6** Click Finish to import the video.

The video of the polar bear appears on the Stage.

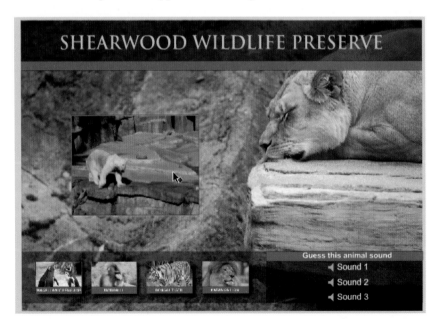

The FLV also appears in your Library.

7  Choose Control > Test Movie to see the embedded video file play from frame 1 to frame 35.

## Using Embedded Video

It's useful to think of embedded video as a multiframe symbol, very much like a symbol with a nested animation. You can convert an embedded video to a movie clip symbol, and then motion tween it to create interesting effects.

Next, you'll apply a motion tween to the embedded video so it fades out just before the zoo director pops up and speaks.

1  Select the embedded video on the Stage, right-click/Ctrl-click it, and select Create Motion Tween.

● **Note:** You will not be able to hear audio in the authoring environment for embedded videos containing sound. To hear the audio, you must choose Control > Test Movie.

**2**  Flash asks to convert the embedded video to a symbol so it can apply a motion tween. Click OK.

**3**  Flash asks to add enough frames inside the movie clip symbol so that the entire video can play. Click Yes.

A motion tween is created on the layer.

**4**  Select the motion tween and click the Motion Editor tab.

**5**  Collapse all the property categories. Click the Plus button next to Color Effect and choose Alpha.

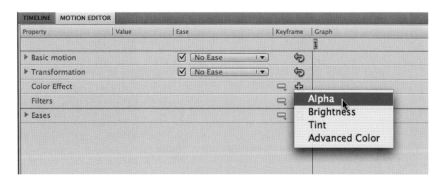

The Alpha property is added to the motion tween.

**6** Select frame 25, right-click/Ctrl-click, and choose Add Keyframe.

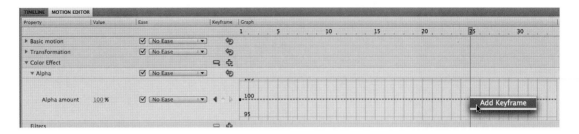

An Alpha keyframe appears at frame 25.

**7** Select frame 30, right-click/Ctrl-click, and choose Add Keyframe.

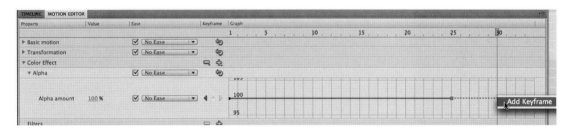

An Alpha keyframe appears at frame 30.

**8** Select the last keyframe at frame 30 and drag it down to 0%.

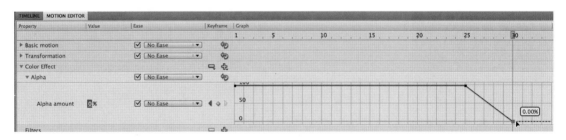

The Alpha is set to 0% at the last keyframe so the embedded video fades out from frame 25 to frame 30.

**9** Choose Control > Test Movie to see the embedded video play and fade out.

## Review Questions

1   How can you edit the length of a sound clip?

2   What is a skin for a video?

3   What are the limitations for embedded video clips?

4   What is a green screen, and how is it used?

## Review Answers

1   To edit the length of a sound clip, select the keyframe that contains it and click Edit in the Property inspector. Then move the time slider in the Edit Envelope dialog box.

2   The skin is the combination of functionality and appearance of video controls, such as Play, Fast Forward, and Pause buttons. You can choose from a wide array of combinations with the buttons in different positions, and you can customize the skin. If you don't want viewers to be able to control the video, apply No skin from the Skin menu.

3   When you embed a video clip, it becomes part of the Flash document and is included in the Timeline. Because embedded video clips significantly increase the size of the document and produce audio synchronization issues, it's best to embed video only if it is less than 10 seconds in length and contains no audio track.

4   A green screen is a solid color background shot behind a video subject. The solid background is then removed from the footage in an application such as After Effects, so that the subject can be placed in front of a different background.

# 8 USING COMPONENTS

## Lesson Overview

In this lesson, you'll learn how to do the following:

- Add a simple component to a project

- Modify a component's parameters

- Configure an interactive component

- Use ActionScript to enable a component

 This lesson will take about an hour to complete. If needed, remove the previous lesson folder from your hard drive and copy the Lesson08 folder onto it.

# ROCK CLASSIFICATION

Rocks are classified by mineral and chemical composition, by the texture of the constituent particles and by the processes that formed them. These indicators separate rocks into igneous, sedimentary and metamorphic. They may also be classified according to grain size, in the case of conglomerates and breccias or in the case of individual stones.

BASALT  SCORIA

RHYOLITE  SHALE

BRECCIA  SANDSTONE

## RHYOLITE

Rhyolite is a colorful and lightweight volcanic rock. It is considered the extrusive equivalent to the plutonic granite rock. Because of its high silica and low iron and magnesium contents, rhyolites polymerize very quickly and form viscous lavas. Rhyolites that cool too quickly do not grow crystals and instead form natural glass, or "obsidian."

Rhyolite weighs roughly one-half as much as limestone and granite, does not crumble, and is virtually impervious to the elements, which makes it a popular choice for decorative building. Additionally recognized for its beauty, this rock is also commonly used today in landscape designs.

Components are prebuilt movie clips that give you a head start, especially when you are creating user interface elements such as scroll bars, menus, and text fields.

# Getting Started

You'll use components to create an interactive display of minerals. When the viewer clicks the image of a mineral, text about it appears. You'll start by viewing the final document.

1  Double-click the 08End.swf file in the Lesson08/08End folder.

2  Click an image in the grid on the left. The text on the right changes. Introductory text appears at the top of the screen.

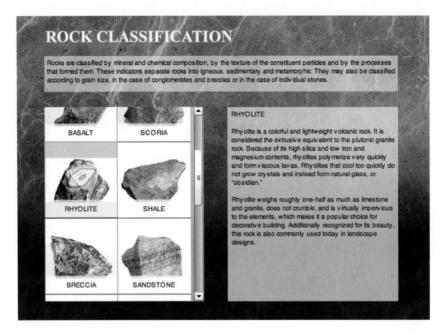

You'll create three components: one for the introductory text, one for the grid, and one for the mineral text. You'll use ActionScript to change the text display when the viewer clicks an image.

3  Close the 08End.swf file.

**4** Double-click the 08Start.fla file in the Lesson08/08Start folder to open it in Flash.

The Flash document contains the background image.

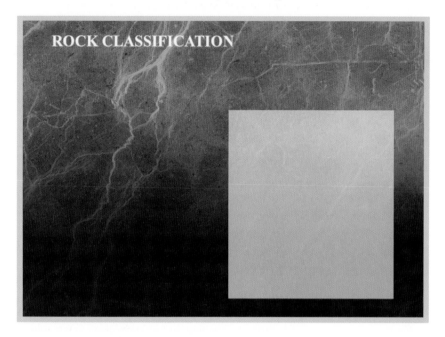

**5** Choose File > Save As. Name the file **08_workingcopy.fla** and save it in the 08Start folder. Saving a working copy ensures that the original start file will be available if you want to start over.

**6** Open the 08End.fla file so you can refer to it when you create ActionScript.

## About Components

Components are prebuilt movie clip symbols with defined parameters that you can use to add user interface elements, such as buttons, check boxes, or scroll bars, to your document. You can modify the parameters to change a component's appearance and behavior.

You already saw and used one component if you worked through the project in the previous lesson. To display and play an external video, you used a playback component. The video playback component provided options to choose the source video file, the skin file, and other optional settings.

You can drag components from the Components panel (Window > Components) onto the Stage and simply modify their parameters. However, for more complex user interface elements, use ActionScript 3.0 to modify the components.

Each component has a unique set of ActionScript methods, properties, and events that make up its application programming interface (API). Learn about the commands that are available for each component in the Actions toolbox category fl.controls or Help > Flash Help. The API also allows you to create new, custom components of your own. You can download components that have been built by members of the Flash community on the Adobe Exchange at www.adobe.com/exchange.

# Adding a Text Component

The top of the document will display a box containing introductory text. You'll create that box using a TextArea component from the Components panel. This is a simple user interface element that doesn't require any ActionScript.

## Dragging a Component to the Stage

All components are listed in the Components panel. You'll drag the TextArea component onto the Stage. When you do so, Flash automatically adds the TextArea component as well as a UIScrollBar component and a Component Assets folder to the Library panel.

1   Lock the Background layer in your working copy of the start file.

2   Select the Background layer and click the Insert Layer icon. Name the new layer **Components**.

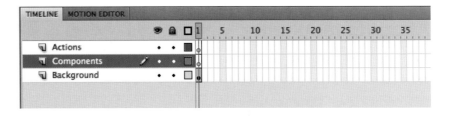

3   Choose Window > Components to open the Components panel.

● **Note:** Which components are listed in the Components panel depends on the version of ActionScript specified in Document Settings. A document can use only one version of ActionScript. This book uses ActionScript 3.0 exclusively.

**4** Select the TextArea component in the User Interface folder in the Components panel.

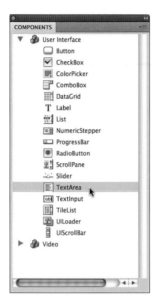

**5** Drag the TextArea component onto the Stage.

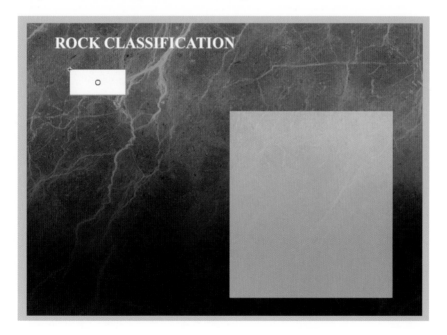

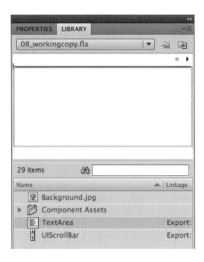

## Inserting Text in the Component

Once we modify this component instance, the text area will fit neatly between the title and the grid, and it should be partially transparent. After you've resized and modified the appearance of the text box, you'll add text from the Intro.txt file to the component using the Property inspector.

1 Select the TextArea component with the Selection tool.

2 In the Property inspector, set the width to **600**, height to **60**, X value to **47**, and Y value to **65**. The text box appears beneath the heading.

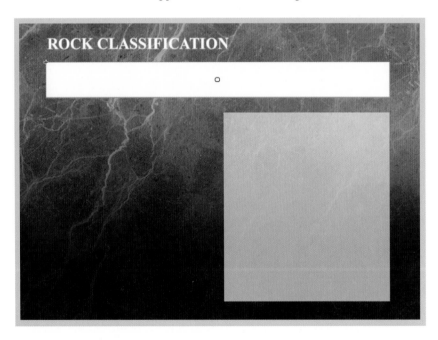

**3** Select Alpha from the Style menu under the Color Effect section of the Property inspector, and select 57 for the percentage.

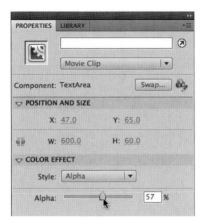

The transparency of the component becomes partially transparent.

**4** Click on the component and open the Component Inspector panel by choosing Window > Component Inspector.

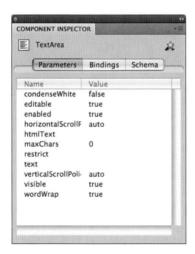

The Component Inspector provides all the options to modify and customize the selected component.

**5** Select the text parameter.

**6** Open the Intro.txt file in a text editor or word processing application. The Intro.txt file is located in the Lesson08/08Start folder you copied from the book's CD.

**7** Select the text and choose Edit > Copy, or use the Copy command for your text editor.

**8** In Flash, click in the text parameter and press Ctrl/Command+V to paste the text.

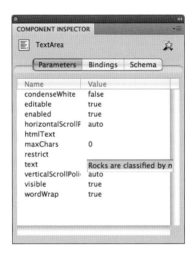

The text also appears on the Stage inside the TextArea component.

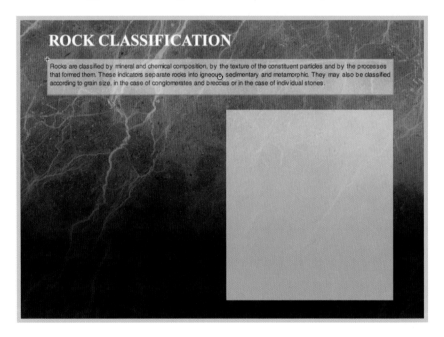

**9** Choose Control > Test Movie. The text appears, and if you click in the text area, you can edit it. Add text, delete text, and change some of the existing text to see what happens.

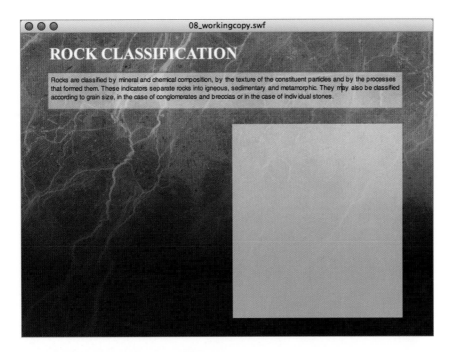

The TextArea component automatically adds a scroll bar if the text exceeds the size of the component that you define on the Stage.

**10** Close the preview window.

## Modifying a Component's Parameters

The introductory text should not be editable for this sample project. You'll change parameters using the Component Inspector to ensure that the text is not editable.

**1** Select the TextArea components on the Stage.

**2** Choose Window > Component Inspector if the Component Inspector is not already open.

**3** Click the editable parameter and select *false* so that the text can't be changed.

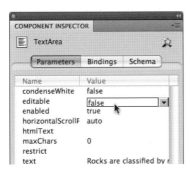

**4** Choose Control > Test Movie. The text is no longer editable.

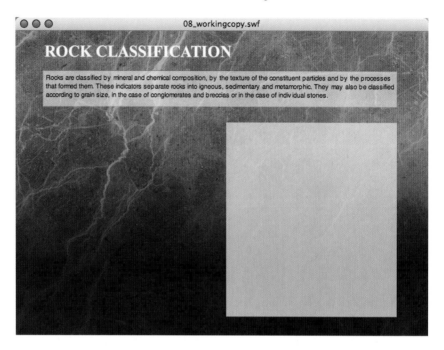

**5** Close the preview window.

# Using Components to Create Interactivity

ActionScript in conjunction with the premade components let you create more complex user interface elements. You'll use the TileList component and another TextArea component to create the grid of mineral types and the area that displays text about each mineral when its thumbnail is clicked.

## Configuring Component Parameters

You will first drag each of the components to the Stage, resize and position them, and then name the instances so you can refer to them using ActionScript.

1   In the Components panel, select the TileList component from the User
    Interface folder.

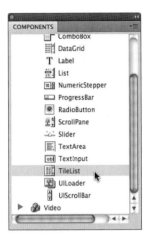

2   Drag the TileList component to the Stage.

3   In the Property inspector, set the width to **270**, height to **318**, X value to **47**, and
    Y value to **150**.

    The TileList component is resized and is positioned on the left side of the Stage.

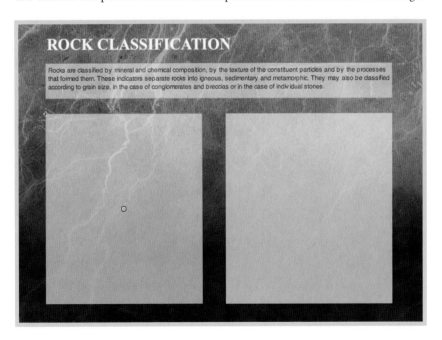

**4** Name the TileList component instance **thumbnails_tl** to represent the thumbnails tile list.

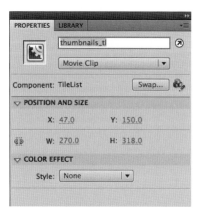

**5** Open the Component Inspector if it is not already open and click on the component on the Stage to select it.

**6** Change the columnWidth value to **125** and the rowHeight value to **125**. These values determine the size of each section in the grid.

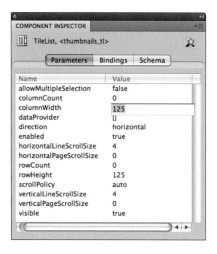
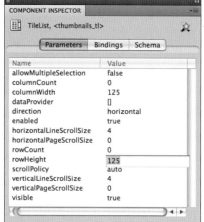

**7** Click the scrollPolicy parameter and select *on* to display a scroll bar.

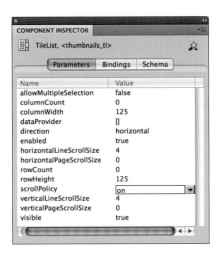

**8** Click the direction parameter and select *vertical* to make the scroll bar vertical instead of horizontal, which is the default.

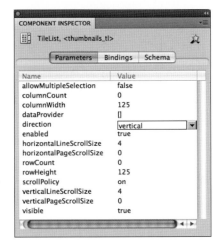

**9** Drag a TextArea component from the Components panel to the right of the grid on the Stage.

**10** Select the new instance of the TextArea component. In the Property inspector, set the text area's width to **290**, height to **318**, X value to **360**, and Y value to **150**.

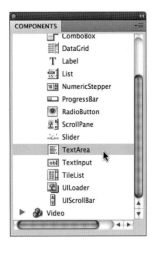

**Note:** The Library contains a single TextArea component and a single Component Assets folder, no matter how many components you drag to the Stage. Just like symbols, you can create multiple instances from a single component.

The TextArea component is resized and positioned on the right side of the Stage.

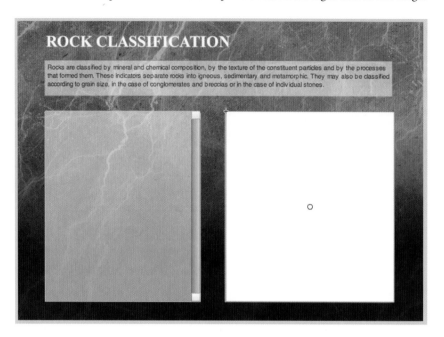

**11** Select Alpha from the Style menu under the Color Effect section of the Property inspector, and select 0 for the percentage.

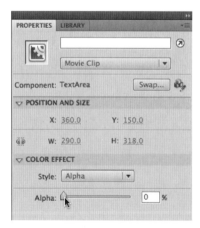

An alpha value of 0% leaves the background of the text area completely transparent, so the original box in the Background layer shows through.

**12** Name the instance **mineral_ta** to represent the mineral text area.

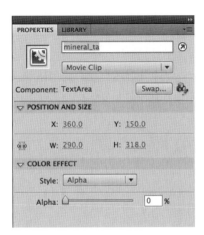

## Enhancing Components with ActionScript

You've created the grid and the text display area. Now you need to add some ActionScript to make this all work. You'll first add images of the rocks to the grid. The images will be pulled dynamically from a folder on your computer. Then you'll add an event listener to trigger a response when a thumbnail is clicked; the response is the display corresponding text. As you write the ActionScript, remember that you named the TileList instance *thumbnails_tl* and the TextArea instance *mineral_ta*. ActionScript uses the instance names to reference the various objects on the Stage.

**1** Select frame 1 in the Actions layer.

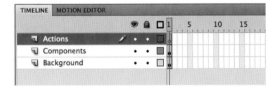

**2** Choose Window > Actions to open the Actions panel.

**3** Type the information to add the first image to the tile list, including the label and source:

```
thumbnails_tl.addItem({label:"OBSIDIAN", source:"thumbnails/
Obsidian.jpg", data:"."});
```

**Note:** If you are uncertain about the ActionScript spacing or punctuation, refer to the 08End.fla file you opened earlier. Select the first frame in the Actions layer to see the final ActionScript in the Actions panel.

```
ACTIONS - FRAME
                                                                    Script Assist
   1   thumbnails_tl.addItem({label:"OBSIDIAN", source:"thumbnails/Obsidian.jpg", data:"."});



  Actions : 1
Line 1 of 1, Col 87
```

For each item in the list, you'll identify the component on the Stage (thumbnails_tl) and use the `addItem()` method. This command is specific to this component. Everything else goes inside parentheses and curly brackets. The label appears as text on top of the box: Include quotation marks around it and type it in all capital letters so it will display that way. Following the comma is the source, which is the path to the image you want to display. The third property is called data. This is the text that will appear in the mineral_ta box. You'll paste that text in later. For now, all you have is a period.

4  Choose Control > Test Movie.

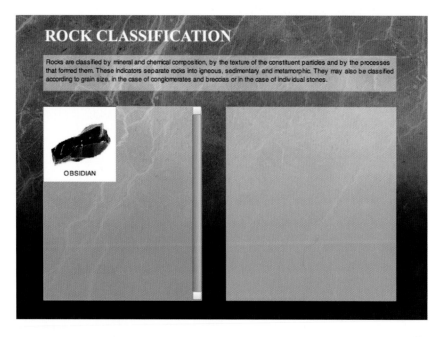

The Obsidian thumbnail should appear on the left. The thumbnail images are pulled from the folder in the 08Start folder called Thumbnails. If the movie doesn't play as expected, check for typos, spaces, or any other errors in your script. You can compare your file to the ActionScript in the 08End.fla file.

5  Copy the line you just typed in step 3 and paste it 14 times to create lines for each of the other minerals.

6  Substitute the appropriate mineral name for the label and source file in each line: Granite, Basalt, Scoria, Rhyolite, Shale, Breccia, Sandstone, Conglomerate, Limestone, Slate, Marble, Quartzite, Gneiss, Schist.

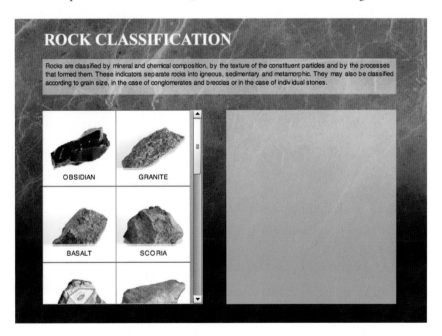

When you test your movie, all 14 of the thumbnail images should be displayed in the component. Each `addItem()` command adds one of the images.

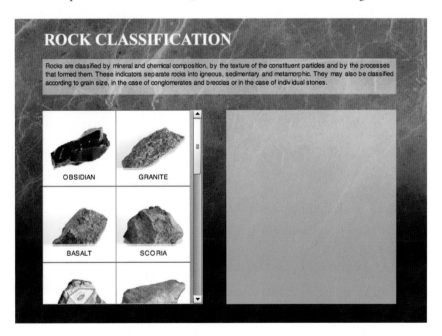

7   Now you'll create a response when the user clicks on each thumbnail image. Create the event listener for the tile list by typing:

```
thumbnails_tl.addEventListener(Event.CHANGE,
thumbnailClicked);
```

In this line, thumbnails_tl, the grid, is the target of the event. You're adding an event listener that listens for a change event, which will trigger the function called thumbnailClicked when a thumbnail image in the grid is clicked.

**Note:** Capitalization is very important in ActionScript. In the code line in step 7, make sure the instance name is lowercase and that other letters are capitalized exactly as they appear in the text.

8   Create the function, or event response, named thumbnailClicked, by typing:

```
function thumbnailClicked(event:Event):void{

    mineral_ta.text = event.target.selectedItem.data;

}
```

```
7   thumbnails_tl.addItem({label:"BRECCIA", source:"thumbnails/Breccia.jpg", data:"."});
8   thumbnails_tl.addItem({label:"SANDSTONE", source:"thumbnails/Sandstone.jpg", data:"."});
9   thumbnails_tl.addItem({label:"CONGLOMERATE", source:"thumbnails/Conglomerate.jpg", data:"."});
10  thumbnails_tl.addItem({label:"LIMESTONE", source:"thumbnails/Limestone.jpg", data:"."});
11  thumbnails_tl.addItem({label:"SLATE", source:"thumbnails/Slate.jpg", data:"."});
12  thumbnails_tl.addItem({label:"MARBLE", source:"thumbnails/Marble.jpg", data:"."});
13  thumbnails_tl.addItem({label:"QUARTZITE", source:"thumbnails/Quartzite.jpg", data:"."});
14  thumbnails_tl.addItem({label:"GNEISS", source:"thumbnails/Gneiss.jpg", data:"."});
15  thumbnails_tl.addItem({label:"SCHIST", source:"thumbnails/Schist.jpg", data:"."});
16  thumbnails_tl.addEventListener(Event.CHANGE, thumbnailClicked);
17  function thumbnailClicked(event:Event):void{
18      mineral_ta.text = event.target.selectedItem.data;
19  }
20
```

The function is named *thumbnailClicked*, and it's the event response that will be executed in the previous line you typed.

This function assigns different text to the text area you named *mineral_ta*. You could type exact text within quotation marks after the equal sign, but for this project the text will change depending on which mineral graphic is clicked. The text is the data for the selected item in the event target, which is the tile list. Currently, you haven't set any text yet.

| Reload Code Hints | |
| --- | --- |
| Pin Script | ⌘= |
| Close Script | ⌘- |
| Close All Scripts | ⇧⌘- |
| Go to Line... | ⌘, |
| Find and Replace... | ⌘F |
| Find Again | ⌘G |
| Auto Format | ⇧⌘F |
| Check Syntax | ⌘T |
| Show Code Hint | ^_ |
| Import Script... | ⇧⌘I |
| Export Script... | ⇧⌘P |
| Print... | |
| Script Assist | ⇧⌘E |
| Esc Shortcut Keys | |
| Hidden Characters | ⇧⌘8 |
| ✓ Line Numbers | ⇧⌘L |
| ✓ Word Wrap | ⇧⌘W |
| Preferences... | ⌘U |

**Note:** To prevent your ActionScript code from running too long in a single line, choose Word Wrap from the options menu at the top right of the Actions panel. Your code will wrap so you can better see the block of text.

9   Open the text document called Minerals.txt (in the 08Start folder) in any text editor. Copy the text from the Obsidian section of the document.

10  In the Actions panel in Flash, select the period between the quotation marks after the word *data* in the first addItem() line and press Ctrl/Command+V to paste the text.

**11** Delete paragraph returns (line endings) from the Obsidian text. Add **\n** where you want paragraph breaks to occur. The **\n** means new line, or end of line. Type **\n\n** where you want space to appear between the paragraphs. There should be no spaces between *\n* and the words that follow it.

```
                                                              Script Assist
1   thumbnails_tl.addItem({label:"OBSIDIAN", source:"thumbnails/Obsidian.jpg", data:
    "OBSIDIAN\n\nObsidian is a naturally occurring glass, produced by volcanoes. When felsic lava
    cools rapidly and freezes without sufficient time for crystal growth, obsidian is
    formed.\n\nObsidian is often found within the margins of felsic lava flows, where cooling is
    more rapid. Obsidian has been used for centuries in making tools and weapons. \n\nMost commonly
    made were arrowheads. Because of the lack of crystal structure, obsidian blade edges can reach
    almost molecular thinness. Today, obsidian can be found in both decorative arts and crafts as
    well as modern day surgical scalpel blades."});
2   thumbnails_tl.addItem({label:"GRANITE", source:"thumbnails/Granite.jpg", data:"."});
3   thumbnails_tl.addItem({label:"BASALT", source:"thumbnails/Basalt.jpg", data:"."});
4   thumbnails_tl.addItem({label:"SCORIA", source:"thumbnails/Scoria.jpg", data:"."});
5   thumbnails_tl.addItem({label:"RHYOLITE", source:"thumbnails/Rhyolite.jpg", data:"."});
6   thumbnails_tl.addItem({label:"SHALE", source:"thumbnails/Shale.jpg", data:"."});
7   thumbnails_tl.addItem({label:"BRECCIA", source:"thumbnails/Breccia.jpg", data:"."});
8   thumbnails_tl.addItem({label:"SANDSTONE", source:"thumbnails/Sandstone.jpg", data:"."});
9   thumbnails_tl.addItem({label:"CONGLOMERATE", source:"thumbnails/Conglomerate.jpg", data:"."});
```

**12** Choose Control > Test Movie. Click the Obsidian image. The Obsidian text should appear. If the movie flickers or returns an error, return to the Actions panel and confirm that you've typed everything correctly and have removed all paragraph returns from the text.

**Note:** To see line endings you might have missed, resize the Actions panel. When the text reflows, line endings (paragraph returns) become more obvious.

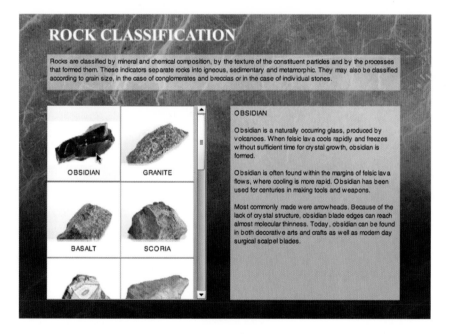

**13** Copy and paste the text for each of the other minerals, removing paragraph returns within the text.

**14** Choose Control > Test Movie. Click each mineral thumbnail to see the corresponding text in the text area. If you encounter any errors, return to the Actions panel to confirm that you've removed all the line endings in the text. Remember that you can refer to the 08End.fla file for comparison.

Using two different types of components, you created an interactive display. You can follow the same basic process when using other components in your own projects.

## Quick Interactivity with Flash Components

Get a head start on a project by using components for standard interface objects, such as radio buttons, Play buttons, scroll bars, and drop-down menus. Drag a component from the Components panel, customize its parameters, and presto, you have a complete interface! Add a little ActionScript to take it even further. Below is a sample interface with some commonly used components along with a list for your reference.

**User Interface Components**

| | |
|---|---|
| 🔲 Button | 🔘 RadioButton |
| ☑ CheckBox | 🗐 ScrollPane |
| 🔳 ColorPicker | 🔅 Slider |
| 🗖 ComboBox | 🗏 TextArea |
| 🗒 DataGrid | 🔲 TextInput |
| T Label | 🔳 TileList |
| 🗒 List | 🗗 UILoader |
| 🔟 NumericStepper | 🗗 UIScrollBar |
| 🗔 ProgressBar | |

**Video Components**

| | |
|---|---|
| 🔳 FLVPlayback | 🔲 MuteButton |
| 💬 FLVPlaybackPationing | 🔳 PauseButton |
| 🔳 BackButton | 🔳 PlayButton |
| ▨ BufferingBar | 🔳 PlayPauseButton |
| 💬 CaptionButton | 🔳 SeekBar |
| 🔳 ForwardButton | 🔳 StopButton |
| 🔳 FullScreenButton | 🔲 VolumeBar |

# Review Questions

1 What is a component?

2 How can you change a parameter for a component?

3 How do you use ActionScript to enhance the functionality of a component?

# Review Answers

1 A component is a prebuilt movie clip symbol with defined parameters that you can use to add user interface elements, such as buttons, check boxes, or scroll bars, to your document. You can modify the parameters to change a component's appearance and behavior.

2 Select the component, and then open the Component Inspector. Scroll through the parameters list, and select the parameter you want to change. Then select a parameter setting from the pop-up menu in the grid or type a new value.

3 You must first name the component that is on the Stage in the Property inspector. ActionScript refers to each object on the Stage by its instance name. Then you create ActionScript code in the Actions panel, combining event handlers, properties, and methods that are unique to each component.

# **9** LOADING AND CONTROLLING FLASH CONTENT

## Lesson Overview

In this lesson, you'll learn how to do the following:

- Load an external SWF file

- Remove a loaded SWF file

- Control a movie clip's Timeline

- Use masks to selectively display content

 This lesson will take less than an hour to complete. If needed, remove the previous lesson folder from your hard drive and copy the Lesson09 folder onto it.

Use ActionScript to load external Flash content.
By keeping Flash content modular, your projects
remain more manageable and easier to edit.

## Getting Started

You'll start the lesson by viewing the finished movie.

1  Double-click the 09End.swf file in the Lesson09/09End folder to view the final movie.

The project is a fictional online lifestyle magazine called Check. A jazzy animation appears on the front page showing four main sections of the magazine. Each section on the front page is a movie clip with a nested animation.

The first section is an article on the star of the upcoming movie called *Double Identity* (whose Web site you created in Chapter 4, "Adding Animation"), the second section is about a new car, the third section presents some facts and figures, and the fourth section is a self-improvement article.

You can click on each section on the front page to access the content. The inside content is not complete, but you can imagine that each section could contain more information. Click again to return to the front page.

2  Double-click the page1.swf, page2.swf, page3.swf, and page4.swf files in the Lesson09/09End folder.

Each of the four sections is a separate Flash file. Note that the front page, 09End. swf, loads each SWF file as needed.

**3** Close all the SWF files and open the 09Start.fla file in the Lesson09/09Start folder.

Many of the images, graphic elements, and animations have already been completed in this file. You will add the necessary ActionScript to make the Flash file load the external Flash content.

**4** Choose File > Save As. Name the file **09_workingcopy.fla** and save it in the 09Start folder. Saving a working copy ensures that the original start file will be available if you want to start over.

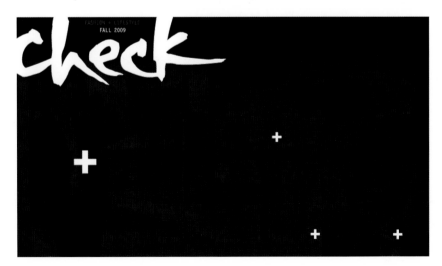

# Loading External Content

You'll use ActionScript to load each of the external SWFs into your main Flash movie. Loading external content keeps your overall project in separate modules and prevents the project from becoming too bloated and difficult to download. It also makes it easier for you to edit, because you can edit individual sections instead of one, large, unwieldly file.

For example, if you wanted to change the article on the new car in the second section, you would simply open and edit the Flash file page2.fla, which contains that content.

To load the external files, you'll use two ActionScript objects: one called a Loader and another called a URLRequest.

1 Insert a new layer at the top and rename it **actionscript**.

2 Press F9 (Windows) or Option+F9 (Mac OS) to open the Actions panel.

● **Note:** To compare punctuation, spacing, spelling, or any other aspects of the ActionScript, view the Actions panel in the 09End.fla file.

3 Type the following line exactly as it appears here.

```
var myLoader:Loader=new Loader();
```

This code creates a Loader object and calls it **myLoader**.

4 On the next line, type the following lines exactly as they appear here:

```
page1_mc.addEventListener(MouseEvent.CLICK, page1content);
function page1content(myevent:MouseEvent):void {
    var myURL:URLRequest=new URLRequest("page1.swf");
    myLoader.load(myURL);
    addChild(myLoader);
};
```

```
ACTIONS - FRAME                                                    Script Assist
1  var myLoader:Loader=new Loader ();
2  page1_mc.addEventListener(MouseEvent.CLICK, page1content);
3  function page1content(myevent:MouseEvent):void {
4      var myURL:URLRequest=new URLRequest("page1.swf");
5      myLoader.load(myURL);
6      addChild(myLoader);
7  };
```

You've seen this syntax before in Chapter 6. On line two, you create a listener
that detects a mouse click on the object called **page1_mc**. This is a movie clip
on the Stage. In response, the function called **page1content** is executed.

The function does several things: First, it creates a URLRequest object with the
name of the file you want to load. Second, it loads the URLRequest object into
the Loader object. Third, it adds the Loader object to the Stage so you can see it.

5  Select the movie clip on the left side of the Stage with the movie star.

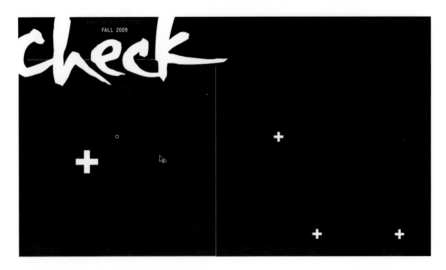

6  In the Property inspector, name it **page1_mc**.

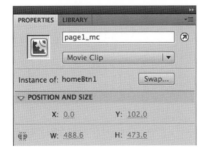

The ActionScript you entered refers to the object called page1_mc, so you need to provide the name to one of the movie clips on the Stage.

**7** Choose Control > Test Movie to see your movie so far.

The front page plays its animation and stops. When you click on the movie star, the file called page1.swf loads and is displayed.

**8** Close the SWF called 09_workingcopy.swf.

**9** Select the first frame of the actionscript layer and open the Actions panel.

**10** Copy and paste the event listener and the function so you have four distinct listeners for each of the four movie clips on the Stage. The four listeners should appear as follows:

```
page1_mc.addEventListener(MouseEvent.CLICK, page1content);
function page1content(myevent:MouseEvent):void {
    var myURL:URLRequest=new URLRequest("page1.swf");
    myLoader.load(myURL);
    addChild(myLoader);
};
page2_mc.addEventListener(MouseEvent.CLICK, page2content);
function page2content(myevent:MouseEvent):void {
    var myURL:URLRequest=new URLRequest("page2.swf");
    myLoader.load(myURL);
    addChild(myLoader);
};
```

```
page3_mc.addEventListener(MouseEvent.CLICK, page3content);
function page3content(myevent:MouseEvent):void {
    var myURL:URLRequest=new URLRequest("page3.swf");
    myLoader.load(myURL);
    addChild(myLoader);
};
page4_mc.addEventListener(MouseEvent.CLICK, page4content);
function page4content(myevent:MouseEvent):void {
    var myURL:URLRequest=new URLRequest("page4.swf");
    myLoader.load(myURL);
    addChild(myLoader);
};
```

```
ACTIONS - FRAME                                                          Script Assist
 1   var myLoader:Loader=new Loader  ();
 2   page1_mc.addEventListener(MouseEvent.CLICK, page1content);
 3   function page1content(myevent:MouseEvent):void {
 4       var myURL:URLRequest=new URLRequest("page1.swf");
 5       myLoader.load(myURL);
 6       addChild(myLoader);
 7   };
 8   page2_mc.addEventListener(MouseEvent.CLICK, page2content);
 9   function page2content(myevent:MouseEvent):void {
10       var myURL:URLRequest=new URLRequest("page2.swf");
11       myLoader.load(myURL);
12       addChild(myLoader);
13   };
14   page3_mc.addEventListener(MouseEvent.CLICK, page3content);
15   function page3content(myevent:MouseEvent):void {
16       var myURL:URLRequest=new URLRequest("page3.swf");
17       myLoader.load(myURL);
18       addChild(myLoader);
19   };
20   page4_mc.addEventListener(MouseEvent.CLICK, page4content);
21   function page4content(myevent:MouseEvent):void {
22       var myURL:URLRequest=new URLRequest("page4.swf");
23       myLoader.load(myURL);
24       addChild(myLoader);
25   };
```

11 Click on each of the remaining three movie clips on the Stage and name them in the Property inspector. Name the yellow car **page2_mc**, name the data section **page3_mc**, and name the self-improvement section on the lower left **page4_mc**.

# Removing External Content

Once an external SWF file is loaded, how do you unload it to return to the main Flash movie? The easiest way is to remove the Loader object from the Stage, so the audience can no longer see it. You will use the command `removeChild()` and specify the name of the Loader object in between the parentheses to remove it from the Stage.

1  Select the first frame of the actionscript layer and open the Actions panel.

2  Add the following lines to your code in the Script pane:

```
myLoader.addEventListener(MouseEvent.CLICK, unloadcontent);

function unloadcontent(myevent:MouseEvent):void {

    removeChild(myLoader);

};
```

```
ACTIONS - FRAME                                                    Script Assist
 1  var myLoader:Loader=new Loader   ();
 2  page1_mc.addEventListener(MouseEvent.CLICK, page1content);
 3  function page1content(myevent:MouseEvent):void {
 4      var myURL:URLRequest=new URLRequest("page1.swf");
 5      myLoader.load(myURL);
 6      addChild(myLoader);
 7  };
 8  page2_mc.addEventListener(MouseEvent.CLICK, page2content);
 9  function page2content(myevent:MouseEvent):void {
10      var myURL:URLRequest=new URLRequest("page2.swf");
11      myLoader.load(myURL);
12      addChild(myLoader);
13  };
14  page3_mc.addEventListener(MouseEvent.CLICK, page3content);
15  function page3content(myevent:MouseEvent):void {
16      var myURL:URLRequest=new URLRequest("page3.swf");
17      myLoader.load(myURL);
18      addChild(myLoader);
19  };
20  page4_mc.addEventListener(MouseEvent.CLICK, page4content);
21  function page4content(myevent:MouseEvent):void {
22      var myURL:URLRequest=new URLRequest("page4.swf");
23      myLoader.load(myURL);
24      addChild(myLoader);
25  };
26  myLoader.addEventListener(MouseEvent.CLICK, unloadcontent);
27  function unloadcontent(myevent:MouseEvent):void {
28      removeChild(myLoader);
29  };
```

This code adds an event listener to the Loader object called **myLoader**. When you click on the Loader object, the function called **unloadcontent** is executed.

The function performs just one action: It removes the Loader object from the Stage.

3  Choose Control > Test Movie to preview the movie. Click on any of the four sections, and then click on the loaded content to return to the main movie.

# Controlling Movie Clips

When you return to the front page, you'll see the four sections, so you can click another movie clip to load a different section. But wouldn't it be nice to replay the initial animation? The initial animations are nested inside each movie clip, and you can control the four movie clips that are on the Stage. You can use the basic navigation commands that you learned in Chapter 6 (gotoAndStop, gotoAndPlay, stop, play) to navigate the Timelines of movie clips as well as the main Timeline. Simply precede the command with the name of the movie clip and separate them with a dot. Flash targets that particular movie clip and moves its Timeline accordingly.

1 Select the first frame of the actionscript layer and open the Actions panel.

2 Add to the commands in the function called **unloadcontent** so the entire function appears as follows:

```
function unloadcontent(myevent:MouseEvent):void {
    removeChild(myLoader);
    page1_mc.gotoAndPlay(1);
    page2_mc.gotoAndPlay(1);
    page3_mc.gotoAndPlay(1);
    page4_mc.gotoAndPlay(1);
};
```

```
ACTIONS - FRAME
                                                                    Script Assist
1   var myLoader:Loader=new Loader ();
2   page1_mc.addEventListener(MouseEvent.CLICK, page1content);
3   function page1content(myevent:MouseEvent):void {
4       var myURL:URLRequest=new URLRequest("page1.swf");
5       myLoader.load(myURL);
6       addChild(myLoader);
7   };
8   page2_mc.addEventListener(MouseEvent.CLICK, page2content);
9   function page2content(myevent:MouseEvent):void {
10      var myURL:URLRequest=new URLRequest("page2.swf");
11      myLoader.load(myURL);
12      addChild(myLoader);
13  };
14  page3_mc.addEventListener(MouseEvent.CLICK, page3content);
15  function page3content(myevent:MouseEvent):void {
16      var myURL:URLRequest=new URLRequest("page3.swf");
17      myLoader.load(myURL);
18      addChild(myLoader);
19  };
20  page4_mc.addEventListener(MouseEvent.CLICK, page4content);
21  function page4content(myevent:MouseEvent):void {
22      var myURL:URLRequest=new URLRequest("page4.swf");
23      myLoader.load(myURL);
24      addChild(myLoader);
25  };
26  myLoader.addEventListener(MouseEvent.CLICK, unloadcontent);
27  function unloadcontent(myevent:MouseEvent):void {
28      removeChild(myLoader);
29      page1_mc.gotoAndPlay(1);
30      page2_mc.gotoAndPlay(1);
31      page3_mc.gotoAndPlay(1);
32      page4_mc.gotoAndPlay(1);
33  };
```

In this function, which is executed when the user clicks the Loader object, the Loader object is removed from the Stage, and then the playhead of each movie clip on the Stage moves to the first frame and begins playing.

3   Choose Control > Test Movie to preview the movie. Click on any of the four sections, and then click on the loaded content to return to the main movie.

When you return to the main movie, all four movie clips play their nested animations.

# Creating Masks

Masking is a way of selectively hiding and displaying content on a layer. Masking is a way for you to control the content that your audience sees. For example, you can make a circular mask and allow your audience to only see through the circular area, so that you get a keyhole or spotlight effect. In Flash, you put a mask on one layer and the content that is masked in a layer below it.

Masks can be animated, and the content that is masked can also be animated. So, the circular mask can grow bigger to show more content.

## Define the Mask and Masked Layers

You'll create a rectangular mask that starts small and grows larger to cover the Stage. The resulting effect is to have the contents of the masked layer be revealed slowly as if a sliding door is opening.

1   Open the file page2.fla.

A single layer called content contains a movie clip of the second section about a new car.

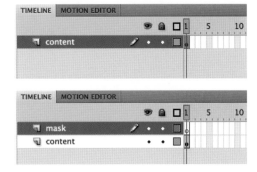

2   Insert a new layer above the content layer and rename it **mask**.

3   Double-click the icon in front of the layer name.

The Layer Properties dialog box appears.

4   Select Mask and click OK.

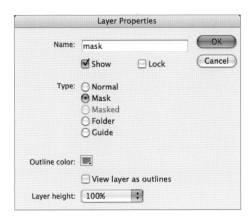

The top layer becomes a Mask layer. Anything that is drawn in this layer will act as a mask for a masked layer below it.

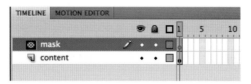

5  Double-click the icon in front of the bottom layer named content.

The Layer Properties dialog box appears.

6  Select Masked and click OK.

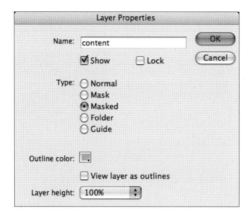

● **Note:** You can also simply drag a normal layer under a Mask layer, and Flash will convert it to a Masked layer.

The bottom layer becomes a Masked layer and is indented, indicating that it is affected by the mask above it.

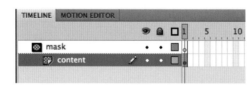

## Create the Mask

1 Select the Rectangle tool.

2 Choose any color for the Fill and no stroke for the Stroke.

3 Select the top Mask layer and draw a thin rectangle just off to the left of the Stage. Make the height of the rectangle slightly larger than the Stage.

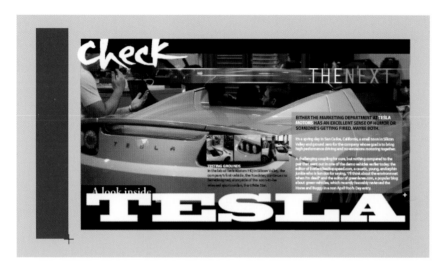

4 Right-click/Ctrl-click the rectangle and select Create Motion Tween.

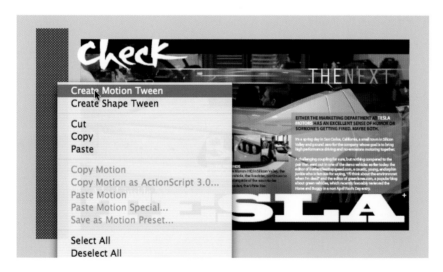

**5** Flash asks to convert the rectangular shape to a symbol so you can apply a motion tween. Click OK.

The top layer becomes a Tween layer, and one second's worth of frames is added to the Timeline.

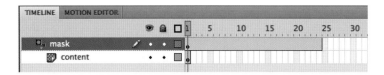

**6** Insert the same number of frames in the bottom layer.

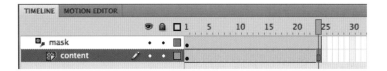

**7** Move the playhead to the last frame, frame 24.

**8** Select the Free Transform Tool.

**9** Click on the rectangular symbol.

The free transform handles appear around the rectangular symbol.

**10** Hold down the Alt/Option key and drag the right edge of the free transform handle to expand the rectangle to cover the entire Stage.

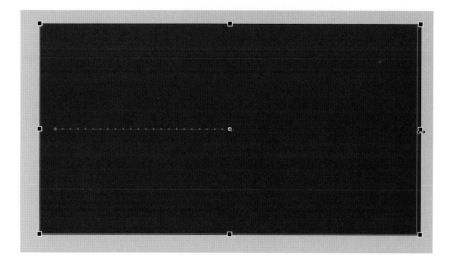

The rectangle becomes wider at the last frame. The motion tween creates a smooth animation of the rectangle growing wider and covering the Stage.

**11** To see the effects of the Mask layer on its Masked layer, lock both layers.

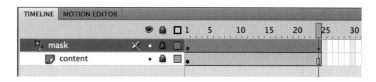

**12** Insert a new layer and rename it **actionscript**.

**13** Insert a keyframe at frame 24 of the actionscript layer and open the Actions panel.

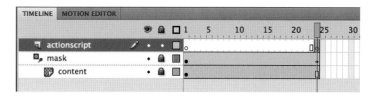

**14** In the Script pane of the Actions panel, enter stop().

**15** Choose Control > Test Movie.

● **Note:** Flash does not recognize different Alpha levels of a mask. For example, a mask at an Alpha value of 50% will still mask at 100%. However, with ActionScript you can dynamically create masks that will allow transparencies. Masks also do not recognize strokes.

As the motion tween proceeds in the Mask layer, more of the Masked layer is revealed, creating a cinematic transition known as a wipe. If you open 09_workingcopy.fla and choose Control > Test Movie, and then click on the car movie clip, you'll see that the masking effect is preserved even as it is loaded into another Flash movie.

# Review Questions

1 How do you load external Flash content?

2 What are the advantages of loading external Flash content?

3 How do you control the Timeline of a movie clip instance?

4 What is a mask and how do you create one?

# Review Answers

1 You use ActionScript to load external Flash content. You create two objects: a Loader and a URLRequest. The URLRequest object specifies the filename of the SWF file that you want to load. To load the file, use the `load()` command to load the URLRequest object into the Loader object. Then display the Loader object on the Stage with the `addChild()` command.

2 Loading external content keeps your overall project in separate modules and prevents the project from becoming too bloated and difficult to download. It also makes it easier for you to edit, because you can edit individual sections instead of one, large, unwieldly file.

3 You can control the Timeline of movie clips with ActionScript by first targeting them by name. After the name, type a dot (period), and then the command that you desire. You can use the same commands for navigation that you learned in Chapter 6 (`gotoAndStop`, `gotoAndPlay`, `stop`, `play`). Flash targets that particular movie clip and moves its Timeline accordingly.

4 Masking is a way of selectively hiding and displaying content on a layer. In Flash, you put a mask on the top Mask layer and the content in the layer below it, which is called the Masked layer. Both the Mask and the Masked layers can be animated. To see the effects of the Mask layer on the Masked layer, you must lock both layers.

# 10 PUBLISHING FLASH DOCUMENTS

## Lesson Overview

In this lesson, you'll learn how to do the following:

- Test a Flash document

- Understand the Bandwidth Profiler

- Change publish settings for a document

- Understand the difference between export file types

- Add metadata

- Publish a SWF file and its HTML file

- Detect the version of Flash Player a viewer has installed

- Publish a self-contained projector file

 This lesson will take less than an hour to complete. If needed, remove the previous lesson folder from your hard drive and copy the Lesson10 folder onto it.

When you've finished your Flash project, publish it as a SWF file for a Web site or as a projector for ultimate portability, or save frames from the animation as image files.

# Getting Started

In this lesson, you'll publish an animation that has already been completed. The project is an animated title page for a cartoon about an alien creature. You'll publish the movie for a Web site, capture specific frames as images, and save the movie so that even viewers who don't have the Flash Player can see it.

1   Double-click the 10End.html file in the Lesson10/10End folder to open the finished project.

A Web browser launches and plays the HTML file, which displays the SWF file. The HTML file tells the browser how to show the SWF file. Quit the Web browser.

2   Double-click the 10Start.fla file in the Lesson10/10Start folder to open it in Flash.

Much of the animation in this project has been created with classic tweens.

3   Choose File > Save As. Name the file **10_workingcopy.fla** and save it in the 10Start folder. Saving a working copy ensures that the original start file will be available if you want to start over.

# Testing a Flash Document

Troubleshooting is a skill you develop over time, but it's easier to identify the cause of problems if you test your movie frequently as you create content. If you test after each step, you know which changes you made and therefore what might have gone wrong. A good motto to remember is "Test early. Test often."

One fast way to preview a movie is to choose Control > Test Movie (Ctrl-Enter/Cmd-Return), as you've done in earlier lessons. This command creates a SWF file in the same location as your FLA file so that you can play and preview the movie; it does not create the HTML file or any other files necessary to play the movie from a Web site.

When you believe you've completed your movie or a portion of the movie, take the time to make sure all the pieces are in place and that they perform the way you expect them to.

1   Review the storyboard for the project, if you have one, or other documents that describe the purpose and requirements of the project. If such documents do not exist, write a description of what you expect to see when you view the movie. Include information about the length of the animation, any buttons or links included in the movie, and what should be visible as the movie progresses.

2   Using the storyboard, project requirements, or your written description, create a checklist that you can use to verify that the movie meets your expectations.

3   Choose Control > Test Movie. As the movie plays, compare it with your checklist. Click buttons and links to ensure they work as expected.

4   Choose File > Publish Preview > Default (HTML) to export a SWF file and an HTML file required to play in a browser and to preview the movie.

    A browser opens, if one is not already open, and plays the final movie.

5   Upload the two files (the SWF and HTML) to your own Web site and give your colleagues or friends the Web site address so they can help you test the movie. Ask them to run the movie and to ensure that all the files are included, and that the movie meets the criteria on your checklist. Encourage testers to view the movie as though they were its target audience.

    If your project requires additional media, for example, FLV or F4V video files, or external SWF files that are loaded, you must upload them along with your SWF and HTML file.

6   Make changes and corrections as necessary to finalize the movie, and then test it again to ensure it meets your criteria.

● **Note:** The default behavior for your movie in the Test Movie mode is to loop. You can make your SWF play differently in a browser by selecting different publish settings, as described later in this chapter, or by adding ActionScript to stop the Timeline.

● **Note:** You can also just choose File > Publish (Shift-F12) to export the SWF file and the HTML file without previewing the movie in a Web browser.

# Understanding the Bandwidth Profiler

You can preview how your final project might behave under different download environments by using the Bandwidth Profiler, a useful panel that is available when you are in Test Movie mode.

## View the Bandwidth Profiler

The Bandwidth Profiler provides information such as the overall file size, the total number of frames, the dimensions of the Stage, and how your data is distributed throughout your frames. You can use the Bandwidth Profiler to pinpoint where there are large amounts of data so you can see where there may be pauses in the movie playback.

1   Choose Control > Test Movie.

Flash exports a SWF and displays your movie in a new window.

2   Choose View > Bandwidth Profiler.

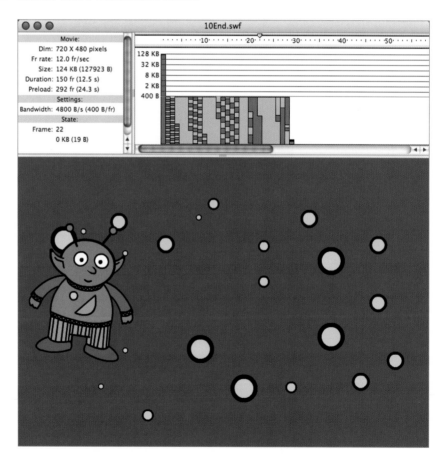

A new window appears above your movie. Basic information about your movie is listed on the left side of the profiler. A timeline appears on the right side of the profiler with gray bars representing the amount of data in each frame. The higher the bars, the more data is included.

There are two ways you can view the graph on the right: as a Streaming Graph (View > Streaming Graph) or as a Frame by Frame Graph (View > Frame By Frame Graph). The Streaming Graph indicates how the movie downloads over the Web by showing you how data streams from each frame, whereas the Frame By Frame Graph simply indicates the amount of data in each frame. In Streaming Graph mode, you can tell which frames will cause hang-ups during playback by noting which bar exceeds the given Bandwidth setting.

## Test Download Performance

You can set different download speeds and test the playback performance of your movie under those different conditions.

1   While in Test Movie mode, choose View > Download Settings > 56K.

The 56K setting is a measure of the download speed that you want to test. It corresponds to a 56K modem. Choose higher or lower speeds, depending on your target audience.

2   Choose View > Simulate Download.

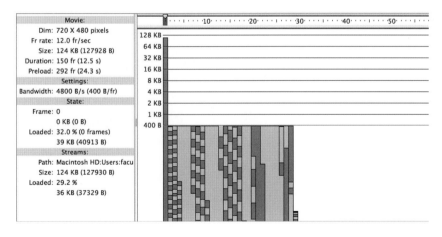

Flash simulates playback over the Web at the given Bandwidth setting (56K). A green horizontal bar at the top of the window indicates which frames have been downloaded, and the triangular playhead marks the current frame that plays. Notice that there is a delay at frame 1 while the data downloads. Anytime a gray data bar exceeds the red horizontal line (the one marked 400 B), there will be a slight delay in the playback of your movie.

Once sufficient data has downloaded, the movie plays.

3 Choose View > Download Settings > DSL.

DSL is a broadband connection, which is faster than a 56K modem.

4 Choose View > Simulate Download.

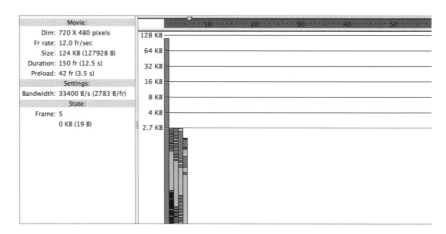

Flash simulates playback over the Web at the faster speed. Notice that the delay at the beginning is very brief.

# Adding Metadata

Metadata is information about data. Metadata describes your Flash file so that other developers with whom you share your FLA can see details that you want them to know, or a search engine on the Web can find and share your movie. Metadata includes a document's title, a description, keywords, the date the file was created, and any other information about the document. You can add metadata to a Flash document, and that metadata is embedded in the file. Metadata makes it easy for other applications and Web search engines to catalog your movie.

1 Choose File > Publish Settings or click the Edit button next to Profile in the Property inspector.

The Publish Settings dialog box appears.

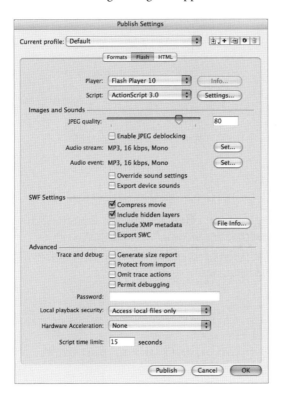

2 Click the Flash tab.

3 In the SWF Settings, select Include XMP Metadata and click File Info.

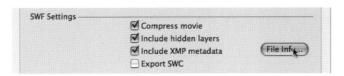

The XMP Metadata dialog box appears.

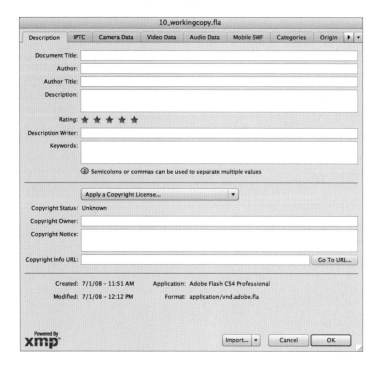

4   Click the Description tab.

5   In the Document Title field, type **Martian Mike Gets Spaced Out**.

6   In the Keywords field, type **Spaced Out animation showcases our favorite outer space buddy, Martian Mike. Animation, Martian, Spaced Out, Martian Mike, Spaceship animation, mini movie, space, science fiction, cute space animation, Flash animation, webisode**.

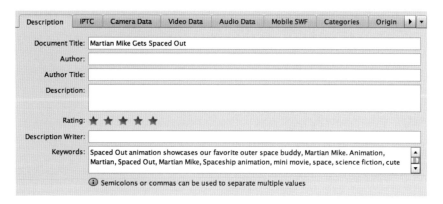

**7** Enter any other descriptive information in the other fields. Click OK to close the dialog box. Click OK to close the Publish Settings dialog box.

The metadata will be saved with the Flash document and will be available for other applications and Web search engines.

# Publishing a Movie for the Web

When you publish a movie for the Web, Flash creates a SWF file and an HTML document that tells the Web browser how to display your Flash content. You need to upload both files to your Web server along with any other files your SWF file references (such as FLV or F4V video files). The Publish command saves all the required files to the same folder.

You can specify different options for publishing a movie, including whether to detect the version of Flash Player installed on the viewer's computer. When you change the settings in the Publish Settings dialog box, they are saved with the document.

## Specifying Flash File Settings

You can determine how Flash publishes the SWF file, including which version of Flash Player it requires, which version of ActionScript it uses, and how the movie is displayed and plays.

**1** Choose File > Publish Settings.

**2** Click the Formats tab and select Flash (SWF) and HTML. You can also choose to publish the file in additional formats.

**Note:** You can change the name of the published file by typing a different filename in the boxes. You can also change the location where the files are saved by clicking the folder icon.

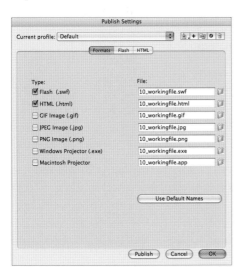

**3** Click the Flash tab.

**4** Select a version of Flash Player.

Some Flash CS4 features will not play as expected in versions of the player earlier than Flash Player 10. If you are using the latest features of Flash CS4, you must choose Flash Player 10.

**5** Select the appropriate ActionScript version. You've used ActionScript 3.0 in lessons in this book, so choose ActionScript 3.0.

**6** If you've included sound, click the Set buttons for the Audio Stream and Audio Event to increase the quality of the audio compression.

7   Select Compress Movie if the file is large and you want to reduce download times. If you select this option, be sure to test the final movie before uploading it.

8   Select Include XMP Metadata if you want to include information that describes your movie.

9   Click the HTML tab.

10  Select Flash Only from the Template menu.

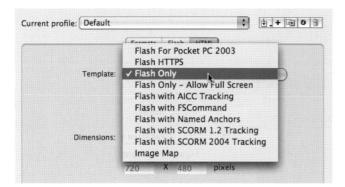

● **Note:** To learn about other template options, select one and then click Info.

## Detecting the Version of Flash Player

Some Flash features require specific versions of Flash Player to play as expected. You can automatically detect the version of Flash Player on a viewer's computer; if the Flash Player version is not the one required, a message will prompt the viewer to download the updated player.

1   Choose File > Publish Settings if the Publish Settings dialog box is not already open.

2   Click the HTML tab in the Publish Settings dialog box.

3   Select Detect Flash Version.

4   In the Version fields, enter the earliest version of the Flash Player to detect.

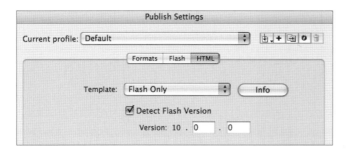

**Note:** Adobe also provides a Flash Detection Kit, which is a series of sample code and files that includes more options for informing viewers about the required Flash Player version and how to obtain it. The Detection Kit is updated when popular browsers make significant changes that affect the way Flash Player is accessed. To learn more about the Flash Detection Kit or to download it, visit www.adobe.com/products/flashplayer/download/detection_kit/.

5 Click Publish, and then click OK to close the dialog box.

Flash publishes the file, creating a SWF file and an HTML file that contains extra JavaScript code that will detect the specified Flash Player version. If the browser does not have the earliest Flash Player version you entered in the Version fields, a message is displayed instead of the Flash movie.

## Changing Display Settings

You have many options to change the way your Flash movie is displayed in a browser. The Dimensions options and the Scale options work together to determine the movie's size and amount of distortion and cropping.

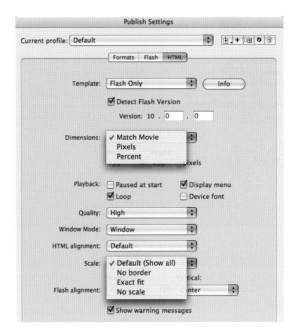

1 Choose File > Publish Settings.

2 Click the HTML tab in the Publish Settings dialog box.

- Select Match Movie for the Dimensions to play the Flash movie at the exact Stage size set in Flash. This is the usual setting for almost all your Flash projects.

- Select Pixels for the Dimensions to enter a different size in pixels for your Flash movie.

- Select Percent for the Dimensions to enter a different size for your Flash movie as a percentage of the browser window.

- Select Default (Show All) for the Scale option to fit the movie in the browser window without any distortions or cropping to show all the content. This is the usual setting for almost all your Flash projects.

- Select No Border for the Scale option to scale the movie to fit the browser window without any distortions but with cropping of the content to fill the window.

- Select Exact Fit for the Scale option to scale the movie to fill the browser window on both the horizontal and vertical dimensions. In this option, none of the background color shows, but the content can be distorted.

- Select No Scale for the Scale option to keep the movie size constant no matter how big or small the browser window is.

## Changing Playback Settings

You can change several options that affect the way your Flash movie plays within a browser.

1 Choose File > Publish Settings.

2 Click the HTML tab in the Publish Settings dialog box.

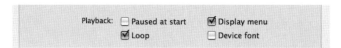

- Select Paused at Start for the Playback option to have the movie pause at the very first frame.

- Deselect Loop for the Playback option to have the movie play only once.

- Deselect Display Menu for the Playback option to limit the options in the context menu that appears when you right-click/Ctrl-click on a Flash movie in a browser.

**Note:** In general, it is a better idea to control a Flash movie with ActionScript than to rely on the Playback settings in the Publish Settings dialog box. For example, add a stop() command in the very first frame of your Timeline if you want to pause the movie at the start. When you test your movie (Control > Test Movie), all the functionality will be in place.

### Dreamweaver and Flash

While Flash provides several options to help display your finished movie within a Web browser, it's best to use a dedicated HTML editor such as Adobe Dreamweaver to position your Flash movie on the page, especially when you want to include other information around it. For example, your Flash movie may be just one component of an overall Web page that also includes information about the animated cartoon, show times, and cast members. Dreamweaver can assemble all the different media components together on a single HTML page.

To insert your Flash movie in an HTML page in Dreamweaver, simply choose Insert > Media > Flash. Select your SWF file and click OK. Dreamweaver creates the HTML code to point to the SWF file and display it in a browser. Many of the same display and playback options are available in the Property inspector in Dreamweaver.

# Alternative Publishing Options

By default, Flash creates SWF and HTML files for your project. However, you can also choose to save specific frames of the movie as images or to save the file as a projector, which can play on computers that do not have Flash Player installed.

## Saving Frames as Images

Sometimes you might not want to share an entire movie but want to display a particular frame. Exporting a frame as a GIF, JPEG, or PNG image might be useful if you need an image for a portfolio or want to provide an end image to a viewer who doesn't have Flash Player. You can also use individual images to compile a storyboard of multiple scenes to share with a client before the Flash file is interactive.

1  Choose File > Publish Settings, and then click the Formats tab. Flash (.swf) and HTML are selected by default.

2  Select GIF Image (.gif), JPEG Image (.jpg), and PNG Image (.png), and click OK to close the dialog box.

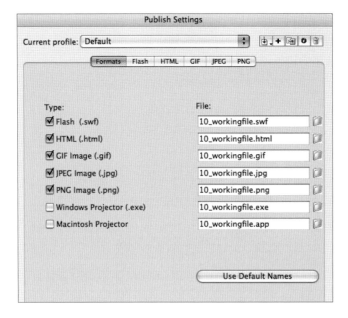

These options export the frame currently selected in the Flash document.

3  Select the last frame in the Timeline (frame 150). This is the frame that Flash will export as image files.

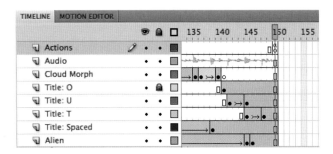

**4** Choose File > Publish. Flash publishes the files to the folder that contains the Flash document file.

**5** Navigate to the Lesson10/10Start folder. In addition to the SWF and HTML files, the folder contains GIF, PNG, and JPEG files. Open the image files to view them.

● **Note:** Which file format you choose depends on the type of content. If the frame contains an illustration with flat, simple colors, GIF is a good option. If the frame is more photographic and you don't mind compressing image data, JPEG may be the best choice. If the frame includes transparency, choose PNG.

# Publishing Movies for Mobile Devices

You can create content for mobile phones and other mobile devices using Flash Lite. To create a Flash Lite document easily, choose File > New, select Flash File (Mobile), and click OK.

The Adobe Device Central launches. Select the target device and click OK.

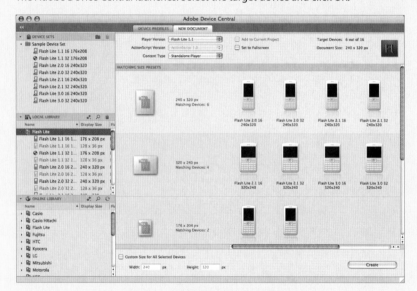

Flash automatically opens the file with the appropriate settings.

Before you publish the file, use Device Central to preview the content in specific mobile devices. To learn more about publishing Flash Lite files for mobile devices, refer to both Flash Help and Device Central Help.

## Creating a Projector

Most computers have the Flash Player installed, but you may need to distribute a movie to someone who doesn't have the Flash Player or who has an older version. You can save your movie as a projector, a stand-alone application that includes all the files necessary to play the movie. Because a projector contains all the data to play your movie, projector files are larger than SWF files.

1  Choose File > Publish Settings, and click the Formats tab.

2  Deselect GIF, JPEG, and PNG. Select Windows Projector and Macintosh Projector.

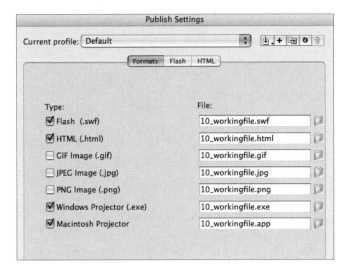

3  Click Publish.

4  When the file has been published, click OK to close the dialog box.

5  Open the Lesson10/10Start folder.

6  Open the projector file for your platform (Windows or Mac OS). The Windows Projector file has an .exe extension.

Both the Windows and the Mac projectors can be double-clicked to play without the browser. You can share the projectors on a CD or DVD. You can use these publishing methods to finalize any Flash projects you create and share them with the world.

# Review Questions

1  What is the Bandwidth Profiler, and why is it useful?

2  What files do you need to upload to a server to ensure your final Flash movie plays as expected in a Web browser?

3  How can you tell which version of Flash Player a viewer has installed, and why is it important?

4  Define metadata. How do you add it to a Flash document?

5  What is a projector file?

# Review Answers

1  The Bandwidth Profiler provides information such as the overall file size, the total number of frames, the dimensions of the Stage, and how your data is distributed throughout your frames. You can use the Bandwidth Profiler to preview how your final project might behave under different download environments.

2  To ensure your movie plays as expected in Web browsers, upload the Flash SWF file and the HTML document that tells the browser how to display the SWF file. You also need to upload any files your SWF file references, such as video or other SWF files, and be sure that they are in the same relative location (usually the same folder as the final SWF file) as they were on your hard drive.

3  Select Detect Flash Version in the HTML tab in the Publish Settings dialog box to automatically detect the version of Flash Player on a viewer's computer. Some Flash features require specific versions of Flash Player to play as expected.

4  Metadata is information about data. Metadata includes a document's title, a description, keywords, the date the file was created, and any other information about the document. Metadata in a Flash document is published with the Flash file, making it easy for search engines to search and share your movie. To add metadata to a Flash document, choose File > Publish Settings, click the Flash tab, and select File Info under the SWF Settings. In the XMP Metadata dialog box that appears, enter the information you want to include.

5  A projector is a stand-alone application that includes all the information necessary to play the movie without a browser, so people who don't have the Flash Player or who don't have the current version can view your movie.

# Appendix: Hexadecimal Color Codes

Throughout the book, colors were referred to by their hexadecimal values, which are commonly used in HTML and other Web programming. Using a hexadecimal value enables you to be very precise about the color you're using rather than referring to it as "blue" or "green." Hexadecimal values are especially useful when you're using the Adobe Color Picker or other tools that don't list color names.

This chart shows 216 standard Web colors and their hexadecimal color codes, as well as the RGB (red, green, and blue) values that combine to create the color. Note that because this is a printed chart, these RGB colors have been converted to CMYK, which changes them slightly from what you see onscreen. To see the true RGB colors, open the file called Appendix.pdf that is on the book's accompanying CD. Use this as a reference to select colors, but consider it a starting point. Many more colors are available. Search the Web for "hexadecimal color codes" to find a variety of tools to help you select colors and find their corresponding hexadecimal codes.

| | | | | | | | | | | | | | | | |
|---|---|---|---|---|---|---|---|---|---|---|---|---|---|---|---|
| 990033 R:153 G:000 B:051 | FF3366 R:255 G:051 B:102 | CC0033 R:204 G:000 B:051 | FF0033 R:255 G:000 B:051 | FF9999 R:255 G:153 B:153 | CC3366 R:204 G:051 B:102 | FFCCFF R:255 G:204 B:255 | CC6699 R:204 G:102 B:153 | 993366 R:153 G:051 B:102 | 660033 R:102 G:000 B:051 | CC3399 R:204 G:051 B:153 | FF99CC R:255 G:153 B:204 | FF66CC R:255 G:102 B:204 | FF99FF R:255 G:153 B:255 | FF6699 R:255 G:102 B:153 | CC0066 R:204 G:000 B:102 |
| FF0066 R:255 G:000 B:102 | FF3399 R:255 G:051 B:153 | FF0099 R:255 G:000 B:153 | FF33CC R:255 G:051 B:204 | FF00CC R:255 G:000 B:204 | FF66FF R:255 G:102 B:255 | FF33FF R:255 G:051 B:255 | FF00FF R:255 G:000 B:255 | CC0099 R:204 G:000 B:153 | 990066 R:153 G:000 B:102 | CC66CC R:204 G:102 B:204 | CC33CC R:204 G:051 B:204 | CC99FF R:204 G:153 B:255 | CC66FF R:204 G:102 B:255 | CC33FF R:204 G:051 B:255 | 993399 R:153 G:051 B:153 |
| CC00CC R:204 G:000 B:204 | CC00FF R:204 G:000 B:255 | 9900CC R:153 G:000 B:204 | 990099 R:153 G:000 B:153 | CC99CC R:204 G:153 B:204 | 996699 R:153 G:102 B:153 | 663366 R:102 G:051 B:102 | 660099 R:102 G:000 B:153 | 9933CC R:153 G:051 B:204 | 660066 R:102 G:000 B:102 | 9900FF R:153 G:000 B:255 | 9933FF R:153 G:051 B:255 | 9966CC R:153 G:102 B:204 | 330033 R:051 G:000 B:051 | 663399 R:102 G:051 B:153 | 6633CC R:102 G:051 B:204 |
| 6600CC R:102 G:000 B:204 | 9966FF R:153 G:102 B:255 | 330066 R:051 G:000 B:102 | 6600FF R:102 G:000 B:255 | 6633FF R:102 G:051 B:255 | CCCCFF R:204 G:204 B:255 | 9999FF R:153 G:153 B:255 | 9999CC R:153 G:153 B:204 | 6666CC R:102 G:102 B:204 | 6666FF R:102 G:102 B:255 | 666699 R:102 G:102 B:153 | 333366 R:051 G:051 B:102 | 333399 R:051 G:051 B:153 | 330099 R:051 G:000 B:153 | 3300CC R:051 G:000 B:204 | 3300FF R:051 G:000 B:255 |
| 3333FF R:051 G:051 B:255 | 3333CC R:051 G:051 B:204 | 0066FF R:000 G:102 B:255 | 0033FF R:000 G:051 B:255 | 3366FF R:051 G:102 B:255 | 3366CC R:051 G:102 B:204 | 000066 R:000 G:000 B:102 | 000033 R:000 G:000 B:051 | 0000FF R:000 G:000 B:255 | 000099 R:000 G:000 B:153 | 0033CC R:000 G:051 B:204 | 0000CC R:000 G:000 B:204 | 336699 R:051 G:102 B:153 | 0066CC R:000 G:102 B:204 | 99CCFF R:153 G:204 B:255 | 6699FF R:102 G:153 B:255 |
| 003366 R:000 G:051 B:102 | 6699CC R:102 G:153 B:204 | 006699 R:000 G:102 B:153 | 3399CC R:051 G:153 B:204 | 0099CC R:000 G:153 B:204 | 66CCFF R:102 G:204 B:255 | 3399FF R:051 G:153 B:255 | 003399 R:000 G:051 B:153 | 0099FF R:000 G:153 B:255 | 33CCFF R:051 G:204 B:255 | 00CCFF R:000 G:204 B:255 | 99FFFF R:153 G:255 B:255 | 66FFFF R:102 G:255 B:255 | 33FFFF R:051 G:255 B:255 | 00FFFF R:000 G:255 B:255 | 00CCCC R:000 G:204 B:204 |
| 009999 R:000 G:153 B:153 | 669999 R:102 G:153 B:153 | 99CCCC R:153 G:204 B:204 | CCFFFF R:204 G:255 B:255 | 33CCCC R:051 G:204 B:204 | 66CCCC R:102 G:204 B:204 | 339999 R:051 G:153 B:153 | 336666 R:051 G:102 B:102 | 006666 R:000 G:102 B:102 | 003333 R:000 G:051 B:051 | 00FFCC R:000 G:255 B:204 | 33FFCC R:051 G:255 B:204 | 33CC99 R:051 G:204 B:153 | 00CC99 R:000 G:204 B:153 | 66FFCC R:102 G:255 B:204 | 99FFCC R:153 G:255 B:204 |
| 00FF99 R:000 G:255 B:153 | 339966 R:051 G:153 B:102 | 006633 R:000 G:102 B:051 | 336633 R:051 G:102 B:051 | 669966 R:102 G:153 B:102 | 66CC66 R:102 G:204 B:102 | 99FF99 R:153 G:255 B:153 | 66FF66 R:102 G:255 B:102 | 339933 R:051 G:153 B:051 | 99CC99 R:153 G:204 B:153 | 66FF99 R:102 G:255 B:153 | 33FF99 R:051 G:255 B:153 | 33CC66 R:051 G:204 B:102 | 00CC66 R:000 G:204 B:102 | 66CC99 R:102 G:204 B:153 | 009966 R:000 G:153 B:102 |
| 009933 R:000 G:153 B:051 | 33FF66 R:051 G:255 B:102 | 00FF66 R:000 G:255 B:102 | CCFFCC R:204 G:255 B:204 | CCFF99 R:204 G:255 B:153 | 99FF66 R:153 G:255 B:102 | 99FF33 R:153 G:255 B:051 | 00FF33 R:000 G:255 B:051 | 33FF33 R:051 G:255 B:051 | 00CC33 R:000 G:204 B:051 | 33CC33 R:051 G:204 B:051 | 66FF33 R:102 G:255 B:051 | 00FF00 R:000 G:255 B:000 | 66CC33 R:102 G:204 B:051 | 006600 R:000 G:102 B:000 | 003300 R:000 G:051 B:000 |
| 009900 R:000 G:153 B:000 | 33FF00 R:051 G:255 B:000 | 66FF00 R:102 G:255 B:000 | 99FF00 R:153 G:255 B:000 | 66CC00 R:102 G:204 B:000 | 00CC00 R:000 G:204 B:000 | 33CC00 R:051 G:204 B:000 | 339900 R:051 G:153 B:000 | 99CC66 R:153 G:204 B:102 | 669933 R:102 G:153 B:051 | 99CC33 R:153 G:204 B:051 | 336600 R:051 G:102 B:000 | 669900 R:102 G:153 B:000 | 99CC00 R:153 G:204 B:000 | CCFF66 R:204 G:255 B:102 | CCFF33 R:204 G:255 B:051 |
| CCFF00 R:204 G:255 B:000 | 999900 R:153 G:153 B:000 | CCCC00 R:204 G:204 B:000 | CCCC33 R:204 G:204 B:051 | 333300 R:051 G:051 B:000 | 666600 R:102 G:102 B:000 | 999933 R:153 G:153 B:051 | CCCC66 R:204 G:204 B:102 | 666633 R:102 G:102 B:051 | 999966 R:153 G:153 B:102 | CCCC99 R:204 G:204 B:153 | FFFFCC R:255 G:255 B:204 | FFFF99 R:255 G:255 B:153 | FFFF66 R:255 G:255 B:102 | FFFF33 R:255 G:255 B:051 | FFFF00 R:255 G:255 B:000 |
| FFCC00 R:255 G:204 B:000 | FFCC66 R:255 G:204 B:102 | FFCC33 R:255 G:204 B:051 | CC9933 R:204 G:153 B:051 | 996600 R:153 G:102 B:000 | CC9900 R:204 G:153 B:000 | FF9900 R:255 G:153 B:000 | CC6600 R:204 G:102 B:000 | 993300 R:153 G:051 B:000 | CC6633 R:204 G:102 B:051 | 663300 R:102 G:051 B:000 | FF9966 R:255 G:153 B:102 | FF6633 R:255 G:102 B:051 | FF9933 R:255 G:153 B:051 | FF6600 R:255 G:102 B:000 | CC3300 R:204 G:051 B:000 |
| 996633 R:153 G:102 B:051 | 330000 R:051 G:000 B:000 | 663333 R:102 G:051 B:051 | 996666 R:153 G:102 B:102 | CC9999 R:204 G:153 B:153 | 993333 R:153 G:051 B:051 | CC6666 R:204 G:102 B:102 | FFCCCC R:255 G:204 B:204 | FF3333 R:255 G:051 B:051 | CC3333 R:204 G:051 B:051 | FF6666 R:255 G:102 B:102 | 660000 R:102 G:000 B:000 | 990000 R:153 G:000 B:000 | CC0000 R:204 G:000 B:000 | FF0000 R:255 G:000 B:000 | FF3300 R:255 G:051 B:000 |

| | | | | | | | |
|---|---|---|---|---|---|---|---|
| CC9966 R:204 G:153 B:102 | FFCC99 R:255 G:204 B:153 | FFFFFF R:255 G:255 B:255 | CCCCCC R:204 G:204 B:204 | 999999 R:153 G:153 B:153 | 666666 R:102 G:102 B:102 | 333333 R:051 G:051 B:051 | 000000 R:0000 G:0000 B:0000 |

# INDEX

working with graphics in, 34–65.
*See also* graphics
working with sound in, 242–255.
*See also* sound files; sounds
working with video in, 256–283.
*See also* video
*Flash CS4 User Guide,* xii
Flash Detection Kit, 338
Flash files, 4. *See also* FLA files
Flash Help, xii, 30–31
Flash Lite, 29, 344
Flash Player, 4, 277, 337–338, 345, 346
Flash Support Center, xii, 30–31, 32
Flash Video format, 256
.flv extension, 256
FLV files, 256, 258, 273, 276, 277–288
ForwardButton component, 306
Frame by Frame Graph mode, 331
frame labels, 226–228
frame rate, 9, 277
frames. *See also* keyframes
adding to Timeline, 246
inserting, 12–13, 107–108
*vs.* keyframes, 32
labeling, 236
purpose of, 9
saving as images, 342–343
selecting multiple, 14
Free Transform tool, 40, 49, 117, 122, 129
FullScreenButton component, 306
functions, 214, 219, 236

## G

garbage masks, 276
GIF files, 77, 342, 343
Global Transform option, 144
gotoAndPlay( ) command, 221, 228, 231–232
gotoAndStop( ) command, 221, 226, 227, 231
Gradient Transform tool, 45
gradient transitions, 43–44
gradients, 42–45
applying, 42–43
changing center of, 45
customizing color transitions in, 43–44
defined, 42
stretching, 45
types of, 42
Graph Size icon, 133
graphic symbols, 73

graphics, 34–65. *See also* images
creating curves, 56–59
creating/editing text, 61–64
creating rectangles, 37–40
creating transparencies, 59–60
drawing ovals, 49–50
making patterns, 50–56
making selections, 45–48
using gradient fills, 42–45
ways of using, 35
green screen, 273, 276, 284
grids, 50
Group command, 46

## H

H.264 format, 256, 258
Hard Light blending option, 89
Help features, xii, 30–31
hexadecimal color codes, 39, 347
History panel, 26, 30, 32
Hit keyframe, 201, 202, 206, 207
HTML editors, 341
HTML files, 28
hyperlinking text, 63

## I

Illustrator, 69–71
image formats, 77, 342–343
images. *See also* graphics
converting bitmap to vector, 78
saving frames as, 342–343
Import to Library command, 8, 71, 242–243
Import to Stage command, 69, 71, 75
Import Video wizard, 268–270, 273–277, 279–281
importing
artwork, 69
Illustrator files, 69–70, 71
layers, 69–70, 71
Photoshop files, 75–77
sound files, 242–243
symbols, 71
video, 268–270, 273–277, 279–281
In point marker, 263, 264
Ink Bottle tool, 60, 173
Input Text option, 23, 61
Insert Keyframes command, 116
Insert Layer Folder icon, 17
instances
breaking apart, 84
changing brightness of, 87–88

changing size/position of, 84–87
changing transparency of, 88–89, 97
defined, 72, 97
naming, 212, 236
*vs.* symbols, 72, 97
instructional movies, xii. *See also* tutorials
interactive buttons, 196, 234. *See also* button symbols
interactive display of minerals, 288–306
adding text component to, 290–296
creating interactivity for, 296–306
viewing final document for, 288–289
interactive movies, 197
interactive navigation, 194–236
checking syntax for, 222
creating animated buttons for, 234–235
creating button symbols for, 201–207
creating destination keyframes for, 223–228
creating event handlers for, 218–221
designing layout for, 197–201
duplicating buttons for, 207
naming button instances for, 212
placing button instances for, 209–211
playing/stopping animation for, 228–233
testing, 211
viewing finished project for, 196
inverse kinematics
articulated motion with, 153–161
defined, 153
purpose of, 151, 153
with shapes, 170–178
invisible buttons, 207

## J

JavaScript, 213
joint speed, 169
joints
changing speed of, 169
constraining rotation of, 162–165
constraining translation of, 166–169
JPEG files, 77, 342, 343

saving as projectors, 345
stopping, 217
testing, 329, 331–332
MP3 files, 8, 242

## N

nav bars, 197
navigation
    commands, 221
    interactive. *See* interactive navigation
    nonlinear, 197
    tools, 25
navigation bars, 197
nested animations, 127–131, 317–318
New Folder button, 79
New Symbol command, 50, 73, 97, 201
news sites, 256, 273
nextFrame( ) command, 221
nodes
    defined, 153
    isolating rotation of, 160–161
    repositioning, 161
nonlinear navigation, 197
Normal blending option, 89

## O

Object Drawing icon, 41
object drawing mode, 41
objects
    aligning, 54–55
    animating, 101. *See also* animation
    breaking apart, 55
    defined, 214
    grouping, 46, 56
    matching color of, 60–61
    positioning in 3D space, 91–96
    scaling, 49
    selecting, 45
ocean animation, 184–192
octopus animation, 152, 170–183
On2VP6 codec, 256, 273
Open command/dialog box, 4
Orient to path option, 125
Out point marker, 264
Oval Primitive tool, 41
Oval tool, 49–50, 65
Over keyframe, 201, 203
Overlay blending option, 89

## P

Paint Bucket tool, 60–61, 173
painting tools, 25
panels, 21. *See also* specific panels
parameters, 214, 218
parenthesis, 215
Paste dialog box, 71
Paste in Place command, 59
Pasteboard, 6, 32
path of motion, 121–125
    changing scale/rotation of, 122–123
    editing, 123–124
    moving, 121–122
    orienting objects to, 125
patterns, 50–51, 53
PauseButton component, 306
Pen tool, 56–57, 58
perspective angle, 95–96
photography portfolio page, 195–235
    adding title/intro text to, 199–201
    checking syntax for, 222
    creating animated buttons for, 234–235
    creating button symbols for, 201–207
    creating destination keyframes for, 223–228
    creating event handlers for, 218–221
    designing layout for, 197–201
    duplicating buttons for, 207
    naming button instances for, 212
    placing button instances for, 209–211
    playing/stopping, 228–233
    testing buttons for, 211
    viewing finished project for, 196
photos. *See also* images
    adding layers for, 17
    adding titles to, 24
    creating transitions between, 229–231
    overlapping, 4
    positioning on Stage, 19
    rotating, 20–21
Photoshop, 5, 68, 75–77, 89
play( ) command, 221
Play buttons, 306
PNG files, 77, 342, 343
polar bear video, 278–281
Polygon Mode icon, 48
poses, 158–159
posterized images, 78

prevFrame( ) command, 221
primitive drawing mode, 41
project files, xi
projectors, 345, 346
properties, 214
Property inspector
    aligning button instances in, 209–211
    applying ease-in/ease-out effects in, 139
    applying filters in, 90
    changing/deleting sound files in, 251–252
    changing instance properties in, 87–89
    changing joint speed in, 169
    changing Stage properties in, 6–7
    changing transparency in, 60, 88
    constraining rotation of joints in, 162–165
    constraining translation of joints in, 166–169
    entering frame labels in, 226–227
    naming button instances in, 212
    opening, 19
    positioning objects on Stage in, 19–21
    setting armature options in, 178–183
    setting brightness in, 229–231
    specifying rectangle dimensions in, 37
    specifying stroke color in, 39
    swapping bitmaps in, 208–209
    swapping target of motion tween in, 127
property keyframes, 116, 148
PSD files, 77
Publish command, 335
Publish Preview command, 329
Publish Settings dialog box, 28–29, 252, 333, 335–345

## Q

QuickTime, x, 256
quotation marks, 215

## R

radial gradients, 42
radio buttons, 306
RadioButton component, 306
RAM, x
Random ease, 141–143

RealPlayer, 256
Rectangle Primitive tool, 41
Rectangle tool, 37
rectangles, 37–40
    adding fills to, 38
    drawing, 37
    merging, 41
    modifying, 40
    rounding corners of, 41
    specifying stroke properties for, 39
removeChild( ) command, 316
Reset Values button, 137
resources, xii, 4, 30
retouching tools, 25
review questions
    Adding Animation, 148
    Articulated Motion and Morphing, 193
    Creating and Editing Symbols, 97
    Getting Acquainted, 32
    Interactive Navigation, 236
    Loading and Controlling Flash Content, 325
    Publishing Flash Documents, 346
    Using Components, 307
    Working with Graphics, 65
    Working with Sound and Video, 284
robot project, 68–96
    adding/positioning text for, 91–96
    applying filters for special effects in, 90–91
    changing brightness of robots for, 87–88
    changing size/position of robots for, 84–87
    changing transparency of orb for, 88–89
    converting graphics to symbols for, 73–74
    editing symbols for, 80–83
    importing artwork for, 69–70
    importing background for, 75–77
    managing symbols for, 78–79
    viewing finished project for, 68
Rock Classification project, 288–306
    adding text component to, 290–296
    creating interactivity for, 296–306
    viewing final document for, 288–289
rocket ship animation, 121–127
    editing path of motion, 123–124
    moving path of motion, 121–122

    orienting rocket ship to path, 125
    replacing rocket ship with alien, 126–127
    scaling/rotating path of motion, 122–123
rotation, constraining joint, 162–165
runtime armatures, 178–179

**S**

Scale options, Publish Settings, 338–340
Script Assist mode, 218
Script navigator, 217
scripting
    languages, 4, 213. *See also* ActionScript
    syntax, 215
    terminology, 213–214
scroll bars, 306
Selection tool, 45–47, 58, 65, 124
selection tools, 25
semicolons, 215
Set In Point icon, 263
Set Out Point icon, 264
shape hints, 188–192, 193
shape tweens
    applying, 186–188, 193
    controlling appearance of, 188
    defined, 184
    establishing keyframes, 184–186
    morphing with, 184–188
    purpose of, 193
shapes. *See also* specific shapes
    adding gradients to, 42–43
    adding text to, 61–62
    breaking apart, 55
    changing transparency of, 59–60
    components of, 36
    converting objects to/from, 41
    defining bones inside, 170–173
    editing, 173–175
    grouping, 46, 56
    matching color of, 60–61
    Shearwood Wildlife Preserve project. *See* animated zoo kiosk
Short command, 18
Simulate Download command, 331–332
skins, 268, 274, 284
Sorenson Spark codec, 256
sound clips, 244. *See also* sound files; sounds
sound files. *See also* sounds
    changing, 251–252

    deleting, 251–252
    editing length of, 247–249, 284
    importing, 242–243
    where to find, 244
sound formats, 242
Sound Properties dialog box, 243
Sound Settings dialog box, 253
sound sync options, 255
sounds, 242–255. *See also* sound files
    adding to buttons, 254–255
    changing volume of, 249–251
    clipping end of, 247–249
    increasing quality of, 252–254
    placing on Timeline, 244–246
    triggering, 255
Spill Suppressor effect, 276
splash page. *See* animated splash page
Stage
    adding items from Library panel to, 8–9
    changing properties for, 6–7
    creating static text on, 61
    displaying frame content on, 9
    dragging components to, 290–292
    positioning objects on, 19–21
    purpose of, 3, 6, 32
    scaling, 6
    swapping bitmaps/symbols on, 208–209
starburst, 50–56
Start sync option, 255
Static Text option, 23, 61
stop( ) command, 221, 233, 235
stop actions, 131, 217, 218
Stop and Start eases, 182
Stop sync option, 255
StopButton component, 306
storyboards, 329
Stream for Sync option, 245
Stream sync option, 255
Streaming Graph mode, 331
strings, 215
Stroke Color box, 39
strokes
    applying to rectangles, 39
    applying transparency to, 59
    defined, 36
Subselection tool, 45, 58, 65, 173
Subtract blending option, 89
Swap Bitmap dialog box, 208
Swap Symbol dialog box, 52
SWF files
    how Flash displays, 147
    loading, 312–315